MYTHS
OF THE WORLD

MYTHS OF THE WORLD

THE ILLUSTRATED TREASURY OF THE WORLD'S GREATEST STORIES

GENERAL EDITOR: TONY ALLAN

DUNCAN BAIRD PUBLISHERS

LONDON

Myths of the World
General Editor: Tony Allan

Distributed in the USA and Canada by
Sterling Publishing Co., Inc.
387 Park Avenue South
New York, NY 10016-8810

This edition first published in the UK and USA in 2009 by
Duncan Baird Publishers Ltd
Sixth Floor, Castle House
75–76 Wells Street
London W1T 3QH

Library of Congress Cataloging-in-Publication Data

Myths of the world : the illustrated treasury of the world's greatest stories / general editor, Tony Allan.
p. cm.
Includes bibliographical references and index.
ISBN 978-1-84483-845-5 (alk. paper)
1. Mythology. I. Allan, Tony, 1946-
BL312.M99 2009
398.2--dc22
2009006468

10 9 8 7 6 5 4 3 2 1

Typeset in Snell Roundhand and Spectrum MT
Color reproduction by Colourscan
Printed in China by Imago

For information about custom editions, special sales, premium and corporate purchases, please contact Sterling Special Sales Department at 800-805-5489 or specialsales@sterlingpub.com.

Contents

Introduction

Mythology represents the world's original database of story. Yet, ironically, as soon as the word "myth" was used, the narratives so described had already lost something of their primordial power. From the time when the term was first introduced, in Greece in the fourth or fifth centuries BCE, it carried the implication that the accounts were untrue, or at the very least not objectively verifiable. Yet the audience that had originally listened to the tales, whether in ancient Greece or in the Celtic lands or Persia or Tibet or Polynesia, for the most part accepted them uncritically as descriptions of real occurrences that had happened in the distant past. Myths started off by being factual for those who heard them, although now we classify them by definition as fiction.

The process of demystifying myth began early, for in many parts of the world the generations that displaced the tales went to considerable lengths to remove all trace of them. While they were accepted as genuine, the narratives had profoundly shaped the way in which people looked at the world and lived their lives. When fresh ideologies arrived, however, usually in the form of a proselytizing new religion, the missionaries' first task was to discredit what had gone before. So, when Christianity became the official religion of the Roman Empire, the last remaining pagan temples were rapidly closed.

Even stronger steps were taken when the new beliefs were imposed by force. In sixteenth-century America, the monks who followed in the wake of the conquistadors enthusiastically set about extirpating all trace of the myths of the indigenous peoples, and it was only through the efforts of a few exceptional individuals that anything at all was preserved.

There was no inevitability about this process of displacement, however. For the most part the world's other major religions proved more tolerant than Christendom of diversity. When Buddhism reached the Far East from India, for example, its proponents proved willing to accommodate the existing bodies of Chinese and Japanese myth, enshrined respectively in the Daoist and Shinto canons; even today, it is not uncommon for Japanese people to make offerings at both Shinto and Buddhist shrines. Although conquering armies carried Islam across the Middle East and North Africa, it too proved comparatively respectful of the other faiths it encountered, and Persia's Zoroastrian heritage of legend was eroded only gradually.

From myth to folktale

Once they had been downgraded to the status of myths, the displaced stories depended for their fate on the treatment they received at the hands of the new political masters. In lands where the old beliefs were suppressed they tended to go underground, often surviving in the distorted form of folktale or legend. One of the most interesting examples of this process was in the Celtic lands and particularly Ireland, whose early gods became transformed in the popular imagination into the fairy folk, believed to inhabit an otherworld that coexisted alongside the everyday one. Accessed through fairy mounds, this alternative realm operated to a different concept of time, and human visitors who stumbled into it by mischance tended to emerge like Rip van Winkle into a world they no longer recognized, many years having passed by without their knowing. A similar fate to that of the Celtic gods also befell the dwarfs of Norse mythology. Originally an industrious underground race of miners and smiths, famed for their craftsmanship, they emerged in Christian times as quaint figures of fun, sufficiently unthreatening to serve decoratively as garden gnomes.

The next great change in attitudes to the myths, at least in the Christian lands, came only after they ceased to be regarded as a threat. Rather like Norse dwarfs, the old stories then became objects of curiosity, survivals of a bygone era that could be appreciated for the intrinsic narrative interest of the tales they told.

The process started earliest with the myths of Greece and Rome. Knowledge of these had never been entirely lost thanks to the prominent part they played in literature, and after classical learning was rediscovered in the Renaissance they rapidly became part of every educated European's mental luggage. The Celtic heritage had to wait longer for rehabilitation, a task largely accomplished by antiquarians and folklorists in the eighteenth and nineteenth centuries. Their counterparts were also at work in Germany and Scandinavia, where the likes of the Brothers Grimm and the Norwegian collectors Asbjørnsen and Moe did much to revive their own countries' heritage of story.

Comparing mythologies

By the nineteenth century a body of myth had started to accumulate from around the world, and the study of comparative mythology was born. Soon academics were researching across cultures, seeking common themes and shared obsessions in tales from different traditions. They came up with rich

This strange enamelled hybrid beast from Ming-dynasty China (1368–1644) was known as a *qilin*. When, in 1414, an East African sultan sent the Chinese emperor a giraffe, it was such a bizarre sight that courtiers presented it as a *qilin*.

pickings. Linguists noticed similarities between the terminology of some classical and Indian myths – the sky god of the Greeks was Zeus Pater and of the Romans Jupiter, for example, while in the Hindu canon he was Dyaus Pitar – that quickly convinced them that the two traditions shared a common Indo-European origin.

Others noted with astonishment that Bible stories could be found in non-Hebrew versions that sometimes long predated their inclusion in the Old Testament. The most widely publicized example involved Noah's Flood, which was eerily paralleled by tales of a similar deluge from Sumerian and Babylonian sources. These too portrayed the cataclysm as divine retribution on humankind, and described how one individual, warned by the gods, built a boat that he filled with animals to ensure that life would continue after the disaster. Very different cultures across the world also had their own traditions of a cosmic deluge; one such from the Aztec tradition is included in this collection (see page 250).

The most ambitious scholars searched for a central theme that could be used to explain the mind of early man, or at least to cast light on the development of society. For Germany's Max Müller, the common substratum was nature worship, and more specifically a cult of the sun. The Scottish anthropologist Sir James

Many of the fairy mounds (see page 7) that dot the Irish landscape are man-made in origin, including the Neolithic passage grave at Knowth, County Meath, in the valley of the River Boyne. Consisting of one large mound and seventeen satellite tombs (visible in the foreground, below), Knowth is the largest passage grave of the region's Brú na Bóinne complex.

Frazer devoted his masterwork *The Golden Bough* to exploring the idea that early religions took the form of fertility cults; he found a repeated pattern of rites focused on the veneration and eventual sacrifice of a sacred king, conceived of as the incarnation of a solar deity who died each winter only to be born again in spring. Frazer's ideas inspired many important writers including T.S. Eliot and Ezra Pound, as well as a group of scholars working in the grey area between literature and religion, who became collectively known as the Myth and Ritual School.

Structures and archetypes

In the twentieth century psychoanalysts took up the hunt, viewing the myths as windows into the darker recesses of the human psyche. Famously, Sigmund Freud coined the term "Oedipus complex" to describe young children's feelings of rivalry with their father or mother for the love of the parent of the opposite sex, taking the name from the legendary Greek hero who unwittingly killed his own father and married his mother. Freud's contemporary Carl Jung combed world mythology for archetypal figures such as the Wise Old Man, the Hero, the Magician, the Orphan and the Wanderer, a cast of universally recognized characters that he believed to be congenitally implanted in the collective unconscious of the human race.

Other researchers employed different disciplines to tease out basic truths. The anthropologist Claude Lévi-Strauss, among others, sought to deconstruct myths in order to expose their underlying structure, which he analysed in terms of the resolution of oppositions through an act of mediation. As Lévi-Strauss himself was

very aware, however, this pattern was far from limited to myth; rather, he saw it as the basis of most narrative, and even as a key to the problem-solving nature of the human mind as a whole.

In recent years students of myth have tended to shy away from such abstract theorizing. They worry that the quest for big generalizations tends to neglect the specificity of each individual story, which needs to be understood first and foremost in terms of its own particular cultural context. In the case of many mythologies, of course, the necessary background information has been lost, giving many of the tales that have come down to us a deeply enigmatic quality. This situation most commonly occurs when myths have been passed down orally, with little in the way of written source material to flesh out the political, social and religious backdrop against which they evolved. It has taken decades and even centuries of research, for example, to make sense of the mythology of ancient Egypt or of the forcibly Christianized lands of Central and South America, and even now holes remain in our understanding that may never be filled.

Particularists and generalists

Two tendencies therefore rub against one another in the modern approach to myth. One can be described as particularism, which focuses on the individual story, studying it in the perspective of the society in which it was framed. The other is generalism, which surveys the body of myth as a whole in search of common themes.

A similar distinction affects scholars' ideas of the ways in which the myths were born. Some view them as the conscious creation of individual human minds, while others prefer to see them as an expression of a collective folk consciousness. The German Idealist thinker F.W.J. Schelling expressed the latter attitude forcibly in the mid-nineteenth century. "Mythological representations have been neither invented nor freely accepted," he wrote. "The products of a process independent of thought and will, they had an irrefutable and incontestable reality for the consciousness that underwent them. Peoples and individuals are only the instruments of this process, which goes beyond their horizon and which they serve without understanding." In other words, the myths had a life of their own that went beyond the power of any individual to consciously shape them.

Most modern commentators, however, take a very different view. While recognizing the sacred status that many myths had for their original audience, they nonetheless prefer to see the tales as narratives that were consciously shaped. Occasionally, the shaping was the work of one man: much of our knowledge of Greek creation myths, for example, comes from the poet Hesiod, whose *Theogony* was composed in about 700 BCE. More often, though, myths were the work not of a single individual but rather of a series of different narrators who passed them down orally from generation to generation, inevitably changing them on the way. Even so, anyone reading a collection of world myths like this one cannot help noticing common themes that appear across different traditions, regardless of the very different circumstances in which each one arose. Similarities can even be found between stories told in remote parts of the world, ruling out any possibility of cultural diffusion.

The most obvious explanation for the common ground lies in the fact that many of the myths were seeking to perform similar functions. The stories that established themselves in the popular memory were never intended simply to entertain, although that may have been a factor in their survival. Rather, they sought to address fundamental questions for which people of all races and in all climes have long sought answers.

Explaining the creation

One of the most basic of these issues concerned the creation of the universe, and a whole branch of mythology grew up around it, becoming known as cosmogony from the Greek words for "birth" and "the cosmos". Although each of the world's major mythologies had its own specific storyline, certain patterns recurred in different regions. Very different cultures imagined a time of primeval darkness, alternatively seen as a shifting mass of water, a cloud, or a featureless wasteland. In most traditions a god or gods duly appeared to bring order to the chaos, but some proposed intermediary stages along the way.

One motif that put in an appearance in lands as far apart as India, Egypt, China, Finland and Tibet as well as in parts of Africa and Polynesia was that of a cosmic egg, which either split in two to create the Earth and

In Norse myth the world was created from fire and ice, a concept that may well have been influenced by the characteristic hot springs of Iceland, settled by Norsemen in the ninth century. It was in Iceland that the Norse oral traditions were recorded for posterity in the thirteenth century as the *Prose Edda* and *Poetic Edda*, from which we have gained an understanding of Viking folklore and mythology.

the heavens or else nurtured primal beings who peopled the universe once they were hatched. Other creation myths reflected the environment of the cultures that produced them. A variant Egyptian tradition saw land emerging from the primeval waters much as it did on the banks of the Nile following the ebbing of the river's annual flood; in Norse myth the world was born from the conjunction of fire and ice, a combination familiar to Viking settlers in volcanic Iceland.

On the whole most mythologies devoted less time to cosmological speculations about the beginnings of the universe than they did to questions concerning the birth of the gods and of humankind. Several traditions proposed rival families of deities that came into conflict in the first times, like the Titans and Olympians of Greek myth or the Aesir and Vanir in the Norse lands. Students of myth have tended to see in such accounts distorted memories of early culture clashes, with a dominant faction's divinities displacing those of their bested foes.

Another common motif involved divine siblings who between them went on to populate the world. Ancient Egyptian myth spoke of the earth god Geb and the sky goddess Nut, but in the Maori version the roles were reversed, with the male Rangi as lord of the skies and his consort Papa as Earth mother. Japanese myth preserved the memory of seven successive generations of twin deities, culminating in Izanami and Izanagi, who between them gave birth to the islands of Japan.

Other common features also found their way into the myths. One was a tripartite division of the universe, with a heaven in the sky, the human world occupying the Earth, and a subterranean underworld often seen as a land of the dead. The Norse realms of Asgard (the home of the gods), Midgard (where humans lived), and icy Niflheim followed this pattern, as did the Japanese vision of a High Plain of Heaven raised above the Central Land of the Reed Plain, focused on Japan itself, with the shadowy realm of Yomi beneath. The three levels of the Norse universe were linked by the World Tree Yggdrasil, a concept also found in Mongolian, Siberian and some Mesoamerican traditions.

Similar parallels cropped up in descriptions of the way in which the first people came upon the Earth. One recurrent theme had them fashioned from clay, with the Egyptian Khnum and the Mesopotamian Nammu as alternative versions of the divine potter. In other mythologies they simply emerged – from caves in Aztec and Inca stories, from a lake in the Chibcha tradition.

Gifts of the culture heroes

Once the world was inhabited, its denizens needed to learn the skills that made civilized life possible. To explain their acquisition, peoples from across the globe had recourse to the figure of the culture hero – an individual, sometimes human but more often divine, who taught his contemporaries the necessary arts of survival. In China Huang Di, the Yellow Emperor, introduced medicine, the martial arts and the Chinese calendar; the Chibcha of Colombia venerated Bochica, a wise old man who perambulated their lands teaching the inhabitants the moral laws; Persia had Kiyumars, a legendary early ruler who introduced religion and weaving, Hushang, who first mastered fire, and Yima, whose many gifts included the mining of precious metals, wine- and perfume-

Izanami (left) and Izanagi (right) standing on the "floating bridge of heaven" and churning the sea below with a jeweled spear. When drops of salty water fell from its tip, Onogoroshima ("self-forming island") was created.

making, and sailing ships. In North American traditions the culture hero often took animal form, as Coyote, Crow or Beaver.

To rationalizing modern minds, many of these origin myths seem readily understandable. People who were used to seeing fledglings emerge from eggs would naturally enough visualize the creation in terms of a cosmic hatching, and cultures familiar with pottery would have had little difficulty in imagining their earliest ancestors being moulded from clay. Knowing that skills had to be learned, individuals from every clime could easily absorb the notion of the culture hero as first teacher.

Even so, an element was missing from these explanations, and that was the presence of an agent to make them work. Someone or something had to lay the egg, breathe life into the clay people, even give the culture hero the knowledge that he or she then transmitted. To fill that gap people turned to the notion of gods or spirits. In this crucial aspect mythology coincided with religion – so much so that a case can be made for claiming that in some respects the term is little more than a holdall name for religious beliefs that have fallen out of use.

A spirit-filled cosmos

Most early religions were animist in their worldview, seeing the universe as filled with spiritual power. There were many different words for the concept, from the Polynesian *mana* and Native American "medicine" to the Chinese *qi*, and each one had its own specific cultural implications. *Qi*, for example, was a life force present in all animate creatures, while *mana* was concentrated in certain individuals and places viewed as having a numinous authority. Similar ideas prevailed in South America, where *huacas* were objects or locations – springs, mountain summits, ancient ruins, even oddly shaped boulders – that were held to have special sacred significance.

The pagan religions for the most part tended to personalize this sense of spiritual force in the form of named beings. These could be spirits of place, like the *genii loci* who haunted woods and streams in classical legend or the Slav *rusalki* (malevolent water sprites) or *leshii* (forest guardians). Similar creatures haunted the hearth and home, whether in the form of German kobolds, British boggarts, Slav domovoi, Roman lares and penates, ancient Egypt's dwarf deity Bes or the Chinese Kitchen God.

Such entities operated on a relatively local scale, though. In most traditions the term "god" was reserved for beings with more universal powers. Given the dependence of early agrarian societies on the weather, it comes as little surprise that the greatest of the gods were those associated with the elements and the changing seasons. Rain deities like the Mayan Chac and the Aztec Tlaloc were undoubtedly important figures, but the paramount chiefs of the early pantheons tended to be linked directly to storms, drawing much of their authority from the terror inspired by thunder and lightning. In the Slav lands the chief focus of worship in pre-Christian times was the thunderbolt-wielding Perun; no Norse god was more widely venerated than Thor; Zeus the Thunderer ruled over the Olympians; and the Hittites and Hurrians worshipped the tempest god Teshub above all others.

Balancing the patriarchal authority of the storm god (and in some societies surpassing it) was the influence of a female figure of power linked to the fertility of the land. This Great Goddess had many different names – for the Sumerians she was Inana, in Anatolia she was Cybele, in Syria and Lebanon Astarte – and she also displayed conflicting attributes. Some traditions emphasized her tenderness and compassion, like the Egyptian Isis or China's Guan Yin; such qualities would later transfer over into the Christian cult of the Virgin Mary. Elsewhere, however, she was fiercely sexual, like the Babylonian Ishtar or the Norse Freyja. One recurrent theme involved her temporary disappearance, a disastrous event that brought barrenness and sterility in its wake. Her subsequent rescue – from the Underworld in the Greek myth of Persephone and the Sumerian tale of Inana and Dumuzi, from the clutches of the giants in the case of the Norse Idun – signalled the return of fertility and (by implication) the coming of spring.

Heroes and tricksters

The old pagan gods and spirits make up a large part of the *dramatis personae* of the myths, but by no means all of it. Another major category consisted of hero legends, and their protagonists were usually human, although often with qualities of strength and endurance far exceeding those of any normal mortal. As the American Joseph Campbell and other scholars have pointed out, hero myths also

The ancient Egyptian deity Bes was a protective god of the household and of childbirth. He was typically represented as a bow-legged, lion-maned dwarf, sometimes clad in a motley of animal skins and a feathered headdress.

The Syrian goddess Astarte was famed for her beauty and her ferocity. She was particularly associated with horses and chariots – as well as owls and lions, as shown in this carving.

followed a repeated pattern, typically involving a portentous birth, a difficult childhood, and an adolescence spent in preparation for some defining quest – Heracles' Labours, Jason's search for the Golden Fleece, Celtic Cuchullain's defence of Ulster, Asian Gesar's campaign against the "four enemies of the four directions". His task completed, the hero then had to adjust to the anti-climactic conditions of normal life, sometimes living out his last years in tranquillity but as often ending up in bitterness and failure.

If the hero myths provided adventure and tragedy, the world of myth also has its comedians in the form of tricksters – pranksters who achieved their ends through slyness and cunning. Sometimes the trouble-maker took the form of a god, like the Norse Loki or West Africa's Legba, or else of a semi-divine culture hero like the Polynesian Maui. In many African and North American traditions, he (for tricksters, like heroes, were usually male) took animal form, as Anansi the spider, Coyote or Hare. In the European Middle Ages, French writers of fables exploited a similar vein in chronicling the adventures of Reynard the Fox.

As an anthology of almost 250 separate stories selected from all the world's major mythologies, this collection includes examples of all the major genres described above. In its pages tricksters rub shoulders with culture heroes, storm gods line up alongside human champions of legend. By bringing together tales from very different traditions, the book inevitably falls within the framework of comparative mythology. Yet its division by geographical regions locates each story within a specific culture, and within the limits of the available space the narratives attempt to supply social and religious context for the wondrous events they describe.

Yet the main attraction of the book lies in the tales themselves, for however great its historical and psychological significance might be, the world's heritage of myth is also a treasure trove of story. Even removed from the framework of shared belief that once sustained them, the best myths still retain their power to amuse, surprise and shock. Generations of readers have been intrigued by their inventiveness and thrilled by their originality. This book seeks to extend those pleasures to a fresh audience.

Cradles of Civilization

Ancient Egypt

Ever since classical times, outsiders have been spellbound by the sheer exoticism of ancient Egyptian religion and its associated mythology. The strange panoply of animal-headed gods – jackal-headed Anubis, ibis-topped Thoth, the Apis bull, the lioness Sekhmet – and the obsession with death, funerary monuments and mummification enthralled the archaeologists who rediscovered the nation's heritage from the late eighteenth century on.

Much about the myths remains puzzling, but one factor scholars have increasingly come to appreciate is the longevity of Egyptian civilization, which flourished relatively undisturbed for more than three millennia – from around 3150 BCE to 31 BCE, when Egypt became part of the Roman empire. Then again, they have learned to understand the importance of local traditions; different towns venerated separate deities, whose status rose and fell with the cities' changing fortunes.

A case in point was the rise of the god Amun. In Old Kingdom days early in Egypt's history, Amun was the local god of Thebes, a relative backwater at the time. From the Middle Kingdom on, however, Thebes assumed central importance as the nation's capital, and Amun's role was similarly magnified. By New Kingdom days around the sixteenth century BCE he had risen to challenge the sun god Re as the supreme deity in the Egyptian pantheon. In the syncretist tradition by which many clashes of divine authority were resolved, the two gods were subsequently worshipped in composite form as Amun-Re, who remained the nation's principal focus of worship until Thebes' own primacy was overthrown.

The focus of the local loyalties underlying much of Egyptian religion fell on temples, which were thought to be the homes of the gods whose statues adorned them. Priests were employed to keep the god daily fed and cleaned, thereby assuring divine goodwill for the town he or she protected. On rare occasions a statue might be sent away so that some other community could benefit from its powers, but in such cases the god's return became a matter of considerable importance (see page 22). Alternatively, pilgrims from the surrounding region might flock to a particularly sacred site to pay homage to the resident deity at an annual festival (see page 23).

Under the later dynasties, citizens found solace in a new, more populist religion. Its central myth concerned a dysfunctional divine family, children of the earth deity Geb and the sky goddess Nut. Chief among them was the compassionate Isis, who took her own brother Osiris as her husband, for in ancient Egypt gods and pharaohs alike were exempted from the incest taboo. But the couple's marital harmony roused the jealousy of another brother, Seth, who murdered Osiris and cut his body into pieces, scattering them across Egypt and the neighbouring lands.

Appalled by her loss, Isis set out to find all the parts of the corpse. It was a long and arduous task, but the goddess devoted tireless energy to achieving it. When she had finally succeeded in reassembling the body, she used her divine magic to bring it briefly back to life, just long enough for the pair to conceive a child, Horus. He in his turn would devote his life to seeking vengeance on the evil Seth, and his ultimate triumph would be seen as the victory of divine justice and order (summarized for Egyptians in the word *maat*) over disruption and chaos (see page 27).

In time Isis came to be viewed as the personification of love and compassion, occupying rather the same role for Egyptians that the Virgin Mary would later play for Christians. As the symbol of *maat* and the social harmony that it implied, Horus became closely associated with Egypt's rulers, the pharaohs, regarded as his earthly incarnations. As for Osiris, he returned after his second death to the Underworld to rule over the kingdom of the dead (see page 24), where the souls of deceased individuals went to be weighed in the balance. Evil-doers faced eternal annihilation, but the righteous could look forward to a new life in the heavenly Fields of Aaru.

The Destruction of Humankind

Before Egypt had human kings, its ruler was the god Re. In his declining years, angered by his subjects' lack of respect, the god sent his Eye, deified as the goddess Hathor, to avenge him. The myth may have been created to explain the failure of a harvest.

Re, as a ruler of men, was past his prime. But his age did not prevent him from hearing that men were mocking him and plotting to overthrow him. Calling the gods to a secret conference, he asked their advice. Nun, as the eldest, was the one to whom he listened most avidly.

Nun advised Re to punish the blasphemers by scorching them with his blazing heat. However, when Re did this, his victims ran for shelter to the rocks and escaped his fury. So he reconvened the gods, who told him to send his Eye in the form of Hathor to punish humankind.

In the guise of the lioness Sekhmet, Hathor perpetrated a savage slaughter. By the time she was recalled by Re, she had acquired an insatiable taste for blood and was determined to return to Earth to destroy the rest of humankind.

Re was alarmed. He had meant only to teach people a lesson, not to wipe them out. While Hathor rested, he sent messengers to Aswan to bring back a consignment of red ochre. He ordered the High Priest of Heliopolis to pound it. As this was done, the god ordered servant girls to brew barley beer. The two elements were mixed together to produce 7,000 jugs of an intoxicating drink that looked like blood. Re ordered the jugs to be emptied over the fields where Hathor had planned her destruction for the next day.

Hathor was taken in by the ruse. Flying over the fields, she saw what she thought to be blood and swooped down for a drink. She imbibed too much and fell into a stupor. On regaining her senses, she had forgotten her original aim and set off home again.

As a reconciliatory gesture, Re decreed that the Egyptian people could drink as much as they liked at Hathor's festivals, in commemoration of Hathor, Lady of Drunkenness.

Isis & the Name of the Sun God

The ancient Egyptians were firm believers in magic. The goddess Isis was considered to be especially potent in the magical arts, and one of her greatest coups came when she persuaded Re to divulge his secret name so that she held power over him.

Isis "was a clever woman," explained one story, "more intelligent than countless gods ... she was ignorant of nothing in heaven or on earth." She wanted to place herself and her son Horus at the head of the pantheon of gods and the only way to do this was to discover Re's secret name.

One day Isis came upon Re when he was asleep, snoring loudly. From the corner of his open mouth hung a long dribble of saliva which gathered weight and fell to the ground. Isis pounced: scooping up the spittle, she mixed it with clay in the form of a poisonous snake. Then she breathed magic into the snake to make it come alive.

Isis had noted Re's movements and knew that every so often he would leave his palace to go for a walk. Each time, on his route, he passed a crossroads. Isis left her snake there and awaited further developments.

Re emerged for his excursion, and – as Isis had planned – the snake bit him. Re saw nothing, but he felt the poison coursing through him. In pain, he called to the other gods for help. Re had a fever and was sweating and shivering, but the gods were helpless: they could do no more than mourn the impending loss of the sun.

Isis then made a dramatic entrance. She could cure him, she said, but only if he would tell her his name. Re refused. She offered again and again, but still he declined. Eventually his agony became so extreme that he could bear it no longer, and he agreed to give Isis the secret, on condition that she should tell it to no one other than her son, Horus. Isis accepted these terms, and speaking aloud the god's true name, she removed the poison. The sun god was cured at once, and Isis and Horus attained the power that they had sought.

Khonsu & the Princess of Hatti

In the late second millennium BCE, Egypt waged a long war with the Hittite empire. The conflict was ended finally in 1256 BCE by the marriage of Ramesses II to the daughter of the Hittite ruler, the king of Hatti. Ramesses bestowed upon his wife the name of Nefrure.

Shortly after the wedding a messenger arrived from the king of Hatti. He brought news that Nefrure's sister, Bentresh, was seriously ill. The pharaoh summoned his top physicians and magicians to ask them their opinion on what this disease might be. When they were unable to reach a diagnosis, he dispatched the royal doctor himself.

Three years later this doctor returned home. The princess, he announced, was possessed by evil spirits and only a god could cure her. Ramesses consulted the priests at the shrine of Khonsu in Thebes. The priests in turn put the question to Khonsu, whose statue nodded its head as a sign that he agreed to be taken to cure the princess.

However, in his role as protector of Thebes, the moon god Khonsu had to stay in his city. The priests therefore sought help from the other, subsidiary form of the god, "Khonsu-the-Expeller-of-Demons".

After a journey of seventeen months, Khonsu-the-Expeller-of-Demons reached the Hittite capital and cured Bentresh on the spot. Bentresh's father, however, was so impressed by the statue's power to heal that he refused to let it go and made a shrine for it in his own kingdom. For almost four years the statue stayed where it was until the king of Hatti was visited by a prophetic dream. In it the statue of Khonsu rose from its shrine in the form of a golden falcon and swooped down at the king before rising into the sky and heading for Egypt.

Realizing his error, the king sent the statue back to Thebes along with a huge tribute. The statue presented the senior Khonsu with the entire Hittite booty – without having even removed any items of treasure as recompense for the priests of its own shrine in Hatti.

The Festival of Bastet

Herodotus told of a festival held annually at the Delta city of Bubastis in honour of the goddess Bastet. His account was widely believed to be a fabrication until archaeologists discovered evidence to confirm that the event did take place.

Daughter of the sun god Re and mother of the moon god Khonsu, the feline deity Bastet was widely venerated throughout ancient Egypt. By the Late Period, Bastet's festival, held in April and May, was one of the most popular in the ritual calendar. For ceremonial purposes the town of Bubastis – fifty miles northeast of modern Cairo – was best approached by water. "They come in barges," wrote the ancient Greek historian Herodotus of the festival, "men and women together, a great number in each boat; on the way, some of the women keep up a continual clatter with castanets and some of the men play flutes, while the rest, both men and women, sing and clap their hands. Whenever they pass a town on the riverbank, they bring the barge close in-shore, some of the women continuing to act as I have said, while others shout abuse at the women of the place, or start dancing, or stand up and hitch their skirts. When they reach Bubastis, they celebrate the festival with elaborate sacrifices, and more wine is consumed than during all the rest of the year."

Herodotus recorded at least 700,000 people – "excluding children" – arriving in similar fashion to pay their respects at the red granite temple erected in honour of the goddess. Again, according to Herodotus, "Cats which have died are taken to Bubastis where they are embalmed and buried in sacred receptacles." Thousands of the dead creatures were mummified and interred in underground galleries here and at other sites so that they might carry their owners' messages all the more swiftly to the realm of the gods.

The sheer scale of the festival seemed incredible to early Egyptologists. But in 1887 a Swiss archaeologist called Henri Edouard Naville, excavating the site, discovered that Herodotus had indeed spoken the truth. He uncovered the site of Bubastis's main temple, the catacombs of mummified cats, and a number of pharaonic shrines which proved that even the highest born venerated Bastet.

Osiris, Lord of the Underworld

Osiris's main function was to rule the Underworld, but he also acted as a god of fertility and agriculture. One of the most enduring deities, he was worshipped throughout Egypt as patron of the dead, lord of the necropolis and the guarantor of rebirth.

Osiris was of prime importance in Egyptian mythology. As a god of fertility, he was seen as the life-force behind all things. Yet, at the same time, he was lord of the Underworld, and this combination of aspects led him to be identified with resurrection.

The connection was spelled out in the most resonant of all Egyptian myths. This told of a time when Osiris ruled the world beneficently with his sister–wife Isis as his consort. This happy state of affairs roused the jealousy of the monarch's brother Seth. According to the best-known version of the story, he constructed a wooden box – in effect, the first sarcophagus – to Osiris's exact measurements, and then at a feast challenged the guests to see who fitted it most closely. When Osiris took his turn to step inside, Seth slammed the lid shut, fastened it with lead, and threw the coffin into the River Nile.

Horrified by her husband's murder, Isis devoted herself to the task of finding his body. When she finally succeeded in tracking it down, Seth intervened again, this time dismembering the body and scattering the parts across Egypt. Isis once again set out on the trail. She eventually traced thirteen of the fourteen separate parts – all but the penis, which had been swallowed by a fish, so Isis had to fashion one from gold. Then she reassembled his scattered limbs in the form of the first mummy and used magical incantations so that his spirit could inhabit his body once again. The couple were reunited long enough for Isis to conceive the infant Horus, then Osiris had to return once more to his underworld domain to take up his duties as merciful judge of the dead.

Osiris's main cult centre was Abydos, in Upper Egypt, where his head was thought to be interred. Some priests went so far as to claim that the tomb of the First Dynasty monarch Djer, who ruled ca. 2900 BCE, was in fact Osiris's burial place. But the god was also described as "he who dwells in Heliopolis", which was the cult centre of Re, thereby linking him with the sun god.

Seth, Lord of Disorder

In very early times, Seth was worshipped at his cult centre, Naqada, and because he was associated with the frightening desert sandstorms of the region, it was important to appease him. He ultimately became a lord of misrule and chaos.

Like most Egyptian gods, Seth was often pictured with the head of an animal – usually the strange "Seth beast", an imaginary creature with a vague resemblance to an ant-eater. Sometimes he was depicted as one of the animals considered to be "unclean" by the Egyptians – such as the hippopotamus or the pig.

As lord of disorder, Seth was the enemy of Horus and the organized world that Horus stood for. This enmity was part of the Egyptian order, a darkness against which the divine light could shine.

For all his villainy, Seth's antecedents were impeccable: as the son of sky goddess Nut, he matched in status his brother Osiris and his sisters Isis and Nephthys (the latter was also one of his wives). Indeed, his strength and rank among the gods gained him Re's support during much of his bitter struggle with Horus. After his defeat on Earth, he journeyed with the sun god during the hours of the night, defending him against the serpent Apophis.

Seth's immense strength and his forceful sexuality guaranteed him the devotion of at least a minority of mortals. Although rarely a popular god, he did have his good points: an appeal to Seth, the lord of chaos, might help keep bad weather away. Indeed, at one point in Egypt's history, during the Nineteenth and Twentieth Dynasties (1292–1075 BCE), he enjoyed a period of general worship and respect.

But Seth was always a dangerous god to venerate. Later dynasties characterized him as the god of harm, and he generally came to be regarded as the personification of evil-doing.

Isis & the Seven Scorpions

Having murdered Osiris, the husband and brother of Isis, their evil sibling Seth kept the goddess and her young son Horus as hostages. One night the captives broke free with the aid of the god Thoth, who provided an escort of seven scorpions to assist them in their daring escape.

The goddess Isis faced great hardships in tracking down the pieces of her dismembered husband Osiris so that she could magically resuscitate him (see page 24). Yet her trials were not over even then, for he died for a second time soon after he had made her pregnant with the child Horus. Then, in her renewed widowhood, she fell into the hands of her husband's killer. Her evil brother Seth imprisoned her, ordering her to weave a shroud for Osiris, who had returned once more to the Underworld kingdom from which Isis's magic had temporarily summoned him.

Yet even at this low point in her fortunes, Isis had friends among the gods. The wise Thoth saw her plight and determined to assist her. Freeing her from the linen mill where she was held, he provided her with an escort of seven scorpions, who each swore to protect the goddess and her unborn son from Seth's vengeance.

The strange band set off for the marshes of the Nile Delta. On their way they came to a village, where Isis determined to seek food and shelter. The first house that she approached belonged to a wealthy noblewoman who, not recognizing the goddess, slammed the door in her face. Unabashed, Isis soon found a poor peasant girl who welcomed her into her humble home.

The scorpions, however, were enraged by the rich woman's treatment of the goddess, and so they prepared to avenge their mistress. One of them crept into the noblewoman's house and stung her young son. As the boy lay dying, his mother ran through the streets crying for help; but in payment for her earlier inhospitality, no one came to her aid.

Isis, however, took pity on the boy, not wishing to see him suffer on his mother's account, and so she cast a powerful spell over him to neutralize the poison. The child recovered at once. His mother, truly repentant, gave all her belongings to Isis and the kindly peasant girl.

Thoth & the Eye of Horus

The conflict between the gods Horus and Seth raged for many decades. On one level it was a struggle in which a son sought just revenge on his father's killer, on another a cosmic struggle to restore universal order.

Born to the knowledge that his father Osiris had been killed by Seth, Horus was fated to be an agent of divine vengeance. From the time of his early manhood he devoted all his efforts to bringing his wicked uncle to justice and thereby restoring order to the world.

The contest between the two gods, one in the prime of his youth and the other still mighty both in strength and cunning, was an epic one that lasted for many decades. At one time Horus, with his mother Isis's help, was on the point of killing Seth when Isis had a sudden change of heart, intervening in her mercy to save Seth's life. In his battle-frenzy Horus turned his wrath on his mother, attacking her savagely and so rousing the anger of the other gods. Swinging wildly with his copper knife, he even managed to sever her head, although as Mistress of Magic Isis was quickly able to repair the damage.

Ashamed of his act, Horus fled into the wilderness while the gods scoured the Earth in search of the miscreant. It was Seth who found him, resting beside an oasis. His old enemy took the form of a black boar to launch his attack. Before Horus knew what was happening, Seth had gouged out his left eye and tossed it beyond the edge of the world. Horus retaliated by ripping off one of Seth's testicles. Given that the two opponents were gods, the injuries had cosmic connotations: Horus's left eye was the Moon, whose light was thereby lost to the world, while Seth's partial emasculation was subsequently used to explain the infertility of the desert, with which he had been associated from early times.

Meanwhile, with the Moon gone, the Earth was plunged each nightfall into the deepest darkness. With disaster threatening, the wise, ibis-headed Thoth came to the rescue. Ever the peacemaker during the conflict between the two rivals, he now scoured the chaos beyond the world's confines until he discovered the missing eye. It had been shattered by its fall, but Thoth pieced it together and restored it to its owner, thereby bringing light back to the night sky. The Eye of Horus was subsequently represented by the *wedjat* amulet, a protective symbol against all forms of evil.

The Wives of Seth

Following Seth's long and unsuccessful battle with Horus for the Egyptian throne, the goddess Neith suggested to the council of gods that Seth be awarded a loser's prize: the "foreign" daughters of Re, named Anat and Astarte, were offered to him as his wives.

One day as Seth was walking by the Nile, he came across the goddess Anat, bathing in the stream. He changed himself into a ram and raped her. But Anat could only be impregnated by divine fire, and so her body expelled his semen with such force that it struck him in the forehead, making him dangerously ill. Seth was relieved of his punishing headache by Re, whom Isis sent to cure him.

In another myth, of which only a part has ever been found, the gods of Egypt were in conflict with the sea god Yamm, and were coming off worse. Yamm demanded tribute of gold, silver and lapis lazuli, which was duly brought to him by the goddess Renenutet. However, having received these treasures, he became greedy for more, and insisted on further tribute. He threatened that, if his demands were not met, he would enslave every god in Egypt. In despair, Renenutet pleaded for help from Astarte, who was famed both for her beauty and her ferocity. The messenger, in the shape of a bird, begged Astarte to carry the extra tribute to Yamm. Reluctantly, Astarte agreed. But when she reached the shoreline, her fiery nature got the better of her and she began to taunt the sea god. Alternately outraged by her impudence and bewitched by her alluring features, Yamm demanded that he be given Astarte as well as the treasure. The goddess Renenutet retired to deliberate with the gods, who acceded to the sea god's demands and furnished Astarte with a dowry consisting of Nut's necklace and Geb's signet ring.

Seth, however, rebelled at the loss of his beautiful wife. Tantalizingly, the remainder of the story is lost. But the outcome, surely, was that, whether by force or by guile, Seth overcame the sea god, saved Egypt's pantheon from slavery, and reclaimed Astarte.

Siosire & the Sorcerer of Nubia

One day, a haughty Nubian appeared before the court of King Ramesses II in Memphis, and issued a challenge to the best scholars of Egypt, testing their abilities in magic. Holding a sealed papyrus up to the king, he asked "Can anyone here read this letter without opening it?"

Perplexed by the Nubian's challenge and fearing humiliation, Ramesses called for Prince Setna, the most learned of his sons. Setna, too, was baffled; but, rather than admit defeat, he asked for ten days' grace to wrestle with the problem.

Setna had no idea how to read the strange letter, and simply fretted anxiously at home. When his young son Siosire tried to comfort him, he said "You are only twelve. A child cannot help me here." Eventually, however, Siosire persuaded his father to explain the problem. "But that's easy," laughed the boy. "I can do that!" He asked Setna to bring him a papyrus scroll. As the boy promised, he was able to read it while his father held it still rolled up.

The next day Siosire went with his father to meet the pharaoh and the arrogant Nubian. At once, the boy proceeded to read from the scroll tied to the Nubian's belt. And what he read shocked the court.

It was a tale from the distant past, when the prince of Nubia had used the powers of his magician Sa-Neheset to bring Egypt's pharaoh to the Nubian court. There he received a brutal and shameful beating. The pharaoh in turn sought magical aid from his own master-magician, Sa-Paneshe, and the struggle between the two nations turned into a battle of wills between two great magicians, which Sa-Paneshe eventually won.

The young Siosire reached the end of his reading. "Now, O king," said the boy, "I can tell you why this Nubian is here. For he is Sa-Neheset, born again. But I, too, have been reborn: I am Sa-Paneshe, and I challenge him once again!" For hours the sorcerers fought spell against spell, the one seeking to destroy Egypt's court, the other to save it. At last, Siosire (or Sa-Paneshe) sent a fire-spell the other could not resist, and Sa-Neheset was consumed in flames.

The Enchanted Island

On his return from an unsuccessful trade mission in Nubia, an Egyptian envoy bemoaned his misfortune – provoking a sailor to console him by telling a tale that began with tragedy but ended happily.

An unnamed sailor was on a voyage on the Red Sea, destined for the royal mines. His 200-foot-long vessel was well appointed, and stoutly manned by more than a hundred crewmen. But then the sky suddenly darkened and a violent storm overwhelmed the ship. She vanished beneath the waves, as did everyone on board – except the narrator.

The survivor managed to stay afloat, bobbing on the now calm surface of the sea, but he was beginning to lose strength. Just in time he found himself washed ashore on an island that had all the appearance of an earthly paradise: it was overflowing with fruits and vegetables, and all the fish and fowl the hungry sailor could wish for. However, a giant serpent, with a body of gold and eyebrows of lapis lazuli, also lived there. The monster threatened the sailor with instant incineration if he did not explain his arrival. But the sailor was rigid with fear. The serpent took him to its lair, whereupon the sailor recounted his tale. The serpent then told its own sorry story. "Once, there were seventy-five snakes here," it said, "including all my kin. But a burning star fell and killed all of them except me. Fate will be kinder to you. A ship will arrive in four months, and you will return safely to your home."

The ship arrived as the snake had promised, and the sailor boarded it, laden with gifts from the now friendly monster. On his return home, the king was so pleased that he made the voyager a royal attendant and granted him many servants.

The Turquoise Pendant

In the second of the three tales of wonder contained in the Westcar Papyrus, Prince Baufre tells of his father's father, King Snofru, and Snofru's lector priest Djadjaemankh.

The day was especially hot. Bored to distraction, King Snofru summoned Djadjaemankh, one of his lector priests, and demanded entertainment. Djadjaemankh (whose name translates as "He who carries the ritual book") came up with a plan. The king should go out in a boat on the palace lake, where he could cool off and take in the beauty of the scenery. To add to Snofru's enjoyment, it was suggested that the boat be rowed by twenty of the most attractive girls from the royal harem.

The king's downcast visage brightened at once. "Let the boat be fitted with gilded oars of ebony and sandalwood," he ordered enthusiastically. The girls were instructed to replace their regular linen shifts with nets of faience beads that scarcely concealed their curves.

At first, all went well. The king reclined happily, enjoying the flowers, the birds and the fish of his lake, but devoting most of his attention to the efforts of his scantily clad crew. After a while, however, the leading rower inadvertently dropped the fine turquoise pendant she wore in her braided hair into the lake. She cried out in dismay, and the rowing stopped. The poor girl was distraught at her loss. Indulgently, the king offered to replace the lost pendant from his own abundant reserves of turquoise, but the girl insisted that nothing other than the return of her own ornament would satisfy her.

"Djadjaemankh!" called the king. "Solve the problem." The lector priest bowed, and at once uttered a powerful spell. Instantly, the waters of the lake rolled back to reveal the amulet lying safely on the dry bed. Djadjaemankh retrieved it, climbed back to the lake bank and used another spell to return the lake to its former level.

Snofru was deeply impressed by Djadjaemankh's prodigious powers and rewarded the servant with riches. The girl put her amulet back in her hair, and the rowing party continued throughout a long and happy afternoon.

Mesopotamia

Mesopotamia may not have had the world's earliest myths, but it was almost certainly the first place where myths were written down. The Sumerian people invented cuneiform writing there around 3500 BCE, and by 2500 the script was being used to bring tales of legend out of the oral tradition.

The stories that the Sumerians (and their Akkadian successors in what is now southern Iraq) recorded told of the epic activities of a multiplicity of rival gods. Some deities may have originated as elemental forces, but others were associated with specific towns, where their statues were cared for and venerated in temples. In a world of competing city-states, the status of individual divinities rose and fell with the fortunes of the locales they represented. The myths recounted the gods' rivalries, which sometimes set son against father in intergenerational strife, as happened in the ruling dynasties of the day (see page 37).

Chief among the elemental forces was the sky god An or Anu. Other important figures included the storm god Enlil, who was also connected with agricultural fertility; the goddess Inana, linked with both sexuality and war; and the divine craftsman Enki, treated in one Sumerian poem both as a creator deity and a culture hero responsible for blessing the world with bountiful harvests as well as the arts of building and weaving (see page 35).

Creation myths seem to have varied from city to city across the Mesopotamian plain. Today the best known is the one contained in the epic poem known from its opening words as the

Enuma Elish (literally, "When on high ..."). Dating perhaps from as early as 1900 BCE but written down in its present form around 1100, it was effectively a work of propaganda celebrating Marduk, the city god of Babylon. Even relatively unimportant centres, however, like the otherwise obscure Dunnu, had origin stories of their own (see page 34).

Ritual life revolved around festivals in which the gods' statues were paraded outside the temples that were their homes. Sometimes the images were borne on barges along the waterways that were the main thoroughfares of Mesopotamia (the region's name translates as the "Land between Rivers", referring to its two great arteries, the Tigris and Euphrates). One such progress is celebrated in the story of the moon god Nanna's journey from Ur to Nippur (see page 36).

Mesopotamia may have been first to write down its myths, but many other areas of the Middle East's Fertile Crescent had traditions of their own. The names of the gods differed from land to land, but in other respects neighbouring mythologies often reflected common themes. One such body of myth came to light only after 1928, when a farmer in the Syrian village of Ras Shamra uncovered an ancient tomb. Subsequent investigation turned up the remains of the ancient port city of Ugarit, part of the culture known to Old Testament scholars as Canaanite. Among the discoveries were thousands of inscribed clay tablets, some containing mythological material.

The principal male deities of Ugarit were the sky god El and the storm god Baal, quite as hot-blooded as his Mesopotamian equivalent Enlil, as the story of his challenge to Mot (Death) shows (see page 38). Inana's counterpart was Anat, who like her Sumerian cousin was associated not just with sexual fertility but also with bloodshed (see page 39). She in turn has been linked with the goddess Astarte, known across the Middle East in early classical times.

Another link was provided by the Hittites of Anatolia, at the Fertile Crescent's northernmost tip. Their storm deity Teshub ruled the heavens as a mighty but unpredictable tyrant who needed to be constantly appeased by his earthly subjects. His duties included looking after the welfare of the sun god Simige (see page 40), whose activities were as vital as Teshub's rain-making to the well-being of Hittite farmers struggling to raise crops in a sun-parched land.

The Gods of Dunnu

In order to create and dominate the world, the gods resorted to incest and patricide. This common mythological motif appears in a Mesopotamian tale that explains the origin of the gods. A minor city called Dunnu provides a backdrop to this dramatic story.

In the beginning, there was the Plough and the Earth; from their union they created the Sea. Soon after, the Cattle God and the eternal city of Dunnu came into being. The Cattle God then made love to his mother the Earth, killed his father the Plough and married his sister the Sea. The same pattern was repeated in the following generation: the Cattle God's son, the God of Flocks, likewise killed his father and married his mother the Sea. For generation after generation a series of male gods, some of them named after the flocks and herds which roamed the land, killed their fathers and married their sisters or mothers, who often represented features of the landscape such as a river, tree or meadow.

Although many details remain obscure, the story can be interpreted as representing the changes of the seasons during the year, each one "killing" or replacing the previous one. Eventually, however, the pattern altered dramatically: one of the gods, instead of killing his father so that he could take over his dominion and marry his mother, merely imprisoned him. This happened at New Year, celebrated by the Babylonians during April, which might suggest that this song was recited at the New Year festival. But because the rest of the text is missing, the significance of this interruption in the cycle of patricides has been obscured.

This myth reinforces the general impression given by the *Enuma Elish* that creation stories were often highly politicized and that they served to glorify a particular city by giving it a pivotal role in the story. In this version of creation, as each god is killed he is laid to rest in Dunnu, a city that was dearly loved by each dead god. Thus, the birth of the world is closely linked to the establishment of the most important social and political institution of all – the city.

Enki, Creator of the World Order

Whereas the *Enuma Elish* credits Marduk as the central figure in the creation and regulation of the world, in an earlier Sumerian source everything is established by Marduk's father Enki, the divine craftsman who presided over life-giving fresh water.

Enki blessed the cities of Nippur, "the place where the gods are born", Ur, Meluhha and Dilmun (probably Bahrain) with abundant crops, flocks, precious metals and success in war. Then he organized the sea, rivers, clouds and rain, turning the barren hills into fields and creating the rivers Tigris and Euphrates by filling their beds with a stream of his own semen. He made the sheep, cattle and crops multiply, and established the skills of building and weaving.

As Enki created each domain, he appointed a god to supervise it. But when he had finished, Inana came to him complaining that he had failed to give her a domain. She described the realms of Nintu the womb-goddess, Nidaba the goddess of surveying, and Nanshe the goddess of the fisheries, and asked plaintively, "As for me, the holy Inana, what is my domain?"

Enki responded by listing the numerous powers and dominions which Inana did indeed have, adding each time, "Young Inana, what more could we add for you?" He reminded her of her dominion not only of the shepherd's crook and staff, but of the bloody business of battle, and certain kinds of cloth and musical instruments that were linked to war, death and funeral rites as well. Enki concluded that Inana's domain was substantial, and finally he told her, "Inana, you have the power to destroy what cannot be destroyed, and to set up what cannot be set up."

A Bountiful Harvest

Several poems describe a god's journey or procession by barge. These accounts probably relate to real-life rituals in which statues of gods were ferried from their home cities to a site of pilgrimage where they received a blessing.

In the springtime, a barge bearing the year's first yield of dairy produce would set out from the city of Ur. At the city of Nippur the goods would be exchanged for produce made by the herders of the south around Ur and those of cultivators in the north around Nippur.

The patron god of Ur was the moon god Nanna (also called Suen or Sin). In a mythical version of this ritual, Nanna decided to visit his parents Enlil and Ninlil at Nippur. He sent men to all the corners of the Earth to gather materials for building a barge and rejoiced as they returned one by one with precious cargos of exotic woods. Nanna then prepared a rich array of gifts for his parents and set off on his journey.

On the way upstream, Nanna stopped at five different cities. At each stop, the patron goddess of the city, seeing his abundant cargo, would welcome him and press him to stay, but at each stop he refused, saying, "I am going on to Nippur."

Finally, the barge docked at the quayside in Nippur and Nanna announced the full list of his offerings to his father's doorkeeper, who was delighted and opened the gates to the temple. Enlil was similarly overjoyed by his son's arrival and staged a banquet, offering him his best beer. In return for his herders' gifts, Nanna asked Enlil for a blessing and some produce from the local fields. Enlil gave him all that he asked for and in great joy Nanna took these blessings home to Ur.

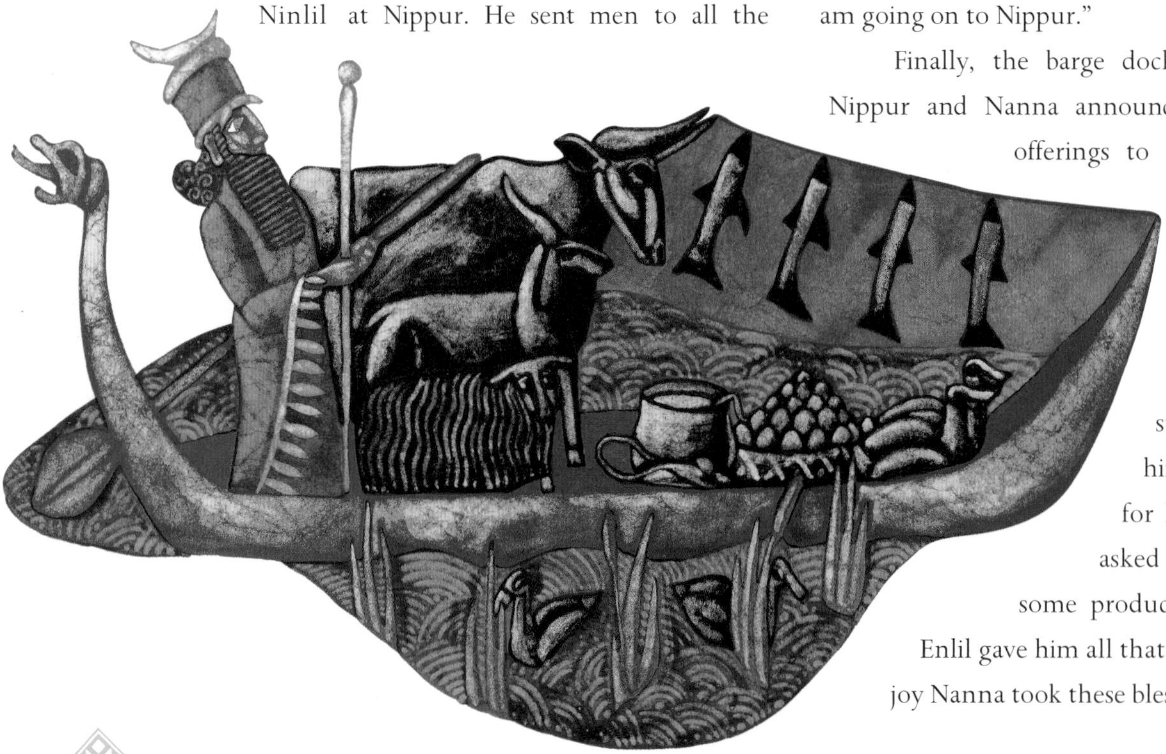

Arrogant Ninurta

This story pokes fun at Ninurta, the god of the thunderstorm, the flood and the plough, who is taught a lesson in humility by his father Enki with the help of a turtle.

To Enki's horror, the formidable Anzu bird stole the precious Tablet of Destinies from his custody. Ninurta attacked the bird and made him drop the tablet back into the *apsu*, Enki's watery domain. Enki was delighted and praised Ninurta as the great conqueror of Anzu, saying that his name would be honoured for ever.

But Ninurta was not satisfied with this blessing. He decided that he wanted to take over the whole universe, and the key to this plan lay with the Tablet of Destinies, which bestowed supreme power on its holder. But Enki guessed what was in Ninurta's heart. As a warning, he stirred up the waves of his *apsu* and sent his minister Isimu to see his son. But Ninurta's arrogance was so great that he even dared to raise his hand against Isimu.

This was too much for Enki. In exasperation, he moulded some clay from the *apsu* to form a turtle. Giving it life, he set it to work scraping out a deep pit with its strong claws. When Ninurta continued to threaten him, Enki retreated gradually toward the trap. Suddenly, the turtle came out from behind him and seized Ninurta, while Enki gave him a shove into the pit.

Ninurta was unable to climb out of the hole. Enki stood on the edge of the pit and looked down at Ninurta far below, where he was still being clawed by the turtle. "You were planning to kill me," he mocked loudly, "you with your big ideas! You have tamed mountains and now you can't even climb out of a pit dug by a turtle! What kind of a hero are you?"

Fortunately for Ninurta, his mother Ninhursaga saw what was happening. She stopped to reprimand Enki and reminded him of a time she had saved his life when he had eaten poisonous plants. "What about you, you plant-eater?", she demanded, "I saved you, so now save your son!"

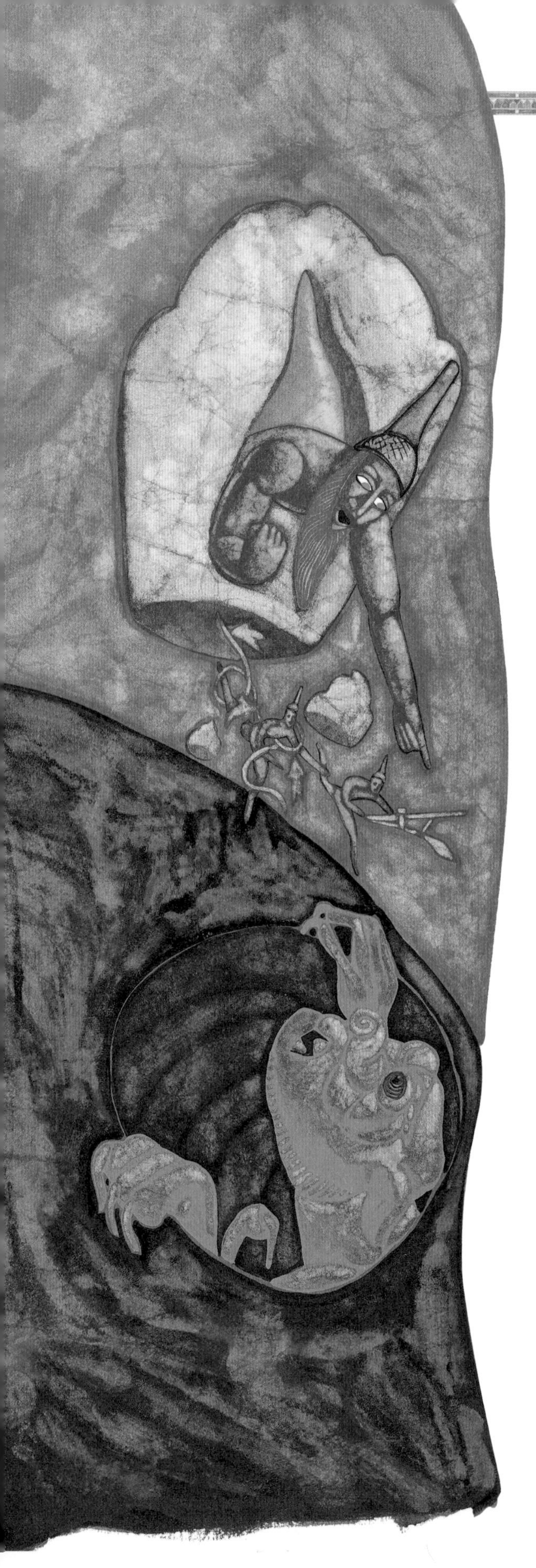

Defying Death

After initially opposing the idea, the Ugaritic storm god Baal agreed to include a window in the design for his new palace. His decision was to lead to a confrontation with Mot (Death).

The divine craftsman Kothar wa-Hasis suggested a window in the royal palace and Baal opposed him. Baal was concerned that his daughters, Dew and Mist, would escape from the palace and fly away. Later Baal must have changed his mind and opted to have a window installed, which provoked words of reproach from Kothar wa-Hasis: "Did I not tell you, Baal, that you would come back to my words?"

The final building did contain a window but its inclusion was to prove a terrible mistake. Although the opening allowed Baal to manifest his power over fertility by pouring rain onto the Earth, it also exposed him to Death, who, it was commonly believed, could only enter a house through a window.

When Baal returned from a triumphal tour of his kingdom, he decided to open the window by making a gap in the clouds. Shouting through the opening, Baal managed to make the Earth below shake as he flung out a defiant challenge to Death: "Enemies of Baal, why do you tremble? Will any king or non-king establish himself on this Earth where I am sovereign? I alone reign among the gods, I alone feed the multitudes on Earth and make them fat!" Baal followed up his challenge by sending two messengers, Gapan (Vine) and Ugar (Ploughed Field), down to Mot's realm in the Underworld. Baal gave his messengers careful instructions for their dangerous mission. "Go down into the dismal, desolate land where Mot reigns. But be careful as you approach him: don't give him a chance to seize you like lambs in his jaws. Go and tell him I have built my palace of gold and silver." The remainder of his message, like the account of the messengers' journey itself, is lost. But the boastful mention of Baal's splendid new palace with its window suggests that the tone was provocative and led to further confrontations between Baal and Death.

Anat, the Bloodthirsty Goddess

The goddess Anat, often identified with Astarte, is the Ugaritic form of a deity who was recognized throughout the ancient Near East. Despite being associated with both sexual love and fertility, in one story she perpetrates a frenzy of bloodshed which led to numerous deaths.

In an episode that can only be described as a digression in the Baal cycle, Anat indulges in two massacres.

The tale begins with Anat's extermination of the populations of two neighbouring cities. Raising her scythe high above her, she stood astride a pile of severed human heads strewn like reaped corn. With mutilated hands flying around her, she wallowed up to her thighs in human blood.

Then she invited an army of soldiers to her palace and slaughtered them as they sat at her dinner table. After calmly rearranging the tables and chairs, she washed and purified herself in Baal's rain and dew.

Baal then spoke to Anat of the powers of his rain and its link to human sexuality. "Lay out delicious fruits of the Earth," he told her, "encourage marriages throughout the land, spread love over the Earth. Hasten to me and I shall tell you something of which the trees speak and the stones whisper, of which the heavens murmur to the Earth and the abyss murmurs to the stars. I know the secret of lightning, unknown to humankind."

This passage may refer to a "sacred marriage" or ritualized sexual union between Anat and Baal, which is described in explicit language in other, more fragmentary texts. It has also been suggested that the vicious massacres by the goddess represent a fertility sacrifice. However, the true interpretation of the story remains uncertain.

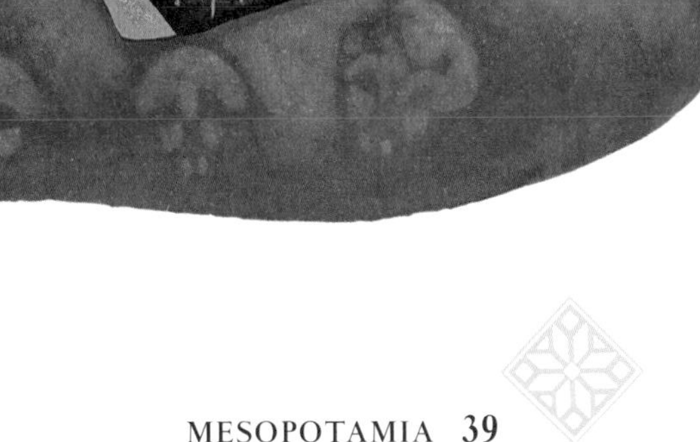

Telipinu & the Sea God's Daughter

The disappearance of the sun god is a common theme in the Hittite myths. In this tale, the mighty deity is dragged down to the depths of the ocean, resulting in devastation on the land.

One day, the sea god found himself quarrelling with the sun god. In his fury, the sea god dragged his rival from the sky to hide him away in the ocean depths. With the sun's disappearance, the land was plunged into darkness. This caused the crops to fail, and famine and hardship reigned.

The storm god Teshub called to his eldest son Telipinu. "You must go to the sea where you will find the sun god. Bring him back so that we can return him to the sky." Telipinu obeyed his father and journeyed to the sea. Seeing the young god draw near, the sea god grew afraid, and offered Telipinu his daughter in marriage, before handing over the kidnapped sun god.

Telipinu returned to the Earth with his bride, and positioned the sun god in the sky. With the sun's light and warmth, the crops grew again, livestock bred and humankind thrived.

But that was not the end. The sea god sent a river with a message to Teshub: "Your son Telipinu took my daughter away with him as his wife. What bride-price are you going to pay me?" Teshub turned to the mother goddess Hannahanna for advice. "The sea god is demanding his bride-price," he told her. "Should I give it to him?" Hannahanna's response was clear: "Of course," she said. "Telipinu took his daughter, the sea god is entitled to his payment." So Teshub gave the sea god a thousand cattle and a thousand sheep, and thus harmony was restored.

The Sun God & the Fisherman

This fragment of a longer tale, now lost, provides a revealing portrait of relations among the gods, animals and man – and affords an intriguing glimpse of the Hittites' wry humour as well as customs surrounding the arrival of new members of the family.

Simige, the sun god, looked down from the sky to see a cow grazing and was filled with desire. Descending to the Earth in the form of a young man, he accosted the cow and demanded to know by what right it grazed in his meadow. He then caught the cow and coupled with it, and nine months later the cow gave birth.

Shocked to discover that her calf had only two legs, the cow tried to kill and eat it, but the sun god, watching from above, intervened. He seized his son, removed him to safety, stroked him tenderly and then left him on a grassy mound, surrounded by poisonous snakes as guards.

A childless fisherman happened to pass by. He rejoiced to find the baby he had so much longed for, and gave thanks to Simige for his good fortune. He took the child home, where his wife was equally delighted. Even in this moment of joy, however, they saw an opportunity to profit: "Take this child into the bedroom, lie down on the bed and wail," said the fisherman to his wife. "The whole city will hear you and assume that you've given birth. Then one person will bring us bread, another will bring beer, and someone else will bring us fat." Sure enough the community responded: "The fisherman's wife has had a baby!" the cry went up. The town flocked to the couple's house, and overwhelmed them with gifts.

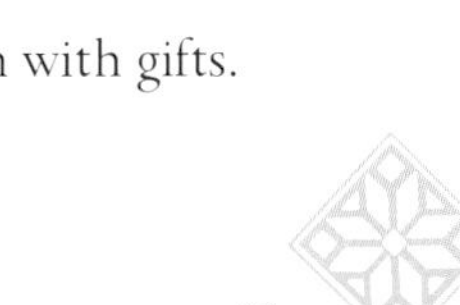

Greece and Rome

Many cultures have myths, but not all mythologies have equal resonance. None has had greater influence than that of the classical world, which has played a huge role in the Western imagination, inspiring writers and artists to the present day.

The classical myths owe their enduring appeal to their epic scope and poetic truth. Yet they did not come out of nowhere; throughout the long history of classical Greece and imperial Rome, foreign influences played a part in shaping the tales. Some gods, like Dionysus, were imported from abroad; the story of Iphigenia's escape from the Crimea bearing the cult statue of the goddess Artemis may hint at another such transfer (see page 55). At other times foreign cults like that of Isis won adherents in the classical world, and even the tale of Io's transformation into a heifer and subsequent flight to the banks of the Nile may reflect stories of the Egyptian cow-goddess Hathor (see page 47).

Whatever borrowings there may have been, though, the corpus of classical myth eventually outstripped all its neighbours in the breadth of its span and its sheer narrative inventiveness. The stories embraced tales of gods, as their Middle Eastern counterparts did, but also legends of heroes; human epitomes of courage, strength and resourcefulness played a greater part in them than in any previous canon.

Hero myths were by no means exclusive to Greece and Rome; they had obvious Middle Eastern predecessors, most notably the Sumerian *Epic of Gilgamesh*. Nevertheless, they formed a distinctive feature of the classical corpus. Mostly conforming to a set pattern that gave the hero a prodigy-filled childhood, an adult quest or time of trial, and a tragic end, they spanned the gap between the human and superhuman worlds. Achilles' mother was a semi-divine sea-nymph (see page 56), yet he made his reputation as a warrior in the semi-historical context of the Trojan War.

Sometimes the stories set out to point an obvious moral: that overbold ambition could lead to a fall, as quite literally happened in the tale of Helios and Phaethon (see page 44), or, as repeated myths made clear, that humans failed at their peril to show fitting respect to the gods. Others had an expository role, seeking to explain natural phenomena like the dangers of the narrow Straits of Messina (see page 46) or even man-made marvels like the massive walls of the cities of Mycenaean antiquity, credited to a past race of one-eyed giants (see page 60).

A lasting strength of classical mythology, however, is its lack of predictability and its constant ability to surprise. Its gods may have been superhuman embodiments of human virtues such as power, beauty and wisdom, but they also had the weaknesses of mortals. In particular they were extravagantly prey to lust, as many stories ranging from Zeus's seduction of Europa and Io to Apollo's pursuit of Daphne suggested. Human heroes too were sometimes shown with feet of clay. Theseus, slayer of the Minotaur, abandoned his helper Ariadne without explanation in the course of his flight from Crete (see page 52). The galaxy of champions assembled to hunt the monstrous Calydonian boar succeeded in their task, but most nonetheless came to a bad end, destroyed by their own vanities and lack of humility before their divine helpers (see page 51).

For the enduring appeal of the classical canon turns above all on the psychological realism of the stories, and their success in addressing great themes that have lost none of their relevance with the passage of time. No myth has dealt more movingly with the pain of bereavement than the tale of Orpheus and Eurydice (see page 48); Antigone's defiance of her uncle King Creon in the matter of the burial of her brother remains a classic statement of the clash between natural justice and state authority (see page 53). Narratives such as these retain their power to move people to this day, bearing witness to the continuing vitality of the culture that gave them birth.

Helios & Phaethon

The Titans and their offspring played a role in establishing the natural order on Earth. Helios, the son of the Titan sun god Hyperion and his partner Theia, drove the chariot of the sun across the sky.

Phaethon was the son of Helios. His friends refused to believe that he was the son of a god, and even though his mother swore that it was true, the boy was not reassured. So his mother advised him to visit Helios and ask him directly.

Phaethon travelled to Helios's magnificent palace to find out the truth. At first the boy could not approach his father because he was dazzled by the solar rays the god wore on his head. Putting the rays aside, Helios greeted his son with great affection and rashly promised to give the boy anything he wanted. Phaethon immediately asked to drive the chariot of the sun for one day.

Although Helios tried desperately to dissuade him, Phaethon was insistent, and Helios was bound by the promise he had made. He coated his son's face in an oil to protect his skin against the heat of the solar rays and tried to teach him the correct way to drive the chariot, but Phaethon was too impatient to listen.

The boy set out boldly, but as the horses rose into the sky they sensed their driver's inexperience and bolted downwards. The terrified boy could not control the chariot and the horses drew the vehicle ever lower, searing much of the Earth with the sun's heat. The Nubian desert, once a fertile land, never recovered from this event, and the peoples of the south were so badly scorched that their skins turned black.

Seeing that the Earth risked total destruction, the gods blasted Phaethon, whose body crashed to Earth in flames. To save other lands from devastation, the gods cooled the world with a drenching cloudburst.

Europa & the Bull

Zeus was famous for his sexual adventures, and many of the stories of classical mythology start with his seduction of a mortal woman. For example, the city of Thebes was said to have been founded as a result of Zeus's desire for Europa, daughter of the king of Phoenicia.

One day Princess Europa went with her friends to gather flowers in a meadow beside the ocean. The group of laughing girls in the hot sunshine was a charming sight, and most delightful of all was Europa herself. She was so appealing that Zeus could not resist her. But knowing everything, he was aware that she was as pure as she was beautiful, and that he would be able to seduce her only through subterfuge.

In the meadows where the girls played, a herd of handsome cows was grazing peacefully. One of the girls noticed a new bull in the herd – a more beautiful, stronger and larger specimen than any they had ever seen. The princess went up to the animal and, despite its strength and size, it turned out to be gentle and playful. It knelt down and she climbed on its back.

Hardly had Europa settled on the bull's shoulders than it charged into the ocean; the princess was out of her depth and all she could do was cling on tightly.

Only when they came ashore on the island of Crete did Zeus reveal to her his true identity. Europa was unable to resist him and eventually bore him three sons, Minos, Rhadamanthus and Sarpedon.

Back in Phoenicia her family continued to mourn their loss. Finally, Europa's brother Cadmus, feeling compelled to take action, set out and wandered over all the world seeking his lovely sister. But he never discovered where Zeus had hidden her. Unable to return home and face his father's profound grief, he built a new city in Greece: Thebes.

Scylla & Charybdis

The channel between Italy and Sicily is dangerous for sailors, with unexpected whirlpools and currents. These natural phenomena inspired tales of Scylla and Charybdis, terrors of the Straits of Messina.

Scylla was a beautiful nymph to whom Poseidon, god of the oceans, became irresistibly drawn, at which Amphitrite, his wife, was seized by jealousy. To punish her rival, she secretly poured the juice of some poisonous herbs into the waters of the fountain where Scylla often bathed.

As soon as the nymph stepped into the pool she was transformed into a monster with twelve feet and six heads, each one with a mouth containing three rows of teeth; the lower part of her body was turned into a pack of dogs who barked incessantly. Terrified and appalled by her new form, Scylla hurled herself from the cliffs at the southern tip of Italy, but even this did not end her suffering. The gods confined her to a cave in the cliffs, from which she snapped at any vessels that came near her, snatching men from the decks.

Sailors were unable to avoid Scylla by steering a course further out to sea, because there Charybdis – once a woman, now a vicious whirlpool – lay in wait. She was the daughter of Poseidon and Gaia, but despite this noble heritage, she was greedy, and had tried to steal Heracles' precious oxen. Heracles complained to Zeus, his father, who struck her with a thunderbolt. She fell into the sea and continued life as a whirlpool, which three times a day sucked down vast quantities of seawater and three times a day spewed it out again. Her greedy maw could pull whole ships down into the depths.

And so "caught between Scylla and Charybdis" became a saying used to describe anyone trapped between two dangerous choices, where to avoid one peril means inevitably confronting another.

The Wanderings of Io

In the story of Zeus's affair with Io, the divine messenger Hermes played a typical role, helping the god out of a difficult situation. The story may reflect myths of Hathor, the cow-headed goddess of ancient Egypt, which were brought back to Greece by early travellers.

Like many beautiful mortals, Io, a priestess of Hera, had been seduced by Zeus, Hera's husband and the king of the gods. Hera herself came upon the couple one day as they dallied in a meadow. Zeus turned his lover into a heifer, hoping that the harmless-looking beast would escape his wife's jealous attention. But Hera at once suspected trickery, and insisted on taking the animal for herself. She led it to her cult site in the Peloponnese peninsula, where she entrusted it for safe-keeping to her monstrous servant, the hundred-eyed Argus Panoptes, who was said never to close all his eyes at once.

To recover his mistress, Zeus turned for help to Hermes, messenger of the gods and also an accomplished musician. Disguising himself as a goatherd he approached Argus, playing such sweet music on his flute that the giant dozed off. As his last eye closed, Hermes saw his chance; snatching up a boulder, he killed him with a single blow to the head. As a memorial to her watchman, Hera later placed Argus's eyes in the peacock's tail.

Meanwhile, Hera had witnessed Hermes' act of violence. Furious, she sent a gadfly to torment the cow, which ran off in a wild flight to escape the insect's stings. Having first swum the Bosphorus, which took its name, meaning "ox passage", from the feat, the beast eventually reached the sea that was later known as the Ionian. Leaping in, it swam all the way to Egypt.

Io's luck changed when she reached Egypt. She was restored to human shape by Zeus, and in due course bore him a son, Epaphus, and a daughter, Keroessa. After the god's interest in her had waned, she subsequently married an Egyptian king. In later times, mythographers would suggest that her story might originally have been inspired by second-hand accounts of Hathor, the ancient Egyptians' horned cow-goddess.

Orpheus & Eurydice

Nowhere in world myth are the themes of love, death and creativity interwoven as poignantly as in the story of the great poet and musician Orpheus, who made music so sweet that it could entrance wild beasts and even rocks and trees, and his beautiful young bride Eurydice.

Orpheus and Eurydice had not been long married when Eurydice stepped on a snake, whose venom killed her. Distraught at the loss of the woman he loved, Orpheus determined to have her brought back to life. Carrying only his lyre, he went to the Underworld to plead with its ruler, Hades, for Eurydice's release. He sang of love as a force that even Hades could not resist, and explained that he was determined not to leave the shades of the dead without his wife.

When even the damned wept at his song, Hades agreed that Eurydice could return with Orpheus on one condition: that he should not look at her until both had left the Underworld. Orpheus guided his wife by striking notes on his lyre as they toiled up the dark path. But at the last moment, his longing to see Eurydice overcame him. He turned to embrace her, only to see her slip back into the shadows with a piteous cry.

Overwhelmed by this second bereavement, Orpheus returned home and hardened his heart against women. This, and his attachment to Apollo, aroused the anger of the wild Maenads, female followers of the rival god Dionysus. In one of their crazed orgies, they fell upon the poet and tore him limb from limb, then threw his head into the river Hebrus. The head floated, still singing, down to the sea. Carried by currents to the island of Lesbos, it was finally laid to rest in a cave, where it served as an oracle for all who came to consult it.

Apollo & Daphne

In the classical myths magical transformations were often awarded as a recompense for virtue or imposed as a punishment for wickedness. However, for the nymph Daphne, daughter of Gaia, metamorphosis was neither reward nor penalty, but necessary protection.

Once Cupid had a quarrel with Apollo. The child god was upset because Apollo told him he was too young for archery and should leave bows and arrows to men. In revenge he shot Apollo with one of the arrows that caused its victim to fall in love with whomever the winged god chose. To perfect his vengeance, he selected Daphne.

Daphne was a virgin nymph, in mourning for the prince Leucippus. He had fallen in love with her, and when she rejected him he disguised himself as a woman so that he could hunt with her. As companions in the chase, they became close, loving friends. Unfortunately, one day after he, Daphne and some other nymphs had been out hunting, the women decided to bathe. The nymphs stripped naked, but Leucippus invented an excuse not to. Teasingly, the assembled nymphs tore off his clothes and his true sex was revealed. The virgin nymphs immediately assumed that Leucippus's intentions were dishonourable. Before Daphne could intervene, they killed him.

After this Daphne not only swore to remain a virgin, but also began to shun all human company, hunting alone. So Apollo had little hope of persuading her to return his intense passion. Nevertheless, the god was determined to have his way with her. Apollo used all his considerable charm to seduce Daphne, but she

rejected him. Then, in frustration, he attempted to rape her. She fled terrified into the forest, but Apollo gave chase and eventually cornered her.

Despairing, she called to her mother for help. Gaia acted swiftly to protect her: just as Apollo reached out to seize her, Daphne was transformed into a laurel tree.

Apollo's lust was replaced by shame, and he humbly broke off a branch of the tree to wear in his hair. From that day on, the laurel was sacred to Apollo, and he awarded a crown made from its branches to the finest musicians and poets, in honour of Daphne's beauty.

The Language of Animals

One day a young healer called Melampus came to the court of King Proetus of Tiryns. Melampus was a man of rare gifts who could understand the language of animals. This had enabled him to cure the son of another king, Phylacus, of impotence.

When Phylacus asked Melampus to heal his son, Iphiclus, he sacrificed two bulls to Apollo, and as two vultures swooped to feed off the remains, he overheard their conversation. They recalled how when Iphiclus was still a boy they had seen Phylacus castrating rams at this spot. The king came toward the boy with his bloody knife and Iphiclus took fright thinking he, too, was to be castrated. Phylacus stuck the knife into a nearby tree while he comforted his son, but the fright had made the boy impotent. The vultures said that Iphiclus could be cured if the knife was pulled out of the tree and the ram's blood was scraped off it and given to Iphiclus in a drink. Melampus did what they suggested and cured Iphiclus.

Meanwhile, Proetus had troubles of his own: his three daughters had taken to roaming the mountainside assaulting travellers. Melampus was able to find them and purify them. He married the one called Lysippe and when Proetus died, inherited his kingdom.

The Calydonian Boar Hunt

When the fearless hunter Meleager was a baby, the Fates told his mother Althaea that her son's life would last only as long as a log then burning in the fire was unconsumed. She snatched it up, doused the flames and hid it.

Each year Meleager's father Oineus, king of Calydon, made a sacrifice to all the twelve Olympian gods, and his kingdom prospered with their favour. But one year he forgot to name Artemis. In revenge, the goddess sent a gigantic boar that ravaged the country, killing cattle and farmers.

Oineus sent out a call for help, promising the tusks and skin of the boar to whoever killed it. Many heroes assembled from all over Greece to hunt the beast under the leadership of Meleager. Some say Jason and Theseus were among them. There also came Atalanta, a girl who had been abandoned as a baby, suckled by a bear and raised by mountain hunters. She was a superb huntress and the fastest runner in the world.

But Artemis was using Atalanta to ruin Oineus. Meleager fell in love with her and while the other hunters complained that a woman would bring them bad luck, he spoke up for her and showed her unfair favour.

Out in the forest, Hylaeus and Rhaecus, two centaurs that were part of the group, tried to rape Atalanta and were shot by her, while the hunter Ancaeus was castrated and disembowelled on the boar's tusks. Atalanta was the first to injure the boar but it was Meleager who finally killed it. He presented its hide to Atalanta, but this act of generosity was too much for some of the other hunters. Toxeus and Plexippus, two of his mother's brothers, disputed Meleager's decision and in a rage he killed them both.

Meleager's mother watched the bodies of her brothers being carried back from the forest and cursed her son. She took the half-burned log from the chest in which she had hidden it and thrust it at once deep into the fire. Immediately Meleager died. His sisters shrieked as they mourned for him and Artemis turned them into guinea fowl. Althaea later hanged herself in remorse.

Ariadne on Naxos

Ariadne gave up her home and family to run away with Theseus, but she found herself abandoned on a remote island, the very archetype of the deserted woman. Her story did have a happy ending, though: her plight was noted on Olympus, and a god came to the rescue.

The intrepid Theseus ventured to Crete to do battle with the fearsome Minotaur in its lair beneath the palace of King Minos. Ariadne, the king's daughter, fell in love with Theseus and decided to help him overcome the monster. She acted under the illusion that the young hero would take her back to Athens and marry her there.

But she was to be cruelly disappointed. On reaching the island of Dia – identified by most scholars with modern Naxos, though some plump for the small island of Dia just off Crete's north coast – Theseus abandoned her. While she slept on shore, he and his comrades sailed away, leaving her to a bitter awakening alone in a strange land.

Luckily, the Olympians heard her complaints, and Dionysus himself came to her rescue. The god of wine arrived on the island accompanied by a festive train of satyrs and maenads. He informed the startled maiden that he had come to marry her forthwith, telling her "Your wedding present is the sky itself!"

The two went back to Olympus, where over the years Ariadne was to bear her divine husband many children. In later times her story would attract the attention of great artists. The sixteenth-century Italian Titian painted a celebrated "Bacchus and Ariadne"; Bacchus was Dionysus's Roman name. In the twentieth century, German composer Richard Strauss composed the opera *Ariadne auf Naxos*, which became a modern favourite.

Antigone's Tragic Defiance

The tragedy of Oedipus, king of Thebes, is one of the most memorable of all the classical myths, but less well known is the drama of his daughter, which was the subject of the play *Antigone* by the fifth-century BCE dramatist Sophocles.

After Oedipus's death, his two sons quarrelled over the succession to the throne. Eventually they decided to rule in alternate years. Eteocles took the first turn, but when his time was up he refused to hand over the kingdom to his brother as promised.

Polynices raised an army to enforce his claim, sharing command with six allied leaders – the famous Seven against Thebes. But their forces were driven back from the city with huge losses. Both Oedipus's sons were killed in a duel. With their deaths, the throne reverted to their uncle Creon.

Creon's first thought was to deter future rebels. So he gave orders that, while Eteocles should be interred in state as Thebes's former ruler, his brother Polynices should be left unburied. He decreed that those who disobeyed would die.

Even so, one person was determined to defy the king's will. That night, Polynices' sister Antigone visited the battlefield and found her brother's body. She covered it with earth, giving him a proper burial. Caught in the act, the princess was taken to her uncle, who upbraided her. She refused to apologize, citing the demands of divine law in her defence. She refused to concede to the king even when he condemned her to death.

The cruelty of the sentence shocked Thebes, but Creon refused all appeals for mercy. Only when the old prophet Tiresias (see page 54) warned the king that the gods would punish him for the deed did Creon finally consider clemency.

But his change of heart came too late: entering the stone room in which he had incarcerated her, Creon found that the princess had hanged herself with her veil. The tragedy did not end there. Creon's son Haemon, who was betrothed to Antigone, threw himself onto his sword upon discovering her fate, dying instantly, and when Creon's wife Eurydice learned of her son's suicide, she too stabbed herself fatally.

Tiresias the Prophet

Tiresias was a unique figure in classical mythology, credited with wisdom beyond that of any normal mortal and with knowledge of the future as well as of all aspects of the human condition. Gods and kings alike sought to benefit from his extraordinary sagacity.

Tiresias was no ordinary mortal. He lived for seven lifespans, in the course of which he spent time as a woman as well as a man. For his pains he was struck blind but also acquired the power of prophecy.

Tiresias's first transformation took place one day on Mount Kyllene in the Peloponnese, where he saw two snakes coupling. He struck them with his staff, killing the female. The act stirred the wrath of the goddess Hera, and instantly he found himself transformed into a woman. Seven years later, he saw another pair of snakes similarly occupied. This time he dispatched the male, and was turned back into a man.

Some time later, Zeus and Hera were arguing over which partner gets the most pleasure from the sexual act, and to settle the dispute they decided to consult the one person on Earth to have had experience of both conditions. Tiresias replied that, judged out of ten, the female gets nine parts of the enjoyment and the man only one – an answer that so infuriated Hera that she struck him blind on the spot. In consolation, Zeus bestowed on him the gifts of long life and of prophecy.

Tiresias became famous for his ability to foresee the future. He was consulted by Amphitryon and Alcmene, Heracles' parents, about the hero's conception and he gave crucial advice to the rulers of Thebes during two successive sieges. According to the dramatist Sophocles, it was Tiresias who revealed to Oedipus, king of Thebes, that he had unwittingly killed his own father.

Tiresias's powers even continued after his death, when he alone of the shades in Hades' underground realm was allowed to retain the gifts of speech and understanding, enabling him to continue his role as a prophet. In the *Odyssey*, Homer describes how Odysseus consulted Tiresias in the land of the dead to learn the outcome of his journey home.

Iphigenia's Escape

Agamemnon, king of Mycenae, had offended Artemis, goddess of the hunt, by boasting of his peerless hunting skills, so she sent an ill wind to hamper the king's efforts to sail his fleet to Troy.

According to the original version of the story, Agamemnon sacrificed his daughter Iphigenia to Artemis to secure favourable winds. But in a more uplifting version, Artemis appeared in person just as the young girl was stretched out beneath the sacrificial knife. The goddess snatched her away to safety, leaving a hind to be killed in her place. Artemis carried Iphigenia to the land of the Tauroi, who lived far away across the Black Sea in what is now the Crimea. There the Greek princess became a priestess in a temple that contained a celebrated image of the goddess.

It was the custom of this barbarous land to sacrifice to Artemis all the strangers who visited the country, and for many years Iphigenia was forced to preside over these bloody rites. Then one day her own brother Orestes came to Taurian shores and was handed over to her in order to be killed.

Recognizing one another, the long-separated pair suppressed their joy at the unexpected reunion only long enough to effect their escape. They took the statue of Artemis with them because they wished to find a more suitable home for it in Greece. Once back at home, Iphigenia became a priestess to Artemis again.

The Childhood of Achilles

Forced by Zeus to marry a mortal, the sea-nymph Thetis feared that her warrior son Achilles would bear her husband's taint. So she did all she could to shield him from danger. But destiny decreed that her efforts were to be in vain.

Thetis cast her first six offspring into fire, hoping to burn out of them all that was not divine. None survived. But when a seventh baby was born, her husband Peleus stopped her and saved the infant's life. The boy grew up strong and handsome, and Thetis soon became reconciled to him, naming him Achilles. Yet, still fearing his human weakness, she made one more attempt to protect him. Taking him to the Styx, the underworld river whose waters conveyed immortality, she dipped him in. His whole body was submerged but for the heel by which she held him – and that small area was to remain fatally vulnerable.

Under the tutelage of the wise centaur Chiron, the young man grew up unmatched in the arts of peace and war. So when news came that all the greatest warriors of Greece were gathering to attack Troy, Thetis at once feared that her son would be summoned. To protect him, she disguised him as a girl and sent him to the island of Skyros. The king's daughter Deidameia was only too happy to learn the truth of the imposture; in time she bore the newcomer a son.

Yet, as Thetis had feared, envoys eventually tracked Achilles down. They had trouble recognizing him, for his real identity was well hidden. But then Odysseus, one of the leaders of the Greek army, employed a ruse. He sent a selection of gifts into the women's quarters that included, alongside jewelry and other adornments, some armour and a sword. When one of the "maidens" was seen practising swordplay, the envoys at once identified their target, Achilles. At their demand he set off to the war, thereby realizing all his doting mother's worst fears.

Troy's Tragic Champion

To modern eyes, Achilles seems a self-absorbed killing machine. The Trojan Hector now appears the more attractive figure, showing concern over the fate of his family and his country.

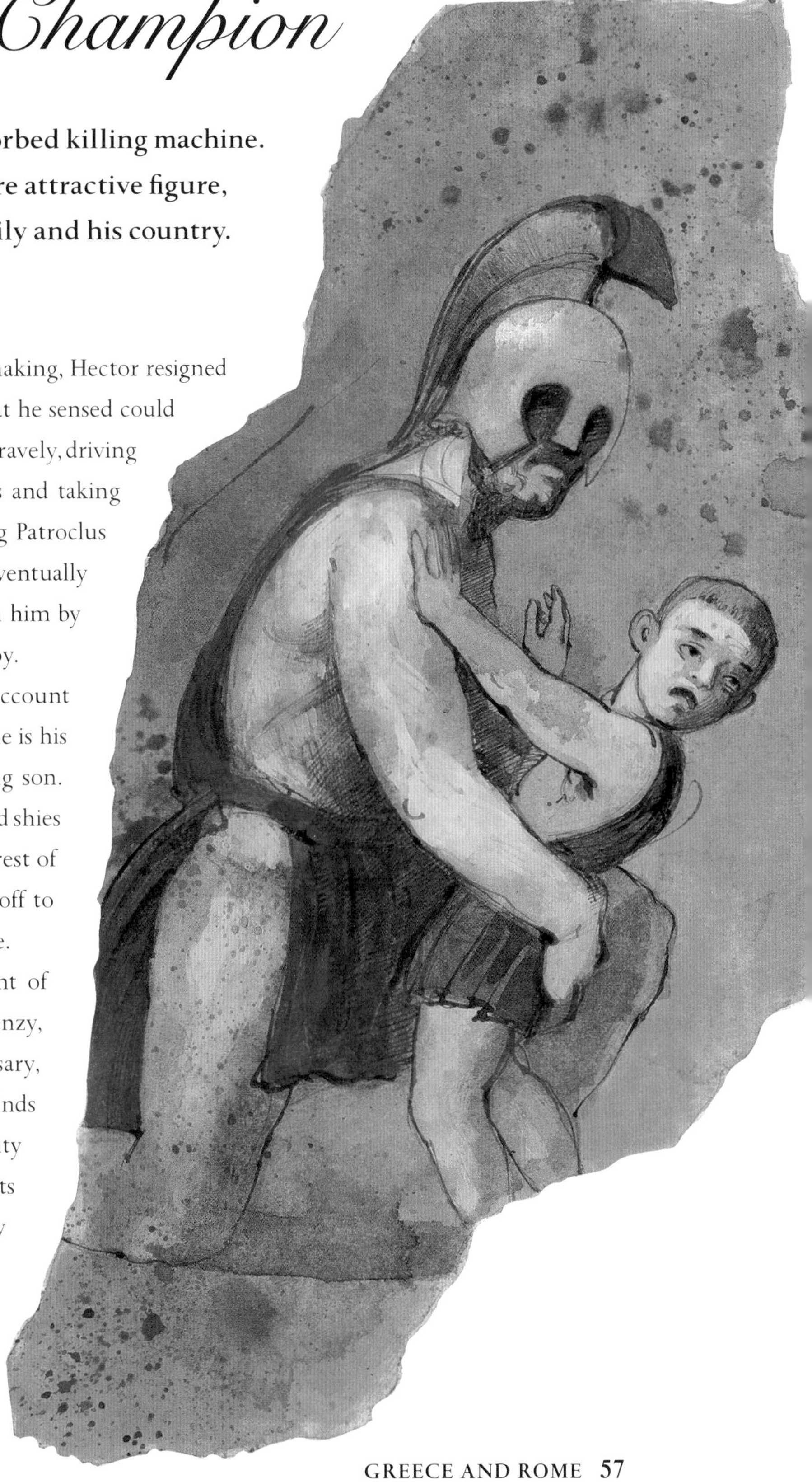

Having exhausted all attempts at peacemaking, Hector resigned himself to seeing through a contest that he sensed could only lead to disaster. He led the Trojans bravely, driving the Greek invaders back to their ships and taking on Achilles' friend Patroclus hand-to-hand. By killing Patroclus he became the target of Achilles' murderous wrath, eventually meeting at the Greek hero's hands the death fated on him by the hatred of the goddess Athene, the deadly foe of Troy.

Two scenes in the *Iliad*, the Greek poet Homer's account of the war, add a note of pathos to Hector's death. One is his leave-taking of his wife Andromache and their young son. When the warrior tries to kiss the boy farewell, the child shies back, terrified by his father's bronze helmet with its crest of horsehair bristles. Laughing, the proud father lifts it off to show his face and then clasps his son in a final embrace.

The other is the hero's one recorded moment of weakness. When Achilles confronts him in his battle-frenzy, the champion's nerve cracks and he flees from his adversary, who chases him round the walls of Troy. Then Hector finds fresh courage to confront his pursuer, going with dignity to the death he knows must follow. Such moments of fallibility, unknown to his mighty adversary, may not have enhanced his military reputation, but they give him a human dimension that his more single-minded opponent signally lacks.

Menelaus Waits for Fair Winds

Having helped to defeat Troy, the Greek hero Menelaus set sail for his kingdom of Sparta with his wife Helen, whose elopement with a Trojan lover had precipitated the war. His refusal to make sacrifices to the goddess Athene before leaving plunged his fleet into trouble at once.

Soon after leaving Troy, Menelaus's fleet was devastated in a great storm. Only five ships survived, including the one in which Menelaus was sailing. They were blown to Egypt, where they were becalmed for eight years.

On the island of Pharos, Menelaus met the sea-nymph Eidoethea. She told him that he must capture her father Proteus, the shepherd of fish and other sea animals, who knew all things, past, present and future. He would tell Menelaus how to raise a wind.

Menelaus and three followers disguised themselves as seals on a beach and when Proteus came out of the waves and lay down to sleep they leaped upon him. The god tried to escape by changing form, becoming a lion, a snake and even a stream, but Menelaus would not let go. Finally, Proteus told Menelaus that Agamemnon had been murdered and that Odysseus was being held captive by the sea-nymph Calypso. He instructed Menelaus to return to Egypt and make a sacrifice to the gods. When he did this, a wind came up that carried him home.

Menelaus and Helen came to Mycenae, where they found that in an act of revenge Agamemnon's son Orestes had killed his father's murderers, Clytemnestra and Aegisthus, and was now facing trial. Orestes appealed for help but Menelaus refused. Orestes and his sister Electra then seized Helen and tried to kill her, but she was rescued by Aphrodite. Helen and Menelaus travelled on to Sparta, where they settled. On his death Menelaus was made immortal by the gods and was allowed to go to the Elysian Fields, the realm of the blessed, with Helen.

Prophetess of Doom

The most tragic of the twelve daughters of Priam, king of Troy, was the beautiful Cassandra, who, like her mother Hecuba and the other Trojans Calchas and Laocoon, had the gift of prophecy. But for Cassandra the gift was a curse, for she was doomed never to be believed.

When Cassandra was visiting Apollo's sanctuary one day, the god himself was struck by her beauty. As a mark of favour, he promised her the gift of prophecy. But when in return he sought to have his way with her, the young princess rebuffed his advances.

Apollo sought revenge. He could not take back his gift, for no divine edict could be undone; so instead he added a cruel rider to his bequest – that no one should ever believe her predictions.

From that time on, Cassandra could see only too clearly the tragedies that lay in store for her people. But whenever she sought to help them – by warning that her brother Paris, who eloped with Helen, would bring calamity on Troy, for example, or that the wooden horse was a Greek ruse – she was greeted only with incredulity. The people of the city believed she was mad. Her name lives on to this day as a generic title for all those unfortunate enough to be able to foresee imminent disaster without being able to avert it.

A Race of Beastly Shepherds

Greek creation myths told of the birth of the fearsome one-eyed giants known as the Cyclopes, who were brothers of the Titans. Later the hero Odysseus had a traumatic encounter with one of their descendants, Polyphemus.

In the *Theogony*, an account of the origins of the gods written by the Greek poet Hesiod in the eighth century BCE, the first Cyclopes were said to have been three sons of the sky god Uranus and the original Earth mother Gaia. Fearing his own offspring, Uranus threw them down into the abyss of Tartarus. In revenge Gaia persuaded another of her sons, Kronos, to castrate her husband. The three Cyclopes were subsequently released by Zeus, whom they in turn helped to attain supreme power.

Thereafter a widespread tradition placed the Cyclopes in Sicily. There their best-known descendant, Polyphemus, was said to have fallen in love with the nymph Galatea, who did not return his affection. In one telling of the tale, Polyphemus crushed his rival Acis to death with a stone. This was the version followed in the opera *Acis and Galatea* by the eighteenth-century composer Georg Friedrich Handel.

Polyphemus played an even more familiar role in the adventures of Odysseus on his way back from the siege of Troy, as described in Homer's *Odyssey*. Cannibalistic in his appetites, he imprisoned the hero and his men in the cave where he guarded his sheep, feeding on them one by one. To escape his clutches, Odysseus got the giant drunk and then put out his single eye with a red-hot stake. The Greeks then strapped themselves to the bellies of his sheep, escaping from the giant's lair when he drove the animals out to graze.

Cyclopes were also said to have built the walls of Mycenae and Tiryns, whose stone blocks were thought too large to have been laid by humans. The term "Cyclopean" is still used to describe massive stone structures.

Telemachus Sets Forth

Odysseus's son Telemachus was a baby when his father left for the Trojan War. He grew up into a fine young man, but he could not control the suitors who invaded his father's palace and pestered his mother Penelope to marry one of them.

The goddess Athene arrived at the palace of Ithaca disguised as a foreign king and told Telemachus to send the suitors home. Then he must sail to Pylos and Sparta in search of news of his father. After she had finished speaking, Athene vanished through the roof – and Telemachus, realizing who she was, was greatly heartened. He summoned the suitors and berated them about their conduct, begging them to go away. Their leader, Antinous, retorted that they would not leave until Penelope agreed to marry one of them.

Telemachus decided to set off secretly to Pylos. Athene went round the city to find a ship and recruit the crew. Then, assuming the form of Odysseus's old friend Mentor, she led Telemachus to the ship and joined him on board.

Telemachus and Athene, in Mentor's disguise, soon reached Pylos, where they were received by King Nestor. He regaled them with tales of Odysseus's bravery, but knew nothing about his fate. Nestor gave Telemachus a chariot and his best horses, with his son as companion. Athene turned back, while the young men drove on to Sparta.

There Menelaus told Telemachus of his encounter with Proteus, the Old Man of the Sea, who had reported seeing a tearful Odysseus trapped on an island with Calypso (see page 58).

The suitors back on Ithaca sent a ship to ambush Telemachus on his return journey and kill him. But Athene warned the prince and he came home by a different route to find his father, disguised as a beggar, already there.

EUROPE: FROM THE ATLANTIC TO THE URALS

The Celtic World

The Celtic peoples spread across much of Europe in the course of the Iron Age, but by Roman times the might of the legions and the advance of the Germanic tribes had driven them westward. There they found a permanent refuge on the continent's edge, in Brittany and Cornwall but above all in Ireland and Wales.

All the evidence suggests that the Celts had an unusually rich mythology, but unfortunately contemporary sources are hard to come by. Our knowledge of the myths has had to be pieced together from archaeological findings or the reports of outsiders, or else from the work of authors writing many centuries later in the Christian era. The patchwork of narrative that has emerged is often infuriatingly vague and hard to follow, but also hugely stimulating in its poetic exuberance and narrative power.

One notable feature of Irish myth is its division into major narrative groupings. One cycle of stories concerns itself with the first inhabitants of Ireland, detailing the strife between successive waves of invaders: Fomorians, Firbolg, the Tuatha de Danaan ("Children of the goddess Danu"). These tales may have enshrined distant historical memories in their details, but mostly belonged firmly in the land of legend; indeed, the Tuatha are generally identified by modern scholars not with any ethnic group but rather with the Celtic gods, who supposedly first established themselves on the island by defeating the Firbolg at the Battle of Moytirra (see page 67). Another group of seemingly historical legends came together in the Ulster Cycle, which turned on the deeds of the hero Cuchulainn, a chariot-borne warrior who defended Ireland's northeastern kingdom from armies attacking it from Connaught. A key tale in the cycle is The Cattle Raid of Cooley, but there are many incidental episodes, such as the apparition of the Washer at the Ford (see page 66). While the Ulster stories belonged firmly to the heroic age, those concerning the warrior leader Finn mac Cumhaill and his followers the Fianna, mostly set further south in Munster and Leinster, were marked by touches of romance, as suggested by Finn's acquisition of supernatural wisdom through a childhood encounter with the Salmon of Knowledge (see page 69).

For modern readers, the prime vehicle of Welsh legend is the *Mabinogion*, a collection of traditional stories compiled by Lady Charlotte Guest in the 1830s. The main section of the book is taken up with a quartet of linked narratives, the so-called Four Branches of the Mabinogion, whose connecting theme is the life of the hero Pryderi. The first of the four contains the story of his birth, abduction and miraculous restoration (see page 74), while the fourth tells of his death at the hands of Gwydion and of that warrior's own subsequent search for a nephew who had been magically spirited away (see page 75). The rest of the work is made up of unconnected romances, including the story of Culhwch and Olwen, much of it taken up with the epic hunt for the gigantic boar Twrch Trwyth (see page 76). At least one of the stories, the Dream of Macsen (see page 77), preserved distant memories of a real-life figure – the Roman general Magnus Maximus, who made a failed bid for the imperial throne while stationed in Britain in the fourth century CE.

The best known of all the cycles, however, was one whose popularity had already spread far beyond the Celtic lands by late medieval times. This was the epic of King Arthur and his knights, believed to have lived and fought somewhere in Britain in the dark time after the ending of the Roman occupation. In their earliest forms the tales had their roots deep in Celtic folklore and magic (see page 78). As embroidered by some of the Middle Ages' finest poets and romancers, they became manuals of courtly etiquette, spelling out a chivalric code of honour (see page 79) and also an unmatched source of poetic imagery that would still thrill the imagination of poets and artists many centuries later (see pages 80 and 81).

The Washer at the Ford

One common theme of Celtic myth is that of the Washer at the Ford – the war goddess who waited at a ford, sometimes in the form of a woman, sometimes as a crow or raven, and determined which of the warriors who passed would perish on the battlefield that day.

On their way to battle, a band of warriors stopped at a ford, where they beheld a terrible sight. A tall phantom woman, her eyes red and angry, glowered at them through grey, matted hair. At her feet, which were awash with blood, lay the mangled corpses of warriors, some so hideously disfigured that not even their mothers would have recognized them.

As the warrior band gaped in horror, the woman let out a hideous, shrieking laugh that sent a shiver of terror down their spines. Slowly, she raised her arm and pointed a bony finger at each man in turn. At last the chief of the band approached the woman. With much effort, he forced himself to speak. "Who are you?" he asked.

"I?" she screeched, "I am the Morrigan, the Phantom Queen. Some call me the Washer at the Ford. My work is to haunt all the streams of Ireland, washing away all the sins of men." "Who, then," asked the band's war-chief, "are the sinful men who lie in this gory heap before us? Are they those you have killed and maimed today?" The Morrigan cackled again. "I did not kill these men, nor have I so much as harmed a hair on their heads!" She peered deep into the warrior's eyes. "Look again at these dead warriors. They are the very men that stand behind you, as they will be this evening, after the battle. I am merely washing the blood from their limbs."

The chieftain looked again at the corpses, and began to make out the features of some of the comrades accompanying him.

The Morrigan slowly bent down to rummage among her gory bounty, then held up an object for the chief to see. He turned to look and beheld, dangling by bloody locks, his own severed head.

The Battle of Moytirra

Moytirra in County Sligo witnessed two of the greatest battles in Irish myth. The first ended in the defeat of the race known to later tradition as the Firbolg and the establishment of the Tuatha de Danaan as rulers of Ireland.

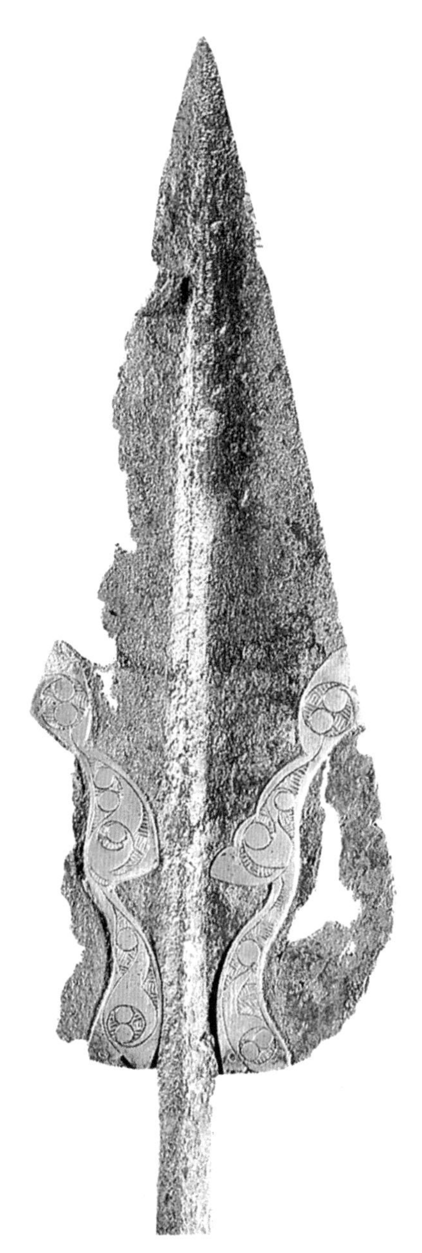

The Firbolg were one of a succession of groups claimed to have ruled Ireland in the days before history was recorded in writing. Before them there had been Fomorian hunter-gatherers and the followers of a leader called Partholon, who had introduced agriculture to the land. When plague wiped his men out, another band under the command of a certain Nemed arrived, supposedly from distant Scythia. But the Nemedians and the Fomorians mostly killed one another off in a great battle, allowing the Firbolg to enter the island unopposed.

The Firbolg evidently reached Ireland's west coast, for it was there that they confronted the next wave of invaders, the Tuatha de Danaan ("Children of the goddess Danu"). When the Firbolg refused the newcomers' demand that they should concede half of the island to them, conflict became inevitable. The battle was delayed for three months, because the Firbolg wanted time to copy the fine javelins of the Tuatha while the latter in their turn spent the interval making heavy spears like those wielded by the Firbolg.

Battle was finally joined on Midsummer's Day. For three days the armies fought and many were slain, but neither side gained the upper hand. Each evening doctors bathed the wounded in healing herbs that restored them in time for the next day's fighting.

On the fourth day the Tuatha finally got the upper hand. At this crucial point, the Firbolg king became so thirsty that he left the field to find water. A Tuatha force set off in pursuit and after a fierce fight killed him. The Tuatha king, Nuadu, now offered peace and the Firbolg accepted. For Nuadu, however, it was a bitter victory. In battle he had lost an arm, and his people could accept only a physically perfect king, giving him no choice but to abdicate.

The Life of Cuchulainn

With his divine connections, supernatural powers and short but brilliant life, Cuchulainn was the epic hero par excellence. His mother, Dechtire, was the daughter of the druid Cathbad. His father's identity, however, was a mystery, although in one story he was the god Lugh.

Lugh is said to have made Dechtire pregnant in a dream while she was staying with King Conchobar and his hunting party. Her child was named Setanta, but became known as Cuchulainn ("Hound of Culann") at a young age, after he had killed the fierce watchdog of Culann the smith and had taken its place until Culann had reared a new one. As a boy, he routed Conchobar's youth brigade and entered the Ulster king's service. He was trained in arms in Scotland by a female warrior, Scathach, who taught him such heroic feats as standing on a lance in flight and also gave him a vicious weapon called the *gae bolg*. A sort of spear, when it struck home its head sprouted thirty darts that coursed through every part of the victim's body, killing him instantly.

When his blood was up, Cuchulainn was gripped by a terrifying battle-frenzy during which his hair stood on end, his muscles bulged and his body rotated within its skin. One eye protruded from his head, the other sank into his skull and his battle-cry drove people insane. He had many lovers, but always returned to his wife Emer.

Cuchulainn appears in many Ulster Cycle tales, most notably The Cattle Raid of Cooley. His death came seven years after the raid, when the goddess Maeve plotted to kill him with six sorcerers. Conchobar tried to keep the warrior out of harm's way. But the sorcerers conjured up an illusion of battle which convinced Cuchulainn that Ulster was being laid waste. As he emerged from his hiding place, he was struck by a magic spear thrown by one of the sorcerers. Mortally wounded, he tied himself to a rock so that he would be able to face his enemies with honour, standing up. For three days none of them dared approach him. In the end a war goddess, Badb, landed on his shoulder in the form of a crow. Cuchulainn did not stir, and so everyone knew that Ulster's greatest hero was dead.

Finn & the Salmon of Knowledge

The turning-point in the life of the great warrior Finn mac Cumhaill came at the age of seven when he apprenticed himself to a bard called Finnegas to learn poetry. Finnegas lived on the banks of the river Boyne, where he tried to catch a salmon imbued with universal wisdom.

Around a well at the source of the Boyne there were nine hazel trees, on which grew nuts that held great wisdom. The nuts had fallen into the river and been eaten by a salmon. Thereafter, the first person to eat the flesh of the salmon would know all that there was to know. It had been prophesied that Finnegas would catch the fish.

For some seven years Finnegas fished for the salmon, but caught nothing. Shortly after Finn's arrival, however, Finnegas landed the salmon and asked Finn to clean and cook it. At the same time, he told Finn that on no account was he to eat even the tiniest bit of the fish, because the first to taste the fish would receive its magic. The boy was careful to obey his master in every respect. While the salmon was cooking, a blister arose on its skin. To burst it, Finn poked it with his thumb, but in doing so scalded himself. He sucked his thumb to ease the pain – and tasted the flesh of the magic salmon.

"What is your name?" asked Finnegas when he learned of this. "Deimne," replied Finn, using the name he had taken to evade his enemies, the sons of Morna. "No, it is not," said the bard. "It was foretold that I would catch the fish, but that Finn mac Cumhaill would be the first to eat it. You are he."

Finn ate the rest of the salmon and received the full power of prophecy. Whenever he wanted to use his gift, all he had to do was suck his thumb. With this talent allied to his battlecraft, Finn became a formidable hero.

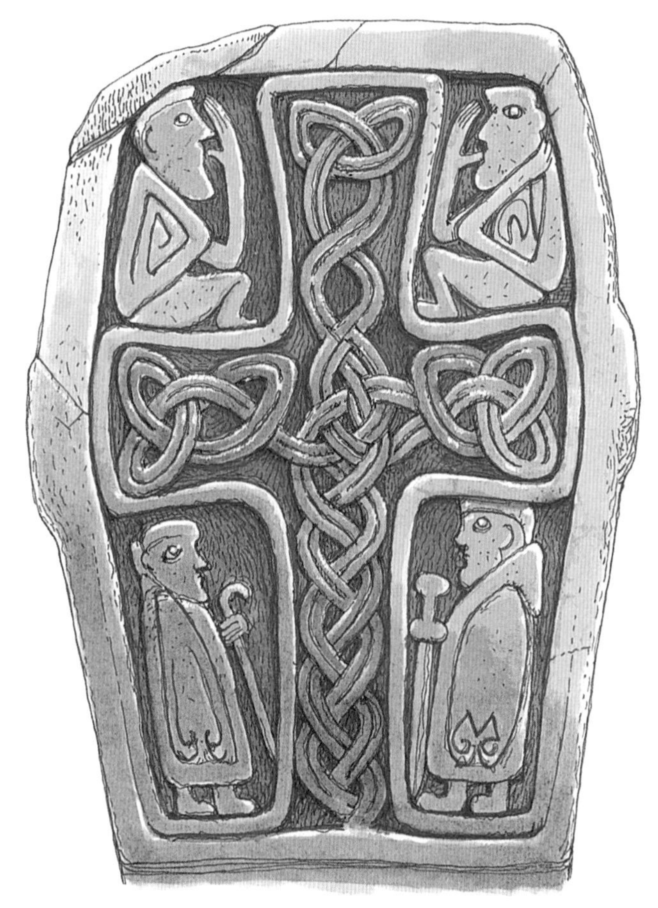

The Dream of Oenghus

The god of love Oenghus himself was not immune to the effects of love. One story relates how, every night for a year, he dreamed of a beautiful woman. She would appear, beckon to him, then disappear as he reached out to her. Oenghus became listless and lost his appetite.

Doctors were summoned but Oenghus was too embarrassed to admit that he was in love with a dream. Finally, one of the best doctors of the Tuatha de Danaan, Fergne, diagnosed his problem.

Oenghus's uncle, Bobd Dearg, was enlisted to find his nephew's dream-woman. After a year's searching, he finally reported success. The woman, named Caer, was the daughter of a Danaan god and lived by a lake in Connacht. Oenghus's father, the Dagda, spoke to King Ailill and Queen Maeve of Connacht on his son's behalf, and Ailill summoned Caer's father, Ethal. He refused to come, however, so Ailill's warriors destroyed the god's home. Even so, Ethal still refused to hand over his daughter. When questioned, he replied that she had powers greater than his: on every day of one year she appeared as a human, but on every day of the next year she took the shape of a bird. In the end Ethal conceded that if Oenghus really wanted her, he must arrange to be at the lake on the feast of Samhain of the following year.

Oenghus did as he was asked and found the lake covered with 150 swans, among them Caer. He called to her from the shore but she said that she would come only if Oenghus allowed her to return to the water as a swan. Oenghus agreed and turned himself into a swan so that he could join her.

The couple embraced and swam round the lake three times, consummating their love as they did so. They then flew away to Oenghus's home at Newgrange. Once there, they regained human form and held a great feast, at which they both sang so beautifully that all their guests were lulled to sleep for three days and nights.

Tadg's Voyage to the Otherworld

A significant body of Irish mythological tales recount journeys to the Otherworld. Their protagonists are usually ordinary people rather than great warriors. Many of the tales revolve around quests, including, in this case, a husband's search for his kidnapped wife.

The Otherworld could be reached in many ways: through a hill, a lake or a mist. For voyagers, however, it consisted of a string of magical islands, which comprised the kingdom of Manannan, son of the sea god Lir.

One voyager to the Otherworld was Tadg, son of Cian of Munster. Tadg's wife and two brothers had been seized in a raid by foreigners, so he mounted a retaliatory raid by sea. Tadg and his crew sailed through raging storms, until finally the waters grew calm and they found themselves on an island of great peace and beauty. They were amazed to find that it was summer there, although it had been winter in Ireland when they had set out. Moreover, despite the hardships they had been through, they felt not the slightest hunger.

Advancing further, they came to three hills. On each hill stood a fort: one was white, one gold and one silver. Approaching the white fort, they were greeted by a beautiful woman. Tadg enquired who lived there and was told it was the home of the Milesian kings of Ireland. At the silver fort they met another beautiful woman to whom Tadg put the same question. It was home, he was told, to everyone else who had once ruled Ireland. At the third hill, they learned that the golden fort was reserved for all the future kings of Ireland, and Tadg himself would find a place there one day. It turned out that the island's ruler was Cliodna, a Danaan goddess of great beauty. When Tadg and his crew left for home, she sent three birds to guide them. En route they defeated the raiders and came home with Tadg's wife and brothers and much booty.

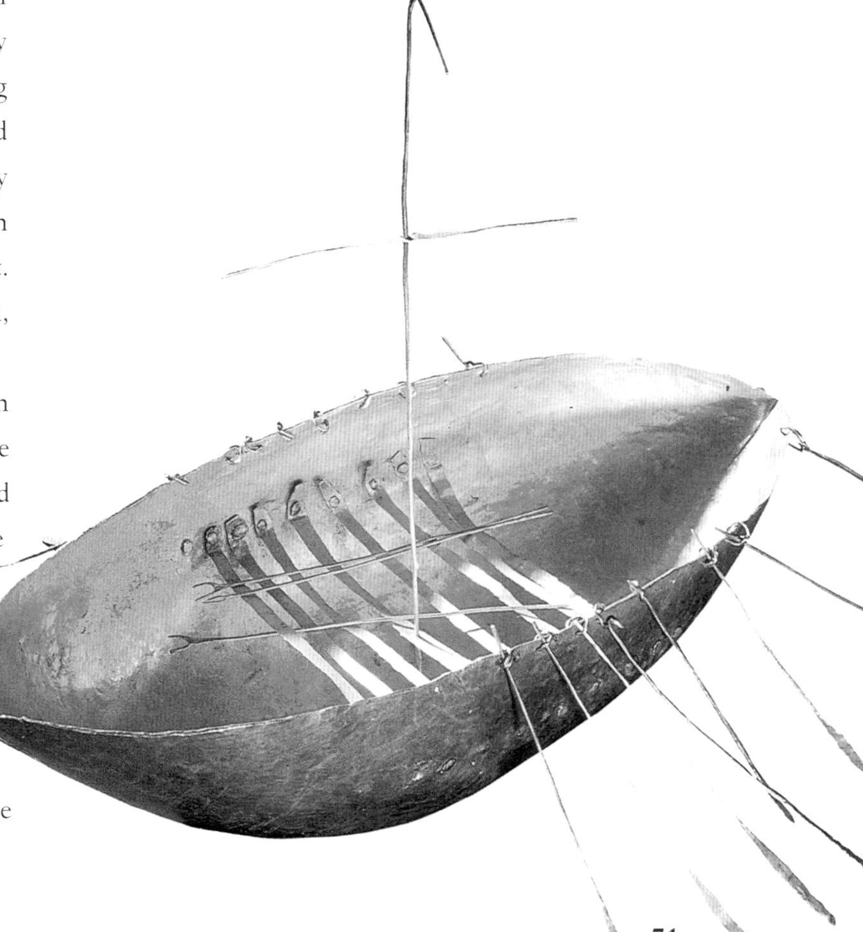

The Birth of Taliesin

Taliesin was to become the greatest of all the Welsh bards. In his famous work *The Boast of Taliesin*, the poet laid claim to omniscience. This legend, which has echoes of the Irish tale of Finn and the Salmon of Knowledge (see page 69), describes how he came by his great wisdom.

To judge from the story, which Taliesin supposedly wrote when he was only thirteen years old, the poet's career began in the most unpromising manner. Afaggdu, "Utter Darkness", was indisputably the ugliest man in the world and all the magic powers of his mother, the witch Ceridwen, could not change that fact. However, Ceridwen decided that if Afaggdu was going to be ugly, he could at least be clever, and so she prepared a potion for him that would reveal all the mysteries of the universe.

It was not a simple process. The brew had to simmer for a year and a day, with herbs added at certain specified times. Toward the end of the year, as Ceridwen was gathering the last of the ingredients, a small boy called Gwion came and watched the boiling pot. As he did so, the mixture bubbled up and spat three drops onto his finger. He licked them off and immediately received the wisdom intended for Afaggdu.

When Ceridwen returned she was furious: Gwion had drunk the three most important drops in the cauldron and the rest was useless. The boy fled, but try as he might he could not escape. He turned himself into a hare, she turned into a hound. He turned into a fish, she into an otter. When he became a bird, she became a hawk; finally, he turned into a grain of wheat, but Ceridwen changed into a hen and ate him.

On resuming her human form, Ceridwen found that she was pregnant, and in due course she gave birth to Gwion. But the reborn boy was so handsome that she could not bring herself to kill him, so she trussed him up in a leather bag and hurled him into the sea.

Two days later, however, the bag was retrieved from the sea by a man of high birth, who gave the child a new name – Taliesin, "Shining Brow" – and fostered him as his own son.

Taliesin & Elphin

The nobleman who was said to have rescued the infant Taliesin (see opposite) was Prince Elphin, the nephew of Maelgwyn, king of Dyfed. Later, when Taliesin had become the prince's court bard, he was able to repay his patron's kindness.

The Taliesin of Welsh myth is often identified with the real-life poet Taliesin Ben Beird, who lived in the sixth century in the service of the historical King Urien of Rheged. By the time the story of his life, the *Book of Taliesin*, was written 800 years later, many legends had gathered around his name. It was said that he became bard to Prince Elphin, one of the local rulers who competed for favour at the court of King Arthur. And the book also told how he came to his patron's rescue when the prince was imprisoned for rashly boasting that he had a more faithful wife and a more gifted bard than any other knight at Arthur's court.

As Elphin lay in a dungeon, a suitor was sent to his palace to disprove the first claim by seducing his wife. But Taliesin's powers of clairvoyance were such that he foresaw what was planned. He persuaded a kitchen maid to stand in for the real princess, dressing her in royal robes. So when the ravisher cruelly sought to prove his conquest by cutting off one of the girl's fingers to take back to court, Elphin had little difficulty in showing that it was not his wife's. It was too fat and the nail was untrimmed; moreover, it bore traces of dough, which a princess would never have had cause to knead.

Thwarted in his first attempt to discredit his prisoner, Arthur next insisted on organizing a contest of bards. But Taliesin's powers were such that he magically reduced all his opponents to mumbling incoherence. Then, when his own turn came, he sang so sweetly that he burst the very chains that held his master captive. The king had no choice but to agree that Elphin had been right in both his boasts, and thereafter he treated both Elphin and Taliesin with the very greatest respect.

Pryderi

A tale from the *Mabinogion* described how Pwyll, lord of Dyfed in southwestern Wales, won the hand of the fairy princess Rhiannon. Yet the marriage was to prove no idyll, as the tale of their first-born child, Pryderi, showed.

Pryderi was abducted shortly after his birth. Fearing for their lives, the nurses charged with looking after him killed a puppy and smeared its blood on the face of the baby's sleeping mother. When the loss was discovered the next morning, the nurses accused Rhiannon of having eaten her own child.

News of this heinous accusation quickly reached Pwyll, who could hardly contain his fury. He condemned his wife to sit outside his castle and greet every visitor with the story of her supposed crime. To complete her humiliation, she was then obliged to carry callers into the castle on her back like a horse.

Meanwhile, near the English border 100 miles or so to the east, a vassal lord named Teyrnon was having trouble with his mare. It foaled annually on the night of the first of May; but, come morning, the foals were always gone. One year Teyrnon decided to solve the mystery of their disappearance by staying up overnight in the stable. No sooner had the mare given birth than, to his amazement, he saw a gigantic, clawed arm reaching through the window to grab the new-born foal. Teyrnon drew his sword and severed the arm at the elbow. There was a howl from outside, but when he went to investigate, he could see nothing unusual. On his return, however, he found a baby boy wrapped in silk.

He took the child home and reared him as his own. As the boy grew up, however, Teyrnon noticed that he looked just like Pwyll. Having heard the tale of Rhiannon, he put two and two together and took the child to the castle. There he told Pwyll his story and presented the king with his son. Rhiannon was at once absolved of guilt, and at the ensuing feast she declared that her newly found son would henceforth be named Pryderi, or "Care", since she had suffered so much for his conception.

The Triumph of Lleu

When the Welsh hero Lleu was speared by his wife's lover, Gronw, he did not die. Instead, he turned into an eagle and flew away. Thereafter, his uncle, the magician Gwydion, searched tirelessly for Lleu. He was about to give up when he stopped for a night at a peasant's house.

During his stay with the peasant, Gwydion heard of a peculiar sow which his host owned. Every morning, the sow would disappear into the countryside, returning only late at night. The peasant had not the faintest idea where it went.

Intrigued, Gwydion waited by the sty the following morning. As soon as the door was opened, he set off after the sow. He followed it upstream to a valley, where it started to gorge itself on something that lay beneath a tree. Coming closer, Gwydion saw that the pig was eating maggots and decayed flesh. And looking up to the top of the tree, he saw an eagle. Every time it shook itself, a shower of rotten flesh fell to the ground.

Convinced that the eagle was Lleu, Gwydion sang it a song. Hearing it, the eagle came down to the middle of the tree. Gwydion sang another song and the eagle came down to the lowest branch. When Gwydion sang a third song the eagle dropped down onto his knee. Gwydion touched the scrawny bird with his wand and, sure enough, it changed back into Lleu. But because of his wound he was in pitiful shape, nothing but skin and bone, and it took him a full year to recover.

As soon as Gronw heard of Lleu's return, he sent him a placatory message, offering compensation for the wrong done to him. Lleu replied that the only reparation he would accept was for Gronw to stand by the river as he himself had done, and allow Lleu to throw a spear at him. Reluctantly – and only after having asked his brothers, nobles and soldiers to take his place – Gronw agreed. Yet he had one hope of survival. Would it be permissible, he asked, since after all he had only been acting on behalf of an evil woman, to hold a stone in front of him as Lleu threw the spear? Lleu agreed. But Lleu's spear passed right through the stone and hit Gronw in the chest, killing him instantly. Lleu regained his lands and in due course became ruler of all Gwynedd. And for ever afterwards, on the bank of the river Cynfael, the stone stood with the spear sticking through it as a reminder of his triumph over Gronw.

The Hunting of Twrch Trwyth

An archetypal Celtic hero, Culhwch was the central figure of *Culhwch and Olwen*, one of the stories collected in the *Mabinogion*. The tale told of the many trials he had to overcome to win the hand of Olwen, beautiful daughter of the chief of the giants.

In his quest for Olwen, Culhwch obtained the help of Arthur, an early Celtic version of the royal hero of later times. It took a year for Arthur's knights to track down Olwen, but when they finally did so she fell in love with Culhwch at first sight. Her father, however, opposed the match, eventually agreeing to allow it only if Culhwch succeeded in accomplishing a number of seeming impossible tasks. Of these, the hardest involved finding a razor, comb and scissors with which the giant could groom himself for the wedding feast – the difficulty being that they adorned the head of a monstrous boar named Twrch Trwyth, actually a prince magically cursed to take animal shape.

So began an epic chase that took the hunting party across much of Celtic Britain. En route they had to contend not just with the boar itself but also with its seven fierce piglets, who razed large areas of Ireland before taking to the sea and swimming over to Wales.

Day after day the pursuit continued, and many warriors died in its course. At last, all the piglets were killed, but by that time Twrch Trwyth himself was heading for Cornwall. There he was driven into a river, where a hunter called Mabon finally snatched the razor and scissors. But the boar regained his footing and rampaged further before the comb could also be retrieved. When that feat too was accomplished, the beast fled into the sea and was never seen again.

The Dream of Macsen

This tale is based on the true story of Magnus Maximus, a fourth-century CE Roman general based in Britain who made a failed bid to become emperor. Macsen, unlike his historical counterpart, is depicted as the true emperor, but one who loses his throne to a usurper.

One night Emperor Macsen dreamed that he had met the most beautiful woman in the world. When he awoke, he set about tracking down the woman. Messengers were sent from Rome to retrace his dream voyage. From the peak of Snowdon, the highest mountain in Wales, they finally spotted the castle in which she lived.

When the lady, whose name turned out to be Elen, was informed of the reason for their coming, she told them that if the emperor was in love with her, then he should come to seek her for himself. Macsen duly arrived with an army, having conquered Britain en route.

Elen agreed to marry him, but asked as a wedding gift that her father should be made governor of Britain. She also requested that the isles of Wight, Man and Anglesey become her personal property.

Macsen lived with his bride in Britain, which experienced a time of great prosperity and peace. After seven years, however, the Romans chose a new emperor in Macsen's place. The usurped ruler hurried back to Italy to reclaim the throne, but all his attempts to capture the city of Rome itself proved unsuccessful.

Then, a year after he had undertaken the siege, a band of British warriors arrived, commanded by Elen's two brothers. They spotted an opportunity: the rival emperors stopped fighting at noon each day so that their troops could rest. Timing their assault for the midday break, the Britons managed to storm the city.

Their reward matched their achievement. Restored to the throne, the emperor gave his British troops a free hand to pillage, and many years passed before they decided to return to their homeland.

Gawain & Dame Ragnell

One of the most humorous Arthurian tales features an unlikely marriage between the courteous knight Gawain and Dame Ragnell, a Celtic-style hag of a type commonly referred to as a "Loathly Lady". Geoffrey Chaucer adapted the story for the *Wife of Bath's Tale*.

One day a hideous hag came to Camelot in order to test the honour of King Arthur's court. The hag challenged the king to engage in a riddle test. He would have one year to answer her riddle, but if he failed to do so he must grant her one wish. Arthur agreed to the challenge and the hag asked her question: "What does a woman want most?"

Arthur's knights spent the next year scouring every corner of his kingdom for the answer to the riddle, but without success. Finally, when the hag returned for her answer, Arthur admitted his failure and, true to his word, asked her to state her wish. "I ask for a husband," said the hag. Arthur felt honour-bound to marry her himself. His knights were horrified and Gawain, the supreme example of chivalry and champion of women, stepped forward to offer himself as the hag's bridegroom in his uncle's place. Arthur readily agreed and Gawain and the hag were married.

On his wedding night, Gawain approached his marriage bed with some reluctance – only to find that his wife had become a beautiful woman, Ragnell, instead of a hag. Ragnell explained to her husband that she was under a curse. "I can be beautiful either by night or by day but not both. The rest of the time I must appear as the hideous hag that you saw. I give you the choice whether to have me beautiful when we are alone at night or when we must face your friends and the whole court during the day."

Gawain gave the matter considerable thought but simply could not make up his mind. In the end he declared, "You must do whatever you will!" Ragnell was delighted. "Your answer has broken the curse," she exclaimed joyfully, "and now I can remain beautiful all the time! For that was the solution to my riddle: what a woman wants most is her own way!"

The Knight of the Cart

Chrétien de Troyes's account of how Lancelot rescued the abducted Queen Guinevere, launched the knight's career as the most popular of Arthur's followers – and as the queen's adulterous lover.

The evil knight Meleagant used trickery to abduct Guinevere from the court of her husband Arthur, taking her by force to his own father's castle. Many of the king's knights set off in pursuit, among them the previously unknown Lancelot. When his steed died under him, he agreed unwillingly to accept a lift in a passing cart, driven by a dwarf who claimed to know the queen's whereabouts. Along the way Lancelot was mocked by all who saw him, for carts were normally used at the time to transport criminals.

As good as his word, however, the dwarf took the young hero to the castle where the queen was held. There he confronted Meleagant in single combat, and the two fought each other to a standstill. Eventually they agreed to a truce by which Guinevere was to be free to go back to King Arthur's court. In exchange, however, Lancelot agreed to meet Meleagant there in combat within the year, and to return the queen if he was defeated.

Guinevere accepted these terms, and she and her rescuer subsequently fell in love, sharing a night of guilty passion. The queen subsequently returned to her husband's court accompanied by a retinue of knights, but Lancelot was not among them. Having treacherously detained his adversary, Meleagant secretly immured the knight in a purpose-built tower. Publicly he gave out that the young man had fled, being too much of a coward to fulfil his pledge to fight for Guinevere a second time.

All who knew Lancelot doubted Meleagant's claim, and a maiden the knight had earlier helped set out to find him, eventually tracking him down and releasing him from his prison. Free at last, he hastened back to Arthur's court, arriving just in time for the promised confrontation. This time Lancelot vanquished and beheaded his evil opponent.

Gawain & the Green Knight

In this tale, New Year is when the supernatural and natural worlds mingle, as on the Celtic feast of Samhain. The Green Knight may derive from Cernunnos, the god of abundance and forests, just as Morgan is related to the Irish goddess the Morrigan (see page 66).

At the New Year's feast, a giant Green Knight with a massive green axe charged into King Arthur's hall on a green horse. He challenged any knight to decapitate him, on condition that he be allowed to return the stroke in a year and a day. Gawain took the axe and cut off the knight's head, whereupon the torso picked it up and departed.

Almost a year later, Gawain set out for the appointed rendezvous at a place called the Green Chapel. He met a man in a forest who invited him to stay at his home, as the Green Chapel was nearby. The host proposed that he and Gawain exchange anything they receive each day and Gawain agreed. For three days the man went hunting, returning with much game for his guest. In the meantime, the man's wife tried to seduce Gawain and gave him one kiss on the first day, two on the second and three on the third, as well as a green belt that prevented its wearer's death. The embarrassed knight passed on the kisses to his host – but kept the belt.

On the fourth day Gawain went to face the Green Knight at the Green Chapel, but the giant's axe merely scratched his neck. "That cut is for the belt," he said. "I am Bercilak, the knight of Morgan Le Fay, your aunt, who sought to test the honour of the Round Table. You did well, but broke our pact by keeping the belt." Bercilak was none other than his host.

Gawain returned home and Arthur ordered all his knights to wear green belts.

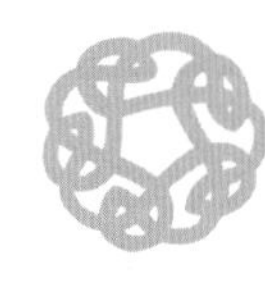

Arthur's Death

For all its glories, King Arthur's life ended in betrayal and tragedy. Sir Thomas Malory's *Morte d'Arthur* described Arthur's final confrontation with the evil Sir Mordred at Camlann and his fate after he was carried fatally wounded from the battlefield.

In Malory's account Mordred provoked a war between Arthur and Lancelot, and took advantage of the strife to seize Arthur's throne. Fighting to reclaim his kingdom, Arthur met the usurper's forces at Camlann on Salisbury Plain. The two rivals met face to face on the battlefield, each mortally wounding the other.

Dying, the king asked to be carried to a waterside chapel. There he instructed Bedivere, his loyal marshal, to take his sword Excalibur and throw it into the depths, then to return and tell him what he saw.

Dazzled by the weapon's splendour, Bedivere at first could not bring himself to do as he was told, and instead hid it under a tree. "What did you see?" Arthur asked him on his return. "Nothing but the wind and waves," Bedivere replied. Hearing his words, Arthur angrily accused him of disobedience and sent him again to accomplish the task. This time too Bedivere's avarice got the better of him, and he returned once more without having done as he was asked. Now the dying king charged him with treachery, saying he had betrayed him twice. Chastened, Bedivere set off once more and finally did as the king wished. As Excalibur flew through the air, an arm emerged from the water to catch the great sword by its hilt, flourishing it three times before disappearing under the surface.

Bedivere ran to tell the king, who now asked to be carried in person to the water's edge. There, out of the mist, a barge appeared bearing three queens. Bedivere gently set Arthur in the vessel. As it drifted away from the shore, Arthur called to the knight that he was bound for Avalon, where his wounds would be healed. Then he disappeared, never to be seen again. Scholars have since speculated that the queens may have reflected the Celtic triple goddess, whose three aspects – maiden, matron, crone – represented the span of human life.

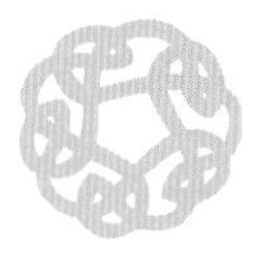

The Viking and Germanic Worlds

The mythology of the Viking and Germanic worlds had its roots in a pagan tradition that survived in the northern lands well into the Christian era. In recent times archaeological discoveries of bog bodies and ship burials have vividly brought home the reality of the old beliefs.

Most of what we know today about northern mythology comes from the Viking lands, largely thanks to compilations like the *Eddas* that were put together in medieval times. These recorded the doings of a range of deities linked in two groups, the Aesir and the Vanir, that were said at one time to have fought a war against one another. Some scholars have seen in the story of the conflict historical memories of the forced merging of two separate bodies of myth, in which the martial Aesir sky gods ultimately predominated over the fertility spirits of the Vanir. Both groups came eventually to live in harmony in the celestial realm of Asgard, located above the human world of Midgard, which in turn topped dark Niflheim, the abode of the dead.

The greatest of the Aesir was Odin, a complex character renowned as much for his foresight as for his skill in battle. Legends told how he sacrificed an eye to win the gift of wisdom, and how he used the cunning for which he was famed to steal the Mead of Poetry (see page 84). Odin's match when it came to fighting, the mighty Thor was in comparison a straightforward character, celebrated more for his brawn than his brain. A typical story has him vying with Jormungand, the monstrous world serpent that straddled the Earth on the oceans' floor (see page 86).

The Aesir's anti-hero was Loki, a trickster figure repeatedly involved in self-serving intrigues that risked bringing disaster on his fellow deities (see page 88). In the tale of Balder, however (see page 93), he played an altogether more sinister role as an active force of evil, scheming to bring about the death of this most loved of gods and so setting in motion the train of events that would lead to the final cataclysm of Ragnarok, the predestined end of the world in its current form.

The chief of the Vanir was Freyr, associated with agriculture and the changing seasons. The stories about him and his beautiful sister Freyja have a different atmosphere to those surrounding the Aesir, being more concerned with love and sexual desire. One told of the passion Freyr conceived for the giantess Gerd and their subsequent marriage (see page 92); another detailed how far Freyja was prepared to go to obtain a matchless necklace from its makers (see page 87).

The giants played a prominent role in Norse myth, locked in rivalry with the gods through the lust for power as well as sexual desire. The antagonism between the two races was fated to have disastrous consequences, for ultimately they were destined to confront one another in the course of Ragnarok. Other significant players in the stories were the dwarfs, wonderful smiths who provided the gods with their greatest treasures (see page 88). Monsters also featured strongly, the worst of them the brood of Loki and the giantess Angrboda, whose unnatural children included not just Jormungand but also the terrible wolf Fenrir (see page 90).

No such coherent body of myth has survived from the Germanic world; what little is known of its gods and goddesses has come down mostly from outside sources, notably the Roman historian Tacitus. There are, however, a number of hero legends, the most famous of them gathered in the Nibelung cycle, dramatized by the nineteenth-century German composer Richard Wagner in the *Ring* operas. Many of these legends, like those of the quasi-historical warrior Ragnar Lodbrok (see page 98), were also shared with the Viking peoples to the north; Old Norse sources even provided their own sanguinary ending to the Nibelung saga, featuring Gunnar and Hogni in place of the Germanic Gunther and Hagen (see page 96).

Odin Wins the Mead of Poetry

The Mead of Poetry conferred the ability to compose poetry or pronounce words of wisdom on those who drank it. Odin had to call on all his powers of cunning and guile to take it from its guardian, the giant Suttung, in order to give it to the gods.

Disguised as a mortal and calling himself Bolverk ("evil-doer"), Odin took up lodgings with Suttung's brother, a giant called Baugi, who had owned nine slaves, all of whom Odin had ruthlessly murdered. He offered to do their work in return for a drink of Suttung's mead of inspiration. Baugi accepted this arrangement.

When he had completed his work, Bolverk demanded his reward and so the two of them set off for Suttung's mountain home. When they arrived, Suttung flatly refused to take any part in Bolverk and Baugi's pact. So Bolverk ordered Baugi to bore a hole into the mountain, which he believed contained the mead.

When a tunnel had been created, Bolverk transformed himself into a snake and slid into it. There he discovered Gunnlod, Suttung's daughter who guarded the precious liquid. He lay with her for three nights, for which she granted him three tastes of the drink. He took full advantage, draining three whole vats of the mead.

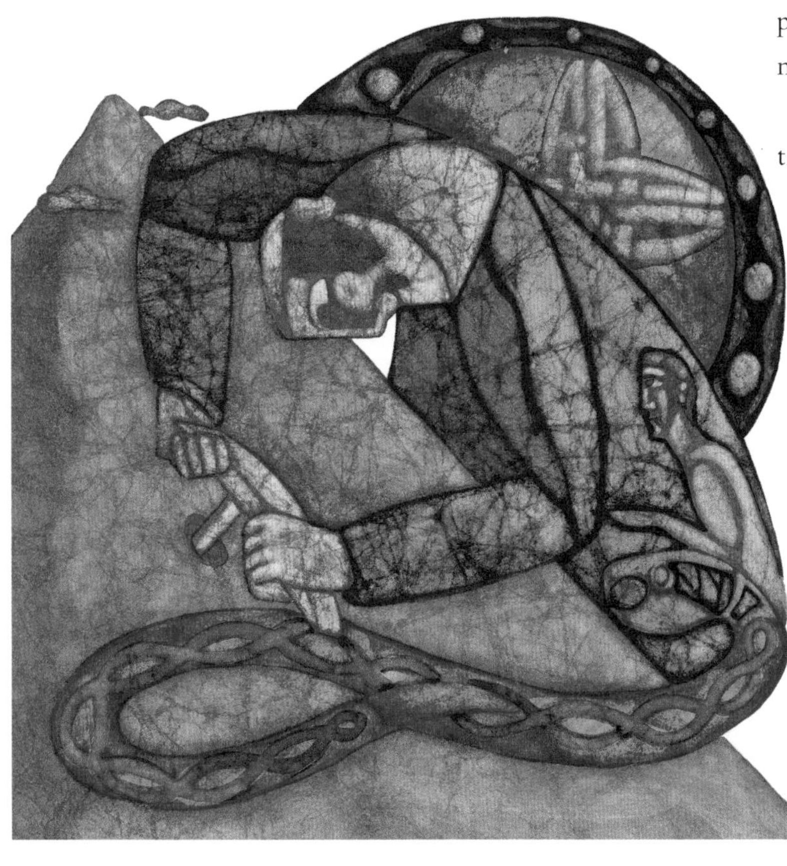

Odin then turned himself into an eagle and escaped to Asgard. Furious, Suttung also took the shape of an eagle and followed in pursuit. When the Aesir saw Odin approaching they placed special containers in the courtyard, so that as he flew overhead he could release the mead into them. Suttung, however, was so close behind his opponent that he caused Odin to spill a little of the mead outside the walls of Asgard, and ever since that time any mortal who so wishes has been free to partake of it there.

Thor Loses His Hammer

Thor's most precious possession was his hammer Mjollnir, a weapon that could never miss its mark and always returned to the hand of its owner. He used it to protect the gods from their great enemies the giants, and so when it was stolen panic quickly spread through Asgard.

When Thor found that his hammer was missing, he went straight to Loki, who soon discovered the culprit: Thrym, Lord of the Giants. Thrym told Loki that he would return the hammer only if he were given the goddess Freyja as his bride. However, when Loki and Thor told Freyja to prepare herself for marriage, she flew into a rage and would not hear of it.

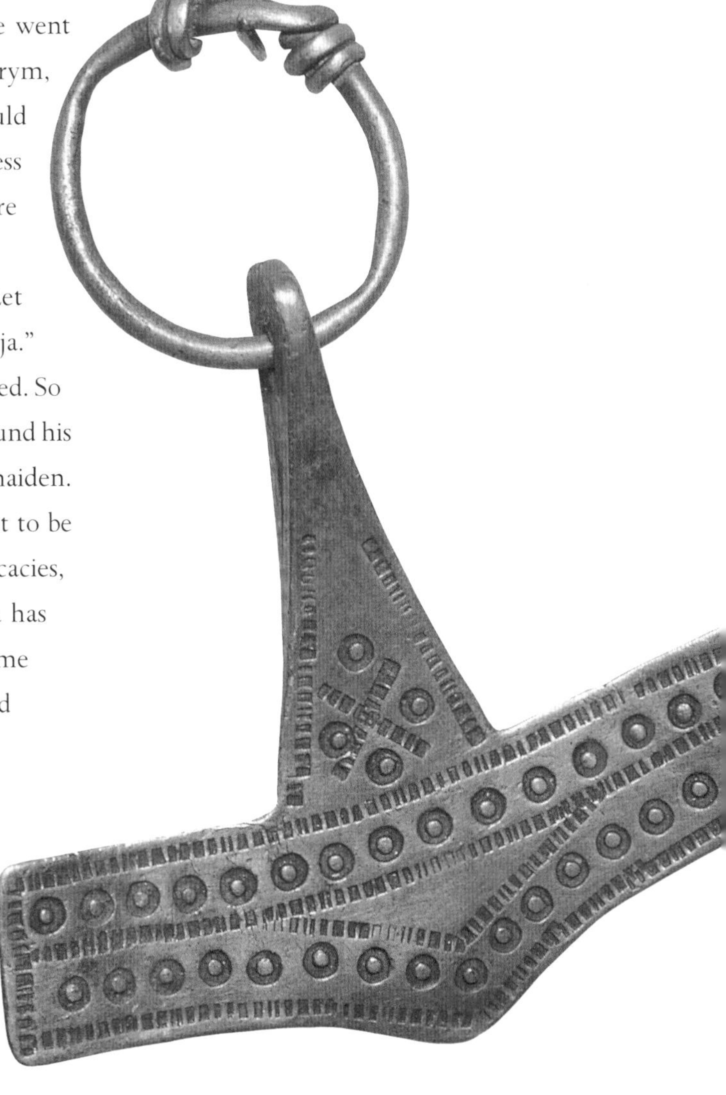

Heimdall came up with a solution to this dangerous situation: "Let us dress Thor in bridal clothes and send him to Thrym in place of Freyja." Thor protested hotly but Loki reminded him of Asgard's fate if he refused. So Thor was dressed in bridal finery, with Freyja's prized gold necklace around his neck and a veil over his head. Loki went with him dressed as his handmaiden.

Thrym was very pleased to see Freyja, and ordered a great feast to be prepared. Thor ate a whole ox, eight salmon and all the other delicacies, washed down with three horns of mead. Thrym was aghast. "Freyja has eaten and drunk nothing for eight whole nights, so eager was she to come to Giantland," explained Loki. On hearing that, Thrym was so pleased he went to kiss Freyja, but reeled back in fright. "Why are Freyja's eyes so red and fierce?" he gasped. Loki quickly replied, "Freyja has not slept for eight nights, so eager was she to come to Giantland."

As gullible as the other giants, Thrym was satisfied and eager to proceed with the wedding. He ordered the hammer to be brought in to hallow the couple. As soon as it was laid on the bride's lap, Thor leaped up, grabbed Mjollnir and tore off his veil. Armed once again, he crushed all the giants in the hall, choosing Thrym as the first of his victims.

Thor Fights the World Serpent

Jormungand, the Midgard serpent – so large it could wrap itself around the world – was Thor's most formidable adversary. The god's meeting with a giant gave him an opportunity to destroy it, which he greatly desired to do.

Thor was travelling across Midgard, having adopted the appearance of a young boy. During this journey he took lodgings at the home of a giant called Hymir who was about to undertake a fishing expedition. Seeing this as an opportunity to confront the world serpent, Thor enquired if he could accompany him. The giant looked him up and down and replied dismissively that he would not be much use as he was so small. Thor, mindful that he needed the boat, had to restrain his temper. Hymir ordered his companion to find his own bait, so Thor tore off the head of the largest ox in Hymir's herd.

The pair launched a boat and rowed fast, until Hymir said that they had reached his usual fishing ground. Thor insisted that they continue further, so they took up the oars again. When Hymir suggested that it would be dangerous to go any further because of Jormungand, Thor ignored him and rowed on. Finally, Thor chose a strong line with a huge hook on the end, to which he fastened the ox-head before throwing it overboard.

Deep under the sea the Midgard serpent went for the bait and swallowed the hook. It pulled away so violently that Thor was flung dramatically against the side of the boat. Summoning up all his strength, he pushed his feet through the bottom of the boat and braced them against the seabed. Then he pulled up the serpent. He was about to lift his hammer to strike the monster when Hymir cut Thor's line so that the creature sank back into the sea. Thor threw his hammer in after it and some say that the serpent's head was struck off, but most people say that it lived on and still encircles the world.

The Lure of the Necklace

As soon as she saw it, Freyja knew she had to have the Necklace of the Brisings. The chain was made by four dwarves, renowned for their prowess in working with gold, and they were not prepared to part with it lightly.

One day Freyja chanced upon the home of four dwarves who were engaged in working gold, their usual occupation. She saw that they were fashioning an exquisite necklace, the like of which she had never seen before. As she looked at the beautiful chain she coveted it. She was certain that no neck other than hers should be adorned by such a jewel.

She offered to buy the necklace from the dwarves, but they replied that it was not for sale. Freyja offered them everything she had of value, but the dwarves were immovable.

The more stubborn the dwarves became, the more Freyja wanted the necklace; she was soon consumed by her desire to own it. Eventually the dwarves named their price: "We have all we want, there is no object you can offer us, Freyja. The only thing we truly desire is you. If you will spend one night with each of us, then we promise to give you the necklace."

Taken aback, Freyja reflected on the dwarves' proposal. Her desire for the necklace was insuperable, and for a goddess whose sexual appetite was the talk of Asgard, four illicit nights did not seem a high price to pay. Besides, thought Freyja, no one would know. So she agreed to the dwarves' terms.

Freyja was as true to her promise as the dwarves were to theirs; the necklace was to become her most prized possession.

How the Gods Gained Treasures

Dwarves were the craftsmen of Germanic mythology. Although they jealously guarded their skill and their gold, the artful Loki persuaded them to make six treasures which he then gave to the gods, to the especial benefit of Thor.

Ever the mischief-maker, Loki decided to cut off all of the goddess Sif's golden hair as she slept. When Thor heard of Loki's prank he threatened to break every bone in his body. So, in terror, Loki promised that he would convince the dwarves to fashion a new head of hair from gold.

The dwarves agreed to help him out of trouble and please the gods. They not only made the head of hair for Sif, but also crafted the ship Skidbladnir, which, when its sail was raised, would always get a fair wind and could be fitted in a pocket when it was not being used. As if this was not enough, they also forged the invincible spear Gungnir.

But Loki could not resist further scheming. He made a bet with two dwarf brothers that they could not make treasures as precious as the first three. They duly produced three more, despite the efforts of Loki who, as a fly, tried to distract them.

Loki took all the treasures to Asgard. He gave the hair to Sif, and it took root on her head. Then he gave Skidbladnir to Freyr and Gungnir to Odin, and both were greatly pleased. Next, he handed over the last three treasures. The first was the gold ring Draupnir for Odin. It is said that eight rings of equal weight and value dripped from it every ninth night. Second, for Freyr, was a golden boar which ran across the sky and sea faster than any horse and shed light from its bristles. The third was the magical hammer Mjollnir (see page 85), which he gave to Thor. The gods thus owe their greatest treasures to Loki, although, in deciding that Mjollnir was the best gift, the gods stated that the dwarves had won the wager with Loki, which he reneged on.

The Golden Apples

Ever the menace, Loki allowed his actions to threaten the gods with extinction. But it was also his resourcefulness that eventually saved them.

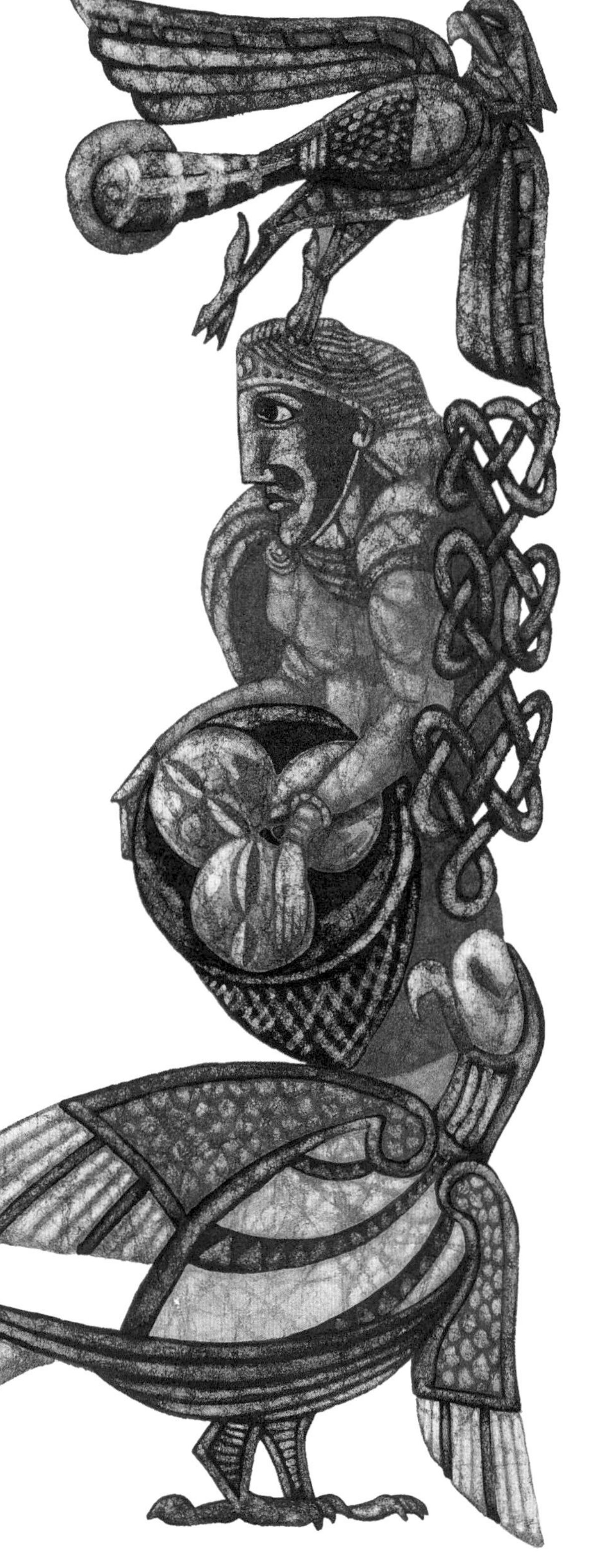

Loki was taken captive by a giant called Thiazi, who would not free him unless he promised to deliver to him the goddess Idunn and her precious apples of eternal youth, which she carried with her at all times. Always thinking of himself, Loki vowed to do this, so the giant released him.

Loki contrived to lure Idunn into a forest beyond the safe confines of Asgard, where Thiazi swooped down on her in the shape of an eagle, snatched her up and took her to his home.

The gods were immediately affected by the loss of the youth-giving fruit and in a trice grew old and grey. Fearing for their lives, they met together to decide what to do. They discovered that Idunn had last been sighted with Loki, so they seized him and threatened him with death if he did not recover her and her apples. Loki promised to find her, and borrowed Freyja's falcon shape to fly to Thiazi's castle in Giantland. Luckily, he found Idunn there all alone, and quickly transformed her into a nut so that he could fly home to Asgard with her grasped in his claws.

When Thiazi returned and discovered his captive had escaped, he adopted the eagle shape again and gave chase. The Aesir saw the falcon flying with a nut gripped in its claws and the eagle following closely behind. They acted quickly and built a fire in Asgard. The falcon flew over the wall and immediately dropped down to safety, but the eagle was not able to take evasive action straight away and flew directly into the flames, where it perished.

Binding the Wolf Fenrir

The gods were afraid that the huge wolf Fenrir – born of an illicit coupling between Loki and the giantess Angrboda – would cause them serious harm, so they attempted to restrain it. But they could not have done so without the selfless bravery of Tyr, the god of war.

When the gods saw how huge Fenrir was growing, they were alarmed and decided to bind the creature. They found a strong iron fetter, called Laeding, and suggested that the wolf pit his strength

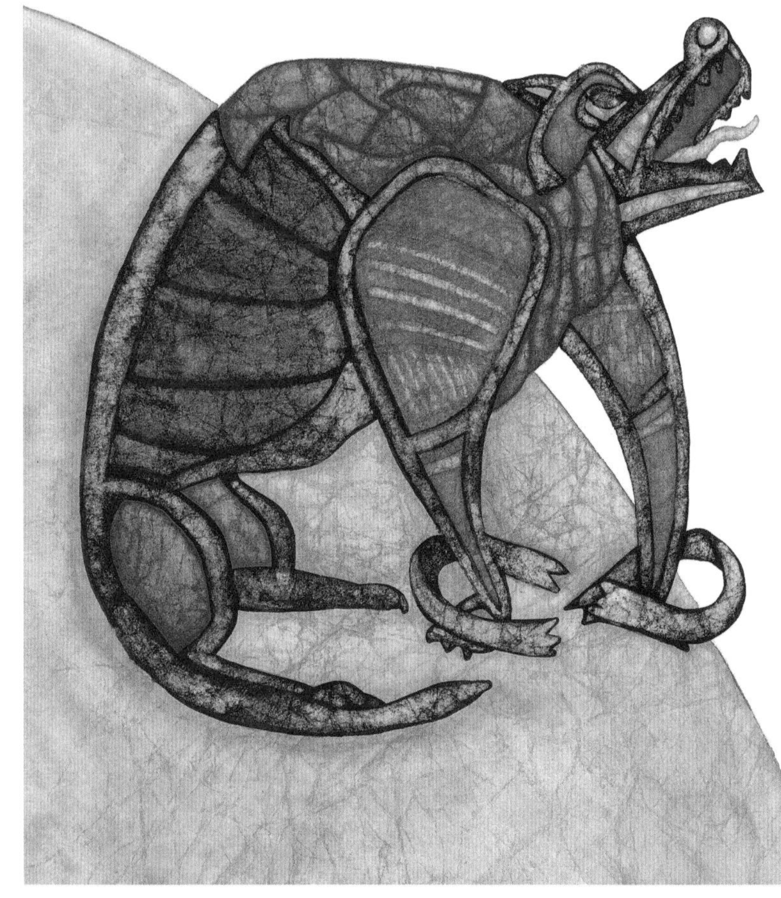

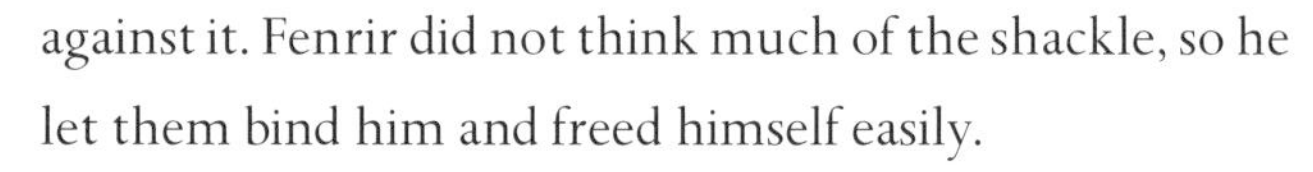

against it. Fenrir did not think much of the shackle, so he let them bind him and freed himself easily.

The gods forged another fetter twice as strong, called Dromi, and urged the wolf to try again. They said that Fenrir would become very famous if he could shake off this binding. Fenrir felt even stronger now and broke from Dromi with ease. The Aesir now feared that they would not be able to restrain Fenrir.

Odin then sent word to the dwarves that they should make another fetter, Gleipnir. It was smooth, soft and silky as a ribbon, but deceptively strong. The Aesir were very pleased. Fenrir looked at it carefully and said, "I do not think I will gain much of a reputation by breaking such a thin ribbon, and if this band is made by magical art then, thin as it is, it is not going around my legs." Fenrir thought again and said, "If I cannot free myself I will have to wait a very long time before you free me. But, lest you think I am a coward, I will take part in this game if one of you will dare to put his hand in my mouth."

None of the gods dared take this risk until at last Tyr volunteered to put his right hand into Fenrir's mouth. At that the wolf allowed itself to be bound, but discovered that the harder he kicked the stronger the fetter became. The Aesir all laughed – except Tyr, who lost his hand to Fenrir's jaws.

Njord & Skadi

The mountain goddess Skadi was the daughter of the giant Thiazi whom the Aesir killed after he had stolen the golden apples of youth (see page 89). She arrived at Asgard determined to avenge her father. The Aesir, hoping to placate her, offered her the pick of the unmarried gods.

In full armour Skadi must have made an impression upon the Aesir. Repenting the death of her father, they were eager to make amends by helping her find a husband. But the gods make nothing easy for the giants or their offspring; a parade was carefully arranged in which only the gods' feet were visible.

Skadi picked the pair that was by far the cleanest, whitest and best kept. She was sure that they must belong to Balder, the fairest and most desirable of all the gods.

Then the owner of the feet was made to reveal his identity. Instead of Balder, Skadi had chosen Njord, god of the sea, whose feet were pristine because the sea continually washed over them. At first, Skadi was taken aback, but she agreed to the marriage anyway.

The partnership was a difficult one; Skadi, the daughter of a mountain giant, longed to live in her peak-top sanctuary, but Njord did not feel comfortable anywhere other than by the sea. They agreed to compromise by residing for nine nights in Thrymheim, Skadi's mountain castle, followed by nine nights at Noatun, Njord's coastal abode.

But this arrangement failed to satisfy either Skadi or Njord – each was desperately unhappy in the other's home. Njord could not bear the dark foreboding mountains, surrounded by the eerie sound of howling wolves, and Skadi could not tolerate the vast expanse of sea and complained about the screeching of the gulls.

Eventually the two were forced to live apart; Njord stayed by the sea while Skadi returned to the mountains, where she was often to be seen roaming the slopes.

Freyr Falls in Love

Gerd personified the cornfield. Held in the clutches of the giants she was unable to flourish and needed the help of Freyr, Lord of Fertility, to break her wintry internment.

One day Freyr sat in Odin's high seat, forbidden to others, from where he could survey the universe. He went away full of woe, for he had seen a beautiful woman, and had fallen hopelessly in love with her.

The woman was Gerd, the daughter of two giants who confined her in their mountain home in the north. It was said that when Gerd lifted her arms, all the worlds were lit up by her beauty.

Freyr withdrew into himself and no one dared approach him. Eventually his father Njord asked Freyr's servant, Skirnir, who represented the sun, to try to discover the source of Freyr's sadness.

Freyr told Skirnir that he had fallen in love with Gerd, "and if I do not have her as my wife I fear I will not live long. You must ask her to marry me, and bring her back here whether her father agrees or not. I shall reward you well for it." Skirnir asked for Freyr's magnificent sword, which could fight on its own, and Freyr handed it to him without hesitation.

Skirnir travelled to Gerd's home, only to discover that she was reluctant to marry Freyr. Initially, Skirnir offered her the golden apples of youth and Odin's gold ring, but she was not swayed.

Skirnir then threatened violence, but still Gerd refused to marry Freyr. Eventually, Skirnir warned that he would curse her with bewitchment and the gods' wrath. At this Gerd yielded and promised to come to Asgard nine nights thence.

When Skirnir returned with the news, Freyr thought he would never be able to survive that long without his beloved. He did, however, and Freyr and Gerd finally married.

The Funeral of a God

Balder was the most beautiful and beloved of the Aesir, so when he died the other gods gave him a magnificent funeral of a kind reserved for the élite of Norse society. The god was placed on his ship and it was launched, engulfed in flames, into the sea.

Beings of many kinds attended Balder's cremation, including Odin with his ravens, Frigg with all the Valkyries, Freyja with her cats, and Freyr in his chariot drawn by the golden boar Gullinbursti.

The Aesir had to summon a giantess named Hyrrokkin to launch Balder's immense ship. She pushed the boat out with just a nudge while flames flew from the rollers and the Earth quaked. Thor was so angry at being unable to accomplish the task himself that he raised his hammer to smash the giantess's skull. But the other gods intervened on her behalf, and eventually placated him.

As Balder's body was carried on to the ship, his wife Nanna collapsed and died from grief, and was laid next to him on the pyre. Then the Aesir set the ship alight and Thor consecrated it with his hammer, Mjollnir.

At the same time, an unfortunate dwarf named Lit happened to run in front of Thor's foot. The god kicked him onto the burning ship, where he perished.

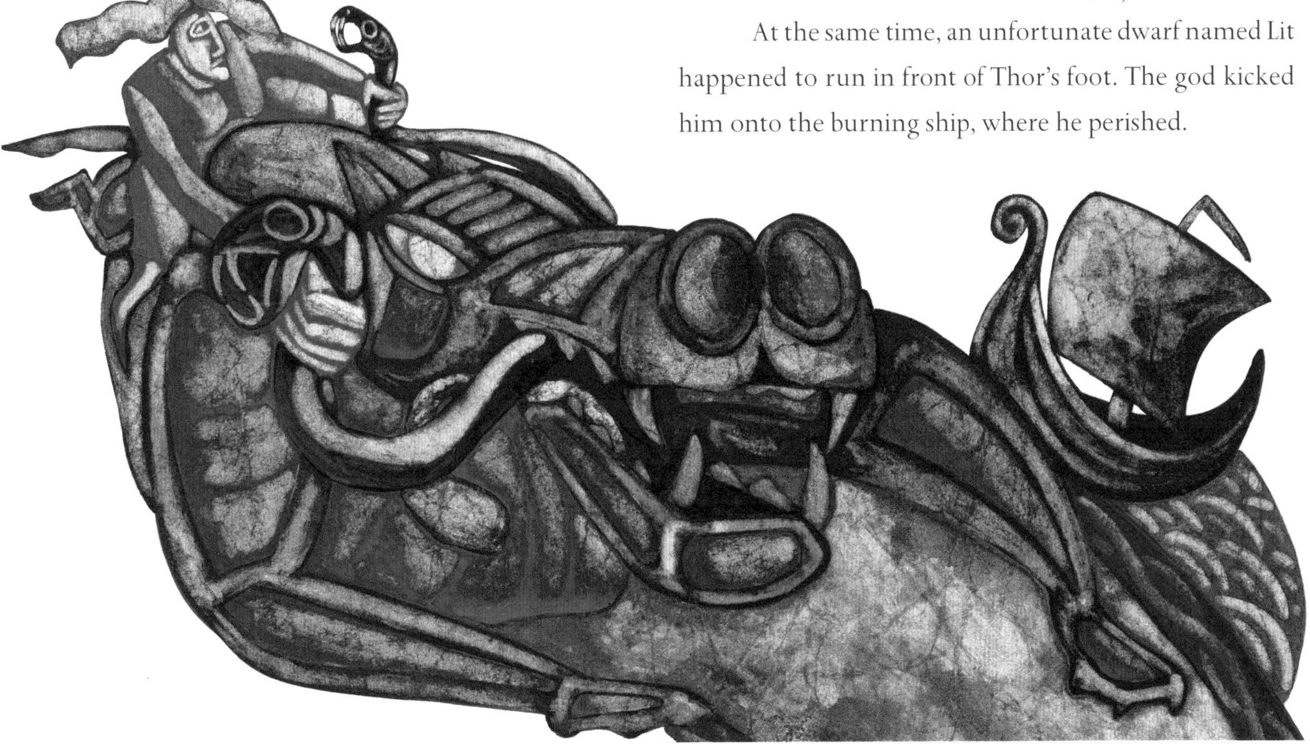

The Ploughing of Gefjun

The origin of the island of Zealand, upon which Copenhagen now stands, is explained in a myth about the goddess Gefjun. It is told that she was responsible for separating the territory from Sweden by tricking the Swedish king with her cunning and magic.

The goddess Gefjun was a minor figure among the Aesir, remembered in medieval times mainly as a patron of chastity. Yet her best-known exploit suggests that in an earlier era she had a very different reputation. For a Viking-age poem by a Swedish royal bard describes how Odin sent her travelling around the human realm of Midgard, where she chanced upon the court of King Gylfi of Sweden. There her beauty won the ruler's favour, and she willingly encouraged his advances. Having taken his pleasure with her, he rewarded her with a grant of land in his kingdom. Knowing nothing of her divine origins, he promised her as much territory as she could plough with four oxen in a day and a night.

Gefjun seized the opportunity with both hands. Setting off for Jotunheim, the realm of the giants, she used her divine powers to transform four sons born to a giant into cattle. These were the beasts with which she chose to take up Gylfi's offer. The four ploughed mightily, bearing down so hard on the earth that they detached the soil from its moorings. Then they took to the water to pull it far out into the Baltic Sea. Moving south around Sweden's tip, they finally deposited it offshore as an island, to which Gefjun gave the name of Zealand.

A huge lake – now called Lake Malar – remained in Sweden where the land had been uprooted. Observers have remarked that its inlets closely match the peninsulas on Zealand.

Walter & Hagen

In contrast with the gods and goddesses of Viking myth, most early Germanic tales that survive involve human heroes. For these courageous mortals, death was no tragedy; far more distressing was the dilemma when a man found himself trapped between conflicting loyalties.

When Etzel (Attila), the fifth-century leader of the Huns, made successful incursions into Germanic territory, he was said to have demanded three hostages as a price for ceasing hostilities: Walter of Aquitaine, Hagen the Frank, and Hildegund, who was to be married to Walter. Walter and Hagen were forced to fight in Etzel's army, where they swore friendship to each other, and Hildegund was put in charge of Etzel's treasure. However, all three escaped, taking Etzel's gold with them.

They reached the Rhine, in Hagen's homeland, and news of their coming was brought to Gunther the Frankish king, who felt he had the right to take the gold from them by force as Etzel had plundered his lands. Hagen, as Gunther's vassal, was bound by oath to assist him and so left the other two.

Walter and Hildegund encamped in a pass among rocks and there Walter prepared to fight. Gunther sent twelve Frankish warriors against Walter, and one by one they were slain, including a young nephew of Hagen. Tragically torn between honouring two sacred bonds, Hagen himself would not fight his friend, though Gunther taunted him with cowardice. He and the king withdrew.

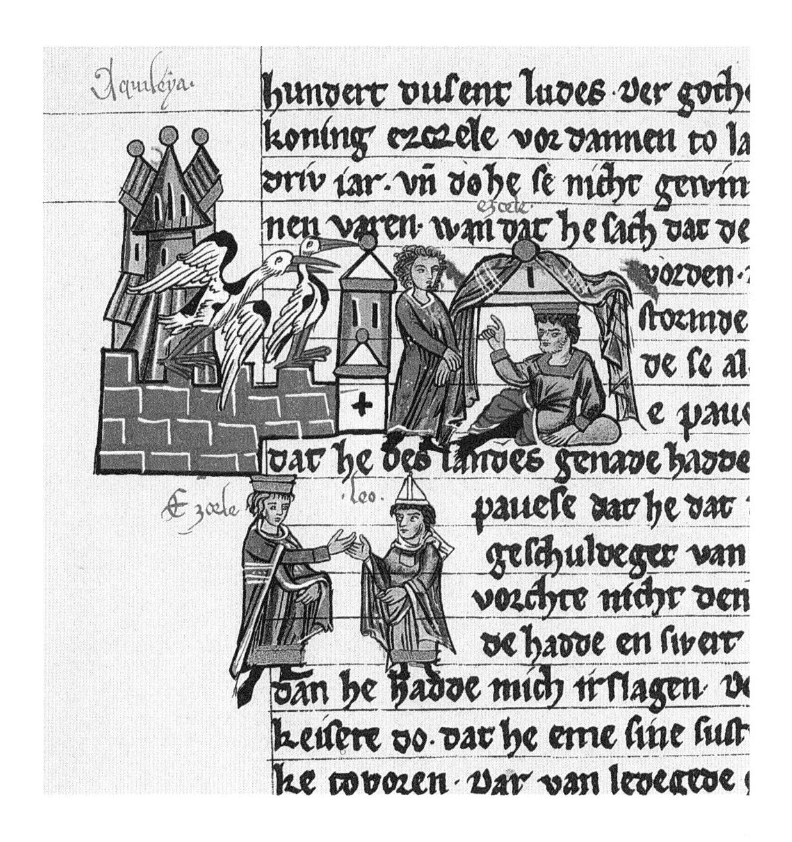

At dawn, Walter and Hildegund left their cave, only to be ambushed in open country by Gunther and Hagen. This time, Hagen joined in the attack, to avenge his nephew. Fierce was the fight of two against one, ceasing only when all three were maimed. Then at last the warriors made peace and Hildegund bound up their wounds.

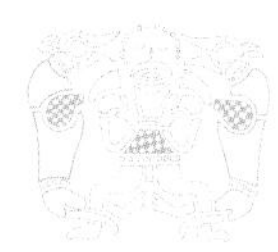

Gudrun's Revenge

In the German Nibelung legend, Gunther and Hagen killed Siegfried, then stole his gold and hid it in the Rhine. In this Norse version, Siegfried's widow (and Gunther's sister) Kriemhild was forced to marry Etzel (Attila) the Hun, whose sole purpose was to discover Sigurd's gold.

Atli (the Norse version of Etzel) invited Gunnar (Gunther) and Hogni (Hagen) to a banquet, but Gudrun (Kriemhild), suspecting treachery, sent them a ring carved with runes to warn them to keep away. Yet Gunnar replied defiantly, "Bring us ale in golden goblets, for this may be our final drink!"

They travelled to Atli's fortress, where armed men overwhelmed and captured them. They were imprisoned apart, and Gunnar was asked if he would buy his life with his treasure. "First bring me Hogni's heart," he said. So Atli's men cut out Hogni's heart and brought it to Gunnar, who cried out, "Now you will never find Sigurd's hoard, Atli! Only I know where it lies. Let the Rhine keep it, rather than Huns enjoy it!" "Take him to the snake-pit," ordered Atli. He watched while Gunnar sat chained among the poisonous creatures, playing his harp, until he died.

When Atli returned, Gudrun greeted him warmly, telling him, "I have had two young deer slaughtered to feast you." But when Atli was half drunk, she jeered at him: "The meat you have eaten and shared with your men was the hearts of our two sons. You will never see them playing again."

That night Gudrun drove a sword through Atli as he slept in a stupor, and burned the hall down, killing all who had helped cause her brother's death. No woman since has done such fearsome deeds to avenge her kin.

How Alboin Obtained a Sword

Mere prowess in battle was not enough proof of valour for the Langobard tribe. The Langobard king Alboin, who was to settle his people by conquest in northern Italy, had to prove himself in his youth by an act of courage that bordered on effrontery.

In his youth, Alboin had fought successfully in his people's war against the Gepids, and had killed their prince, Thurismod. Returning home, the warriors asked that Alboin should sit in honour at the table of his father, King Audoin, during the victory feast. But Audoin refused him this privilege, saying it was a Langobard custom not to let a prince eat at his father's table until he had managed to obtain a sword from a foreign king.

Hearing this, Alboin at once rode off with forty companions to the stronghold of Thurisend, king of the Gepids, where he claimed hospitality as a peaceful guest. Thurisend could not in honour refuse; he welcomed the Langobards to his banqueting hall, and seated Alboin at his side, where his dead son Thurismod used to sit, although he knew well that it was by Alboin's hand that Thurismod had met his death.

Others among his entourage were less patient. One of the king's younger sons mocked the Langobards because they wore white leggings: "You look like white-legged mares – have many men ridden you?" To this, one of the Langobards retorted: "You there, whose prince's bones lie scattered on the meadow like those of a wretched old pack-horse, go back to the battlefield, and learn how hard these mares can kick!"

Both sides reached for their weapons. But King Thurisend put himself between them and ordered his men to keep the peace, saying it would be an offence to God to attack guests in one's own hall. After the feast he took his dead son's sword and presented it to Alboin.

Then Alboin triumphantly returned home, and was granted a seat at his father's table. When he told what had happened, the Langobards marvelled at Alboin's boldness, and at Thurisend's great wisdom and magnanimity.

Laughing in the Face of Death

One of the most celebrated hero's deaths was that of the Viking champion Ragnar Lodbrok, who, like Gunnar (see page 96), had his fearlessness put to the supreme test by being left in a pit filled with deadly snakes.

A familiar figure in Northern epics, Ragnar Lodbrok is thought to have been modelled on a real-life raider of the ninth century. In the tales, he was a fearless warrior who mounted the Danish throne at the age of fifteen and married the lowly ward of a peasant couple only to find out later that her true parents were the Germanic heroes Siegfried and Brynhild. He rescued another of his four wives from a castle entirely entwined in the coils of a huge dragon. The name Lodbrok or "Leatherbreeches" comes from the oxhide armour he is said to have worn for that exploit.

He is probably best known, though, for the manner of his death, which occurred after a raid on England. Captured by King Ella of Northumbria, he was condemned to die in a pit of adders. At first he was shielded by a magic shirt given to him by his mother, but when this was removed he had no protection from the snakes' venom. Accepting his fate with equanimity, he bellowed forth a death-song proclaiming that he went to his end laughing.

Even so, Ragnar was to be ferociously avenged. His sons later captured King Ella and disembowelled him by opening up his back and internal organs to form the image of a spread eagle.

The Triumph of Wolfdietrich

The Germanic tale of Wolfdietrich is a classic hero legend, involving childhood rejection, dragon-slaying, a period of exile and a triumphal return. The legendary Wolfdietrich may be based on Theodoric the Great, a real ruler who seized power in Italy in the sixth century CE.

Wolfdietrich was the son of Hugdietrich, emperor of Constantinople, and the beautiful Hildeburg. But their marriage was a secret one, for Hildeburg's father Walgund would permit no suitors, and the child was born while Hugdietrich was away at the wars. One time when Hildeburg had to hide the baby to prevent her parents from discovering him, he disappeared, only to be found days later in the forest nearby playing with wolf-cubs. From that incident he won his name.

In time Walgund did learn of the marriage and accepted it. Wolfdietrich grew up to be a fine man, in every way a suitable heir to the throne. But in Constantinople a faction refused to accept him, spreading the rumour that he was not Hugdietrich's child. When the old emperor died, this group drove Wolfdietrich from the city, setting his two younger brothers on the throne in his stead.

From then on, Wolfdietrich's life was devoted to regaining his rightful inheritance. He had to suffer many trials on the way. At one point he fell into the hands of a hideous witch, Rauch-Else, who took the form of a she-bear; but when he consented unwillingly to marry her, she turned into a beautiful princess with whom he lived happily for many years. Then he sought to enlist the aid of Ortnit, king of the Lombards, in his cause, only to find that his intended ally had been killed by a dragon. Wolfdietrich confronted the beast, and succeeded in killing it with the aid of a magic shirt of invulnerability and a sword that had been tempered in dragon's blood.

Eventually, he returned to Constantinople and triumphed over his enemies. Then he returned to Lombardy to be crowned Holy Roman Emperor.

The Middle Ages

By the time of the Middle Ages, the stories by which the peoples of Europe sought to understand and interpret their lives had moved out of the realm of myth and become part of folklore and legend. The population of the continent was by then firmly Christian, and the tales in favour at the time dealt not with gods and spirits but rather with heroes, villains, and the abuses of feudal power.

Many of the narratives revolved around famed champions of the past. One such was Charlemagne, creator and first ruler of the Holy Roman Empire, who became the central figure in a cycle of epics concerned with the daring deeds of the knights of his court. This Carolingian Matter of France paralleled the Arthurian Matter of Britain, providing role models for aspirant warriors. Elaborated by Italian romancers, the cycle was given a fantastic twist in the Orlando epics, recounting the adventures of Charlemagne's paladin Roland (Italianized as Orlando) in pursuit of honour and love. The story of Bradamante and Ruggiero (see page 103) captures the playful inventiveness of Ariosto's *Orlando Furioso*, involving as it does enchanters, magical illusions, spellbound lovers, and even a hippogriff – the poet's own creation, a blend of griffin and horse.

The Spanish equivalents of the Charlemagne stories turned on El Cid. Like his Frankish counterpart, he too had some basis in reality, in his case in the figure of the eleventh-century warlord Rodrigo Díaz de Vivar, who played a prominent role in the struggle between Christian and Moorish forces on the Iberian peninsula. While the real Cid was a pragmatist, happily allying with the Moors when it served his purpose, the legendary figure became a paragon of the Christian virtues, as the story of his charitable treatment of a leper shows (see page 104).

Other romancers looked back further, to antiquity and the career of the Macedonian conqueror Alexander the Great. Initially inspired by classical accounts of his life, the medieval Alexander epics were spiced up with travellers' tales brought back from the East by the crusaders, including accounts of giant scorpions and prophetic talking trees (see page 105).

Many stories stood on their own, appealing to an audience deeply versed in the codes of chivalry and romance. Some existed in a dream-world of poetic reverie, like the legend of Thomas the Rhymer, which drew on Celtic notions of fairyland as a subterranean realm ruled over by a beautiful princess with a roving eye for human lovers (see page 107). Others, like the Lohengrin story later turned into an opera by Richard Wagner, had a Superman-like element of wish fulfilment, with a swan-borne knight arriving magically to answer the call of a damsel in distress (see page 106). A folktale that Boccaccio retold in the *Decameron* told of the struggle of a chaste wife accused wrongly of infidelity, who was vindicated only after a sequence of improbable adventures that took her to Egypt and the Muslim sultan's court (see page 112).

The combating of injustice was in fact a favoured theme across many lands throughout the Middle Ages. Often the initial wrong sprang from an abuse of feudal power. One group of stories highlighted the plight of noblemen dispossessed of lands that rightly belonged to them. This subject underlay the legends of Wild Edric (see page 109), inspired by the misfortunes of a real-life Saxon lord who lost his estates following the Norman conquest of Britain. Similar concerns also informed the tragedy of Raoul de Cambrai, incorporated into one of the Charlemagne epics, whose only redress lay in inflicting similar wrong on another rightful heir (see page 102).

The injured parties in the familiar story of Lady Godiva were the people of Coventry, subjected to extortionate taxes by the lady's own husband (see page 110). Even better known was the legend of the Pied Piper of Hameln, who took a terrible revenge on the burghers of the German town when cheated of his promised reward for services as a rodent remover (see page 113).

The Tragedy of Raoul de Cambrai

The tale of a French knight, Raoul de Cambrai, dispossessed as a child of his inheritance by Charlemagne's son King Louis I, is one of the best-known episodes in the colourful late twelfth-century French epic *Les Quatre Fils Aymon* ("The Four Sons of Aymon").

The Count de Cambrai died while his wife Aalais was pregnant with their son, Raoul. King Louis tried to force Aalais to marry Gibouin le Manceau, but she refused. The furious Louis then seized Raoul's inheritance and gave it to Gibouin in perpetuity.

Raoul grew up to be a skilled knight and a favoured member of court, but one day two young brothers were killed while under his supervision. Although Raoul was not to blame, he was too proud to explain and the boys' father, Ernaut de Douai, declared undying enmity.

Raoul pressed Louis to restore his inheritance, but the king refused, offering him instead the lands of the next knight to die. Raoul accepted these terms, though they were highly unchivalrous.

Herbert de Vermandois soon died leaving four adult sons, one of them the father of Raoul's squire, Bernier. Raoul demanded that Louis keep his promise and the king assented but said that Raoul would have to win the land in battle.

Both Bernier and Aalais tried to dissuade Raoul from rendering unto another the wrong he had suffered himself. He would not listen, and after a fierce quarrel with his mother the proud Raoul rode fully armed into the Vermandois territories. Bernier himself came to blows with Raoul but fled, hurt, to his father's camp. Then Raoul met his sworn enemy Ernaut de Douai, alongside Bernier, in battle. As the three fought Raoul declared that God Himself could not save Ernaut – a blasphemy that sealed his fate. Raoul was killed by Bernier and his body borne sorrowfully home.

Bradamante & Ruggiero

In *Orlando Furioso* ("Roland Maddened") by Lodovico Ariosto, the chaste warrior maiden Bradamante, who rode as the Virgin Knight clad in white armour, won the heart of the pagan champion Ruggiero – but there were many twists and turns in their romance.

Ruggiero was said to be descended from Hector of Troy. Nursed in infancy by a lioness, he was a ward of the magician Atlas, who kept him away from harm because a prophecy had foretold his early death.

Bradamante freed Ruggiero from Atlas's castle, which was spun from spells – only for Atlas to sweep the hero away once more on a hippogriff, a winged horse with a griffin's head. He was then freed again by another knight and travelled far and wide, but Atlas always worked to bring him back to safety.

One enchanted day, deep in a forest glade, Ruggiero encountered a knight and a giant locked in single combat. The giant downed and prepared to dispatch his opponent, but just then the knight's helmet came loose and Ruggiero saw that the fallen champion was none other than his beloved Bradamante. As he leaped forward to save her, the giant swept her up and ran deeper into the forest with the knight over his shoulder, leading Ruggiero to an enchanted castle. There he searched for her but without success, for Atlas had had his way once more: both the maiden in the likeness of Bradamante and the castle itself he had created by his magic.

The time came when the real Bradamante rode by the same glade and Atlas used a phantom in the form of Ruggiero to lure the virgin champion into his lair. She too searched vainly for her beloved. When they were later freed from the spell, Bradamante and Ruggiero embraced passionately. The pagan knight converted to the Christian faith to win her hand. Eventually, the two were wed at Charlemagne's court; splendid pavilions were raised and the fields decorated with garlands.

El Cid & the Leper

Preserved in medieval Spanish ballads and chronicles, the legend of El Cid was based on the life of the eleventh-century nobleman Rodrigo Díaz de Vivar. El Cid's generosity toward a roadside beggar is one of many episodes celebrating Don Rodrigo's piety and knightly virtue.

The great El Cid rode at the head of a company of twenty knights, to pay his respects at the shrine of James, Spain's national saint, at Santiago de Compostela.

When he came upon a leper in the road, calling in a frail voice for Christian charity, El Cid stopped his horse, dismounted and helped the leper to his feet. He lifted the man into the saddle, then climbed up himself and rode on with the leper sharing his mount.

Later they stopped for the night at an inn. Don Rodrigo insisted that the leper be admitted and even brought him to his own table to eat. As the candles were lit at the end of the day Don Rodrigo led the leper into the chamber he himself had been allocated and there allowed him to share his bed.

In the darkest hour of night the Christian warrior woke with a start, feeling a cold breath between his shoulders. He leaped from his bed and called for a light; when the shadows were banished neither he nor the manservant could see the leper anywhere in the chamber.

Then the great champion fell to his knees, for he saw an apparition blazing with the light of Heaven. The ghost declared itself to be Lazarus, the corpse raised from death by Christ himself. He, Lazarus, had taken the form of the leper whose suffering El Cid had relieved the previous day. Then he foretold a wonderful future for the warrior, an honourable death and welcome into Paradise. The vision faded, and for the rest of the night Don Rodrigo remained on his knees praising the Virgin Mary and God the Father, Son and Holy Ghost.

Alexander's Letters to Aristotle

The exploits of the fourth-century BCE Macedonian general Alexander the Great were the basis of a series of romance narratives that were familiar throughout medieval Europe. Some of the more exotic stories take the form of letters written by Alexander to his tutor Aristotle.

One of Alexander's missives describes how, on a visit to an untamed part of the world, the general's army saw a great city that seemed to float in the air – for it was constructed on top of reeds that thronged a riverbank. When they tasted the river water it was foul, and some of the men who tried to bathe there were eaten by reptiles.

Later, when they were thirsty after a long march, they came across a lake with sweet waters and camped beside it. That night, horned snakes and scorpions the length of a man's forearm emerged from the ground and attacked the soldiers. Fierce beasts came to drink at the lake; they included foul-breathed animals with the faces of women but the jaws and fangs of dogs.

On another campaign, in India, Alexander was shown a sacred garden filled with talking trees. They stood at the centre of the garden, surrounded by a hedge. One, sacred to a sun god named Mitora, spoke three times each day – at dawn, noon and dusk; another, the tree of a moon god called Mayosa, spoke twice, at midnight and in the early morning. At sunset, Alexander heard words emerge from the first tree. It made its utterance in the local language, and Alexander had to pester a priest to reveal what the oracle had said. In fact, it had warned Alexander that he would soon be killed by his own men.

Later that night he returned to the precinct close to the time when the moon tree was due to pronounce, and again he was not disappointed. A deep voice sounded from the timber, revealing more dread news – great Alexander would die at Babylon, far from home. In truth the gods spoke wisely for he was to face a mutiny that would force him to retreat from India, and in 323 BCE at Babylon on the Euphrates Alexander would die – of fever, rather than treachery.

The Mysterious Swan Knight

On his deathbed, the Duke of Brabant left his daughter Else in the care of a much-feared knight called Frederick, who wished to marry her. She refused, but Frederick got permission from the emperor to win her by right of combat, against any champion she chose.

Hard as she tried, Else could not find anyone prepared to fight Frederick. However, her predicament started a magic bell ringing in the blessed land of the Holy Grail, the cup used to offer the first communion at the Last Supper. The sound of the bell summoned Lohengrin, the son of the Grail's guardian, to aid her.

Lohengrin was about to mount his horse and set off when he saw a swan on the river, pulling a shallow boat, and he realized that it had come for him.

In Brabant, the day for the contest arrived, and, without a challenger, Frederick was about to claim Else. Whereupon the swan-drawn boat pulled up to the riverbank, with the sleeping Lohengrin inside. Waking, he leaped onto the shore, and the swan swam off.

Lohengrin then fought and killed Frederick, and Else offered herself and her lands to him. He accepted, but only if she agreed never to ask where he came from.

They lived happily for several years, but after Lohengrin broke a knight's arm in a tournament, the man's wife began to question his past. When Else heard this, she cried every night until at last she asked Lohengrin where he was from. He told her, but at dawn the next day the swan came for him and he departed.

True Thomas of Erceldoune

Thomas the Rhymer, or True Thomas as he is also known, was a famous character from Scottish folklore, said to have been based on the historical Thomas Learmont, a thirteenth-century laird. It was said that an elf-queen granted him the gift of always telling the truth.

Thomas was resting on the banks of a ravine when he saw a woman riding toward him. She was so lovely that, when she came near, he asked if she were the queen of heaven. "No," she answered, "I am the queen of elfland." She then explained that she had come to take Thomas to live with her for seven years, and that if he kissed her he would be under her spell.

Thomas promptly climbed on to the back of her horse. The pair flew like the wind until they came to a fragrant garden. Thomas wanted to eat some of its fruit, but the elf-queen warned him that it contained the plagues of all humankind. She gave him bread and wine, and after he had eaten she pointed out the three paths that led from the garden.

The first one, winding through prickly briers, was the path of righteousness. The second, running through a lily field, was the way of wickedness. The third led to elfland – but before they took it the queen warned Thomas not to say a word while in her country, or he would not get back to his own land.

They travelled for forty days and nights before finally they reached the elf-queen's garden. There she gave Thomas an apple which, once eaten, would prevent him from ever telling a lie when he went back home.

Thomas ended up staying in elfland for seven years. When he returned home, he won a reputation as a great prophet, for all the predictions he made came true.

The Worth of Hynd Horn

While there were medieval stories about love across class boundaries, most romance occurred between social equals. Birth-status notwithstanding, in a number of tales a knight would go on a quest in pursuit of glory so that he might deserve his beloved when he returned.

Although he was of noble birth, Hynd Horn was not rich and worked as a servant at the court of the king. One day he was spotted by the king's daughter, who immediately fell in love with him. She begged him to marry her, but he protested that he was not wealthy enough to marry a princess, and would only agree if her father knighted him first.

The girl persuaded her father, and as soon as Hynd was a knight, she pestered him again to marry her. This time, though, he insisted that he must first prove himself in combat before he could be deemed worthy of her.

Before he departed, the princess gave him a special ring. If it ever lost its gleam, she warned, he would have lost her to another man. For seven years he travelled in foreign countries, often checking the ring, until one day he noticed that it had become tarnished.

Returning home swiftly, he met a beggar, who told him that the princess had been married for nine days, but she was refusing to go to her husband's bed until she heard news of Hynd Horn. Hearing this, Hynd swapped his clothes for the rags belonging to the beggar and went promptly to the palace where the couple lived.

At the gate, he asked for a drink served by the bride's own hand. The princess brought him a goblet, and after draining it he slipped the ring inside. She asked who had given him the ring, and he replied that she had, long ago. At that, the princess recognized him, and left her husband to run away with Hynd Horn.

Tales of Wild Edric

The Saxon resistance to the Norman conquest spawned legends across England, notably the Fens saga of Hereward the Wake. On the Welsh border another dispossessed nobleman took up arms against the invaders, winning a lasting place in local folklore by his deeds.

In real life, Edric was a Saxon nobleman who rose in revolt against the Normans to defend his lands in Shropshire and Herefordshire. He waged a guerrilla campaign that won him the nicknames "Edric of the Woods" and "Edric the Wild". After three years' struggle he reportedly came to an accommodation with King William, even accompanying him on a punitive raid into Scotland. The arrangement evidently did not last, however, for the Domesday Book revealed that he had indeed lost most, if not all, of his lands.

History then forgot him, but legend kept his memory alive. Medieval chroniclers claimed that, lost in the forest one night, he abducted a fairy bride, only to lose her years later when he broke a promise never to mention her supernatural origins. In later times people insisted that he did not die but lived on with his men in the lead mines of Shropshire, ready to ride forth at their head whenever England needed him. Another tradition even maintained that he bequeathed his sword to a great fish, which was sometimes seen in Bowmere Pool near Shrewsbury with the weapon strapped to its side.

A Woman's Ride for Justice

One famous English tale relates how it took a lady to make common cause with the people. In an age when women had little political influence, she used the only weapon available to her – her beauty.

There really was a Lady Godiva – more correctly, Godgifu or "Gift of God" – though there is no contemporary record of the ride through the city of Coventry for which she became famous. The earliest record of the event comes in the chronicle of Roger of Wendover, writing more than 150 years later, who gives the date as 1057.

As he told the story, Godiva was constantly pestering her husband, Earl Leofric of Mercia, to reduce the taxes on the people of Coventry, where the two had jointly founded a monastery in 1043. Tiring of her ceaseless pleading, he eventually told her he would do as she wished – but only if she would ride naked through the town's busy marketplace. No doubt he intended merely to put an end to her cajolery, but if so he misjudged his wife. For she duly did as he required, taking care to cover her nakedness with her long flowing hair.

The detail that all townsmen were ordered to stay indoors behind shutters for her ride was a later addition, as was the story that one, Peeping Tom, disobeyed and was struck blind for his effrontery. But there is at least some evidence that Coventry really did pay little tax in the early Middle Ages – an enquiry carried out in the late thirteenth century established that the only toll in force there was one on horses.

The Weasel & the Baby

Bestiaries were a distinctive feature of medieval intellectual life, scanning animal behaviour in search of human morals. Something of their spirit showed up in folk tales that drew emotional parallels between people and animals, as a Welsh tale about a weasel showed.

The medieval fascination with animals also expressed itself in fables, a well-developed literary genre at the time. Geoffrey Chaucer included the tale of the strutting cockerel Chanticleer, lured through vanity into the fox's mouth, in his *Canterbury Tales*. Foxes were favourite anti-heroes of the time, starring in animal tales from across Europe. Many of the best stories found their way into a mock epic, the *Roman de Renart*, compiled in France in the thirteenth century but bringing together folk material from a much earlier time.

Much of Reynard's appeal came from his cartoon-like antics, relying on quick wits to get the better of his adversaries. Yet the compiler of the *Roman* framed the tales in terms of the fox's supposed trial before a Council of Animals, thereby setting the scene for a series of satirical digs at the society of the day.

The fox's only rival for slyness was the weasel, thought at the time to be venomous. Yet as one story from a medieval chronicle revealed, it could also show very human emotions. According to Gerald of Wales, a man found a weasel's nest inside a sheepskin in his house in Pembroke and carefully removed it with the weasel's young still inside. When the mother returned and found her litter gone, she determined to take revenge. So she went to the jug of milk set aside for the man's infant son and, raising herself on her hind legs, spat poison into it.

The man saw her doing so, and hurried to put the sheepskin back in its place. When the mother weasel saw that no harm had been done to her young, she squeaked with delight, then rushed back to the jug and knocked it over so that all the milk was spilt. In her gratitude at the return of her own offspring, she vowed to ensure that no harm should come to the human child.

A Faithful Wife Vindicated

One story of changing fortunes from Giovanni Boccaccio's *Decameron* told of a wife's revenge on the man who had wronged her. And although it took several years to enact, it nonetheless tasted sweet when it finally came.

When Bernabo of Genoa boasted of the fidelity of his wife Zinevra, his fellow-merchant Ambrogiuolo wagered him 5,000 florins that he could seduce her – for, he argued, no woman was chaste. Then he cheated to win the bet. He had himself carried into her chamber concealed in a chest. Emerging at night when she was asleep, he was able to note enough details of the room and of her own uncovered charms to convince Bernabo that she had indeed been unfaithful. Furious, he paid up the money, then gave orders that his wife be killed.

But the servant deputed to carry out the deed had not the heart for murder. Instead he let her go. Disguised as a boy, she found her way to Egypt and took service with the sultan, rising to a position of authority in his court.

Then one day several years later, her betrayer Ambrogiuolo came to Egypt on a trading venture. Recognizing some former objects of hers among his merchandise, Zinevra wormed the story of his duplicity out of him. Using a stratagem to draw Bernabo from Italy, she summoned both men before the sultan and then, under threat of torture, forced Ambrogiuolo to reveal the truth.

Bernabo was overcome with guilt, bemoaning the terrible wrong he had done his wife. At that point Zinevra revealed her true identity, and the two were reconciled.

As for the wicked Ambrogiuolo, the sultan sentenced him to death: covered in honey and tied to a post in the sun, he was left to the flies and mosquitoes.

The Pied Piper of Hameln

On 26 June 1284 a strange figure attired in multi-coloured costume approached the town fathers of Hameln in the Brunswick region and offered to solve a problem that had been troubling them: a plague of rats that infested their larders and cellars.

The burghers agreed on terms with the stranger, and he proceeded to play his pipe from street to street, charming the vermin into following the music. Then he led the rats to the nearby river, where they all drowned.

The council was delighted to be rid of the pests, but not so eager to pay the bill. The mysterious musician ended up cheated. So sometime later he returned to the town to take a terrible revenge. Once more he played his pipe, only this time to a different tune. Now it was the town's children that pursued him, all the way to a hill called Koppen. And there they and their leader vanished, apparently into its slopes, never to be seen again.

The legend was so firmly entrenched in Hameln by the late Middle Ages that councillors dated documents "from the year of the transmigration of the children" and banned musicians from their streets. Today scholars suggest that some actual incident may have become confused in the folk memory with a genuine migration out of Saxony to Hungary, or even with the Children's Crusade of 1212. Then, thousands of children from the Rhine Valley set out on a hopeless mission to liberate the Holy Land; most starved to death or were sold into slavery and, like the children of Hameln, never came home.

The Slavic East

The Slavs entered history in the fifth and sixth centuries CE, moving westward from the lands north of the Black Sea and settling in eastern Europe and the Balkan peninsula. Later incursions by Magyars and other invaders would split them geographically between Western Slavs, inhabiting Poland, the Czech lands and Slovakia, Eastern Slavs in Russia and the Ukraine, and the Southern Slavs of Bulgaria and the Balkans.

Over time different groups developed their own languages, all derived from a Proto-Slavic tongue spoken across borders as late as the seventh century CE. Cultural differences also emerged as the separate groups found their own way to Christianity from a shared paganism that centred on the worship of powerful nature gods. The Eastern Slavs of Kievan Russia were converted by the Byzantine missionaries Cyril and Methodius, who won them over to the Orthodox version of the faith and also endowed them with the Cyrillic script used in Russia to this day. The Western Slavs in contrast adopted Roman Catholicism. As for the Southern Slavs, they split between the two, with Bulgarians, Serbs and Macedonians settling for Orthodoxy and Croats and Slovenes choosing Catholicism, thereby implanting cultural differences that still continue to echo.

The old pagan beliefs, however, lived on, although hidden under a Christian veneer. Russian folklorists who studied the phenomenon in the nineteenth century coined the word *dvoeverie* ("dual faith") to describe the way in which the two traditions intermingled. Odd couplings continued to crop up in folktales, among them a curious one describing a carpenter, representing the Russian Everyman, outwitting his two housemates: Perun, the old Slav storm god, and the Christian Devil (see page 117). Memories of Perun also lay behind Tsar Medvyed, King of the Bears, a figure of power who, like the storm-bringer, used thunderbolts as weapons (see page 128).

Unreformed attitudes also found expression in supposedly Christian stories of the patriarchs and saints. One such had the prophet Elijah behaving with all the vindictiveness of an unappeased pagan god toward a peasant farmer, who was only saved through the good offices of kindly St Nicholas, the original Santa Claus (see page 118).

Santa Claus was in fact only one of several iconic figures that Slav legend passed on to the wider world. Vampires were largely products of the Slavic imagination, although the ones met with in folktales there were often more to be pitied than feared (see page 125). Much the same applied to werewolves, who generally either inherited their condition or had it imposed on them by hostile magic (see page 127). Another character who won international fame was the evil witch Baba Yaga, a fearsome bogeywoman who lived in a forest hut raised on chicken's legs, and who in the stories was generally bested by the smart thinking of her peasant victims (see page 126).

Slavic stories were in fact an important source for the fairytales that became popular in western Europe from the nineteenth century on. Familiar elements from Jack and the Beanstalk crop up in the tale of the Fox Physician (see page 123), although the Slav version has an ending that would be too grotesque for the average pantomime audience today.

Other recurrent figures in the Russian folk lexicon included a range of domestic and nature spirits that folklorists generally consider to be the distant descendants of ancient Slav gods. The household sprites known as *domovoi* had their equivalents in Britain's boggarts, Sweden's *tomte*, and German kobolds; generally benevolent in their attitude toward the humans who shared their homes, they could turn hostile if treated thoughtlessly (see page 120). The *leshii* were forest guardians, feared by solitary travellers for their malicious pranks (see page 122). As for the *bogatyr*, they were legendary figures once celebrated in the *byliny* oral epics of Kievan Russia, remembered in later times as fairytale heroes who killed dragons and rescued princesses (see page 129).

A Hero from the Holy Mountains

The epic hero, or *bogatyr*, Svyatogor, a warrior of apparently peerless strength and courage, met his match when he least expected it. His tale comes from one of the earliest extant cycles of *byliny*, or songs, celebrating the mythical "Elder heroes".

One day Svyatogor prepared to set out on a long journey across the steppes. He whistled a familiar tune and stroked his steed as he strapped on his favourite saddle. Then he leaped up and set off at a gallop.

Svyatogor felt full of life. He clenched his hands on the reins, exalting in his own strength – so great that it was like a weight he carried around. He laughed as he looked across the immense plain and shouted a boast that he was strong enough to lift the Earth in his bare hands.

Then he saw a saddle bag on the ground before him. Curious, the great warrior brought his horse to a halt and tried to flick the bag up with his whip handle: but it would not move. Next he leaned down and attempted to raise it with his finger: but it was as heavy as a boulder. Still in the saddle, he tried to shift the bag with one hand, without success. Again Svyatogor laughed, for he realized the bag was enchanted and that meant a challenge.

Down he leaped and took the sack with both hands. Roaring with the effort, he succeeded in lifting the bag to the level of his knees. But when he looked down he saw that he had sunk deep into the earth and that the bag still rested on the ground. Red drops splashed onto his arms – for tears of blood were pouring from his eyes.

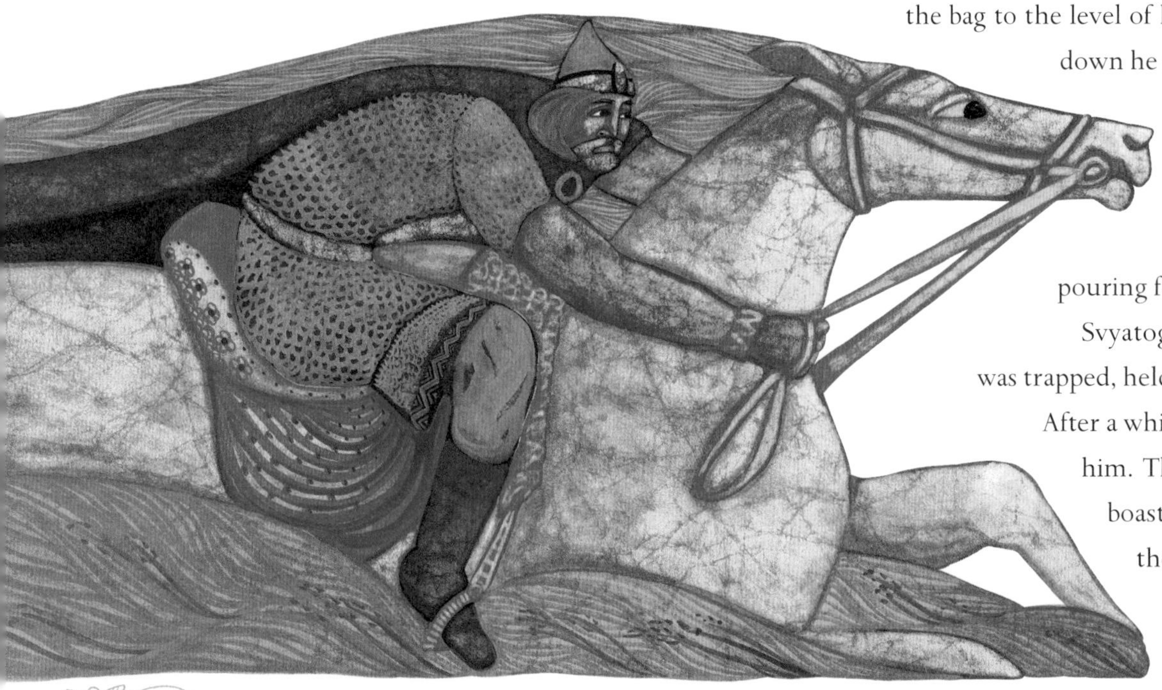

Svyatogor tried to clamber out but he was trapped, held magically by the clinging soil. After a while his faithful horse abandoned him. The *bogatyr* bitterly regretted his boast. And there in that lonely place, the great man met his demise, slowly wasting away under the unheeding sky.

The Carpenter, Perun & the Devil

The foremost deity in the pantheon of pre-Christian Russia was Perun, god of thunder and war. In a folktale of the Christian era, Perun becomes the companion of the Devil and a humble carpenter.

The three found a place to live in the forest, and the carpenter built a hut for them. They began to grow vegetables until, one night, a thief came and stole all their turnips.

The following night Perun lay in wait for the robber. He heard the creak of wagon wheels and flung himself into the darkness, but he was caught by a stinging whip and brought to his knees. The Devil laughed at this and promised to gain revenge. But on the following night he too was thrashed by the mysterious miscreant.

On the third night the carpenter sat up, armed only with a violin. At midnight he began to play a folk dance. Instantly the thief appeared, a withered old woman, and begged to be taught the tune.

The carpenter promised the hag that he could make her old fingers supple enough to play the notes. Leading her to a tree that he had split with an axe, he placed her hands in the crack, then knocked the wedge away, trapping her fingers. He made the witch vow never to return to the hut and then drove her away in her cart, which he then kept for his own use.

Perun, the Devil and the carpenter decided to part soon afterwards. All three wanted to stay in the hut so they agreed to hold a contest, with the prize going to the one who was able to frighten the other two. The Devil went first, whipping up a raging wind. Perun fled, but the carpenter was unmoved. The next night Perun unleashed a deafening thunderstorm. This time the Devil decamped, but the carpenter sat calmly through it.

When it was his turn, the carpenter rode up to the hut in the witch's wagon, taunting the others with their failures. The Devil and Perun fled, never to return – and the carpenter settled down to a happy life on his own.

The Peasant & the Saints

Famed for his kindness, St Nicholas was the inspiration for Santa Claus. In this Russian folktale, his clemency contrasts with the punitive anger of the prophet Elijah, who, in the dual faith of medieval Russia, was identified with the pagan storm god Perun.

There was once a peasant who loved St Nicholas but who had no time for the prophet Elijah. He would devoutly light a candle before the icon of Nicholas on the saint's feast days, but when Elijah's festival came around he went about his business as usual, instead of observing the holiday. Angered by this impertinence, Elijah vowed to Nicholas that he would send hailstorms and lightning blasts to destroy the peasant's crops.

Nicholas went to the peasant and advised him to sell the crops to the priest at the village church dedicated to Elijah. The peasant did as he was told. Within a week, a hailstorm had devastated the peasant's field.

Elijah boasted to Nicholas that he had taken revenge on the disrespectful peasant but Nicholas pointed out that the blow had fallen not on the peasant but on Elijah's own priest, who had bought the crop while it was standing. So Elijah vowed to restore the field to its former glory. On hearing this, Nicholas told the peasant to buy the field back; the priest was only too happy to sell.

Elijah sent sunshine and gentle rains and the field sprouted a new crop of tall rye. But when the prophet learned that he had been tricked again, he flew into a fury. He promised that no matter how many sheaves the peasant put on the threshing floor they would not yield a single grain.

Nicholas now told the peasant to thresh one sheaf at a time, and by doing this the man was able to amass a vast store of grain. When Elijah saw this he realized that Nicholas had been helping the peasant, so this time he refused to tell Nicholas what he was going to do next. Nicholas gave the peasant one last piece of advice.

The very next day Elijah and Nicholas, disguised as poor pilgrims, met the peasant on the road near his field. He was carrying one large and one small candle. When Nicholas asked him where he was going, the man said he planned to light the large candle before an icon of Elijah for he had given him such a wonderful crop, while the small one was for St Nicholas. Elijah was finally pacified and from that day onwards the peasant honoured both men and lived a fine and contented life.

Why the Dnieper Flows So Swiftly

Long, long ago the rivers Volga, Dvina and Dnieper were poor orphaned children, who had to labour hard in the fields to feed themselves. One day Dnieper, who was a boy, and his sisters Volga and Dvina resolved to transform themselves into rivers to escape their lives of drudgery.

For three years they wandered and finally found a swamp that seemed a good starting point for three great rivers. They settled down to rest, intending to begin their new lives the following day. But Volga and Dvina wanted a head start on their brother and as soon as they heard him snoring they found a gentle incline and began to flow away.

The next morning Dnieper could see no sign of his sisters. Flying into a fury he set out after them, running as fast as he could. But then it dawned on him that he would catch them sooner if he were flowing between banks – for no runner alive could outpace a river. Striking the ground with all his might, he became a stream.

His anger was a powerful force, driving him between tall banks and sending him gushing down steep slopes where rapids formed. His sisters, hearing his pursuit, ran away from each other and into the sea. Dnieper himself grew calm when he neared the shore and flowed gently into the waters of the Black Sea.

The Ungrateful Farmer

Although the *domovoi* was considered the most benevolent of the domestic spirits, his behaviour was by no means predictable. To overlook his hand in a family's fortunes was unwise, but to spurn him altogether was pure folly, as this tale of a farmer who moved house suggests.

Outside the city of Kupiansk, in the Ukraine's Kharkov province, lived a young peasant. Hard-working and self-reliant to the point of stubbornness, he never stopped to consider how others had helped him – the advantages his ancestors had left him with, or even the assistance his *domovoi* had given him around the farm.

Soon the farmer came to feel cramped in the house his family had lived in for generations, and he thought nothing of leaving it for another he had built nearby. It did not for a moment occur to him to invite his *domovoi* to join him in his move. Without a thought for the past or the future, he pulled down the old house and chopped up its timbers for firewood.

From the first, the move proved a disaster. The crops withered in the field, the livestock sickened in the stalls, and the young man's own health started to suffer. His fortunes went steadily into decline.

One night he walked past the site of the old homestead. From the heap of ashes which lay where the stove had once stood, a mournful voice could be heard complaining how the previous occupants had abandoned their grandfather. Startled yet strangely moved by this mystical voice, the young man went on his way wondering what it might mean. He went to the village elders to ask them how his old *domovoi* might be appeased.

On their advice he returned to the ash-pile one night with an offering of bread and salt and begged the *domovoi* to make his new home his own. From that day forth he never looked back. His health recovered, as did the state of his farm. Once more his house flourished, restored by the protection of the *domovoi*.

The Tsar of the Sea

This famous story tells of Sadko, a poor man from Novgorod who owned nothing but a traditional harp-like instrument called a *gusli.* In his hands this simple instrument produced the most enchanting music.

One day Sadko sat by Lake Ilmen playing the *gusli* when he noticed a disturbance in the water. The waves parted, and there before him stood Morskoi, the Tsar of the Sea. The monarch thanked Sadko for his playing, and bade him cast a net into the lake. Sadko did as he was told and made a wondrous catch of glistening treasure.

Some years later Sadko, now a wealthy merchant, was voyaging across the Caspian Sea when his ship was suddenly becalmed. The fearful crew drew lots to find out who on board could be the cause of the disaster – and Sadko drew the shortest. The trader then confessed: he had for years neglected the observance he owed to the Tsar of the Sea. When they heard this, the seafarers threw him overboard. Even before he hit the water, a brisk wind filled the ship's sails and off they went once more.

The merchant sank to the seabed where he found Tsar Morskoi. He had been waiting twelve years to hear Sadko again, he said; and he must play to him now, and enchant his heart once more. Sadko took his *gusli*, and strummed out his sweetest music. Tsar Morskoi danced in delight, causing storms for miles around. The happy water king then offered Sadko the pick of his thirty daughters in marriage. But Tsar Morskoi's wife told him to choose the plainest, Chernavka, and warned him not to kiss her. Sadko did as he was told and the following morning awoke to find himself on the lush banks of the Chernava River, in Novgorod, where he was soon reunited with his own beloved wife.

The Happy Hostage

The *leshii* were forest guardians of Slav legend, tree spirits that inspired awe and fear in equal measure. Accomplished shapeshifters, they often took the form of wizened old men, but if threatened they could swell to enormous size, wreaking havoc on all around them.

One day, a young girl wandered off into the forest and disappeared. Despite their best efforts, her family failed to trace her and eventually gave her up for dead.

Three years went by before a hunter from the girl's village happened to find himself once more in the sector of the woods where she had been lost. There, on a log across the path, he saw an odd-looking figure. Realizing from its glowing eyes that it was a *leshii*, the hunter quickly raised his gun and fired. He saw the *leshii* fall, then crawl off into the undergrowth. So the hunter followed.

The trail led him to a hut in a clearing, and inside the hut he found the *leshii* stretched out in death. Beside him a young woman stood weeping. When the hunter asked her who she was she looked at him blankly, so he took her back with him to the village, where her parents recognized the daughter they had lost long ago.

At first the girl could not understand anything that anyone said to her, all remembrance of her past life having been erased. In time, however, she recovered her memory and with it her zest for human company. She married the hunter who had found her, and the couple lived together happily for many years. As they got older, they took to wandering in the forest, looking for the hut where she had been so long confined. Search as they might, they could not find it: it had vanished as if it had never existed.

The Fox Physician

A macabre variation on the Jack and the Beanstalk theme evokes the image of the mighty Heaven Tree, which in old Slavic myth connected Earth and sky and was the key to the Creation.

Once an old man planted a cabbage-head in his cellar and was astonished at the speed with which it grew. He had to cut a hole first in the floor of his cottage, and then the ceiling, as the amazing stalk thrust itself into the sky. Curious to see where it led, the old man scrambled up it until he found himself in a strange land.

There he found a handmill, out of which came a pie, a cake and a pot of porridge. The old man ate heartily before stretching out to sleep off his meal. He then slid back down the tall cabbage-stalk to tell his wife what he had found.

Amazed at the story, the old woman insisted upon seeing for herself. As she was too weak to climb the whole way, however, they decided that she should slip into a sack which the old man would grip tightly in his teeth. This would leave both his hands free for the arduous climb.

As they neared the clouds, the old woman called out, demanding to know whether they had much further to go. Her husband tried to answer, but the sack slipped from between his teeth. It hurtled to the ground and when the old man climbed down fearfully after it he found his wife lying dead.

Just then a fox came by and offered to use its special healing powers to bring the woman back to life. All the husband needed to do, it said, was to place his wife in the bathhouse and stoke up the fire until it was nice and hot; then he must wait outside while the fox performed its merciful work.

The old man did as he had been instructed, waiting patiently for several hours. At last the fox came out and told him he could open the bathhouse door and take a look at his spouse. As he did so the fox suddenly raced off, laughing wickedly. To his horror the husband saw why: for all that was left of his beloved wife was a pile of well-gnawed bones.

City of Lost Souls

In Slav legend, vengeful spirits could plague whole cities as well as individuals and households – and, as one tale of the city of Slavensk shows, they could also drive people to make desperate sacrifices.

Long ago, the city of Slavensk was founded by slaves from the Danube valley. Legend has it, however, that it was built without the ritual offerings that were the spirits' due. In a few short years the unfortunate city was devastated by plague. The surviving city fathers decided to establish the colony anew, this time taking care to offer the prayers and sacrifices that would ensure a future of good fortune.

One morning they sent out messengers in every direction, charged with bringing back the first living creature they met – for this would be the sacrifice to propitiate the spirits. After a short while, one of the envoys returned with a young child. The elders would not allow pity to sway their judgment, resolved as they were to omit no part of the rites. The child was thus buried alive beneath the foundation stone of the new city, which was renamed Dyetinets. But the ill-luck which had attended the city's first incarnation persisted until Dyetinets was at last ravaged by fire. Its terrified inhabitants knew better than to stay there and fled the accursed site to found a new city, Novgorod, nearby, which, finally freed from misfortune, flourished for many generations.

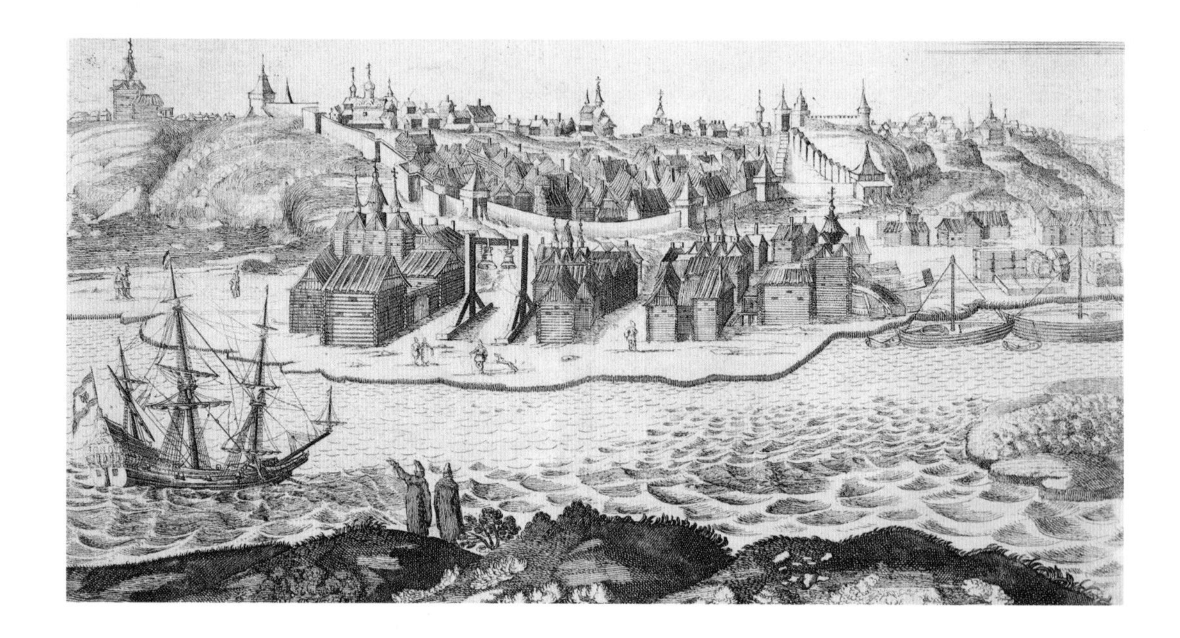

The Dead Mother

The vampire of many Slavic folktales is a very different figure from the Dracula of popular fiction. Rather than a vengeful spectre of fear, the undead could be a tragic ghost lost through fate rather than misdeed. And as the following story shows, the fiend is not always male.

A young married couple lived happily together, the envy of all for the love they had for each other. Before long, the woman bore a child – a fine, healthy boy. But within hours of the birth, his mother had died. Her husband grieved sorely for her loss, and agonized over what should become of the baby. While he could offer the child his love, the boy needed a mother's milk and tenderness and these he could not give.

An old woman was found to take charge of the boy, but he would take no food from her. He showed no appetite for milk, but simply cried and cried. Yet somehow as the weeks and months passed he seemed to be thriving, and for a short time each night his complaints would somehow cease.

One night the boy's father resolved to keep a vigil to find out what was happening. That evening, he lay down as if to sleep, with a candle by his bed, its flame concealed in an earthen pot.

For some hours all that could be heard was the incessant sound of the baby's crying, but at midnight the door creaked and a dim figure crept in. It made its way across the floor to the cradle where the baby lay complaining; it raised the child up and he lay silent and still.

The father uncovered the flame to reveal the strangest sight imaginable: there sat the dead mother, calmly suckling her living son. She looked up sadly as she saw the candle for she could not endure its light. She walked wordlessly from the room without so much as a backwards glance; then the father rushed to the cradle and found the baby dead.

Baba Yaga & the Brave Youth

Terrifying though she was, the forest-dwelling bogeywoman Baba Yaga did not always triumph over her adversaries. Indeed, in some stories she was outwitted by the simplest cunning, as the tale of the youth who lived with a cat and a sparrow illustrates.

One day the cat and the bird went into the forest to cut wood, warning the youth that should Baba Yaga appear he must say nothing. Baba Yaga duly arrived, and rummaged through the kitchen drawers. The youth kept quiet until he saw her taking one of his spoons. But as he cried out in anger, Baba Yaga saw him and bore him away. He called out to the cat and sparrow and after much pecking and biting, they managed to set him free.

Next day they went off to the woods again, leaving the youth with the same warning, but once more he cried out at the hag as she counted out the spoons. Again she abducted him, and he had to be rescued once more.

When this happened on the third day, however, he was not so lucky. As Baba Yaga carried him off, he called out in vain – for his friends had ventured out of earshot.

The old woman took him to her house, where she told her eldest daughter to roast him while she went out on an errand. Asked to lie in the roasting pan, the youth pretended not to understand. How was he to arrange himself? he asked. Exasperated by his stupidity, Baba Yaga's eldest daughter got in herself to show him: and he promptly pushed her into the oven and slammed the door. She was roasted to a crisp. The young man played the same trick on the witch's second daughter. And when the youngest daughter met the same fate, Baba Yaga saw that she would have to do the job herself. But she too fell for the youth's simple deception, and was roasted in the oven as well.

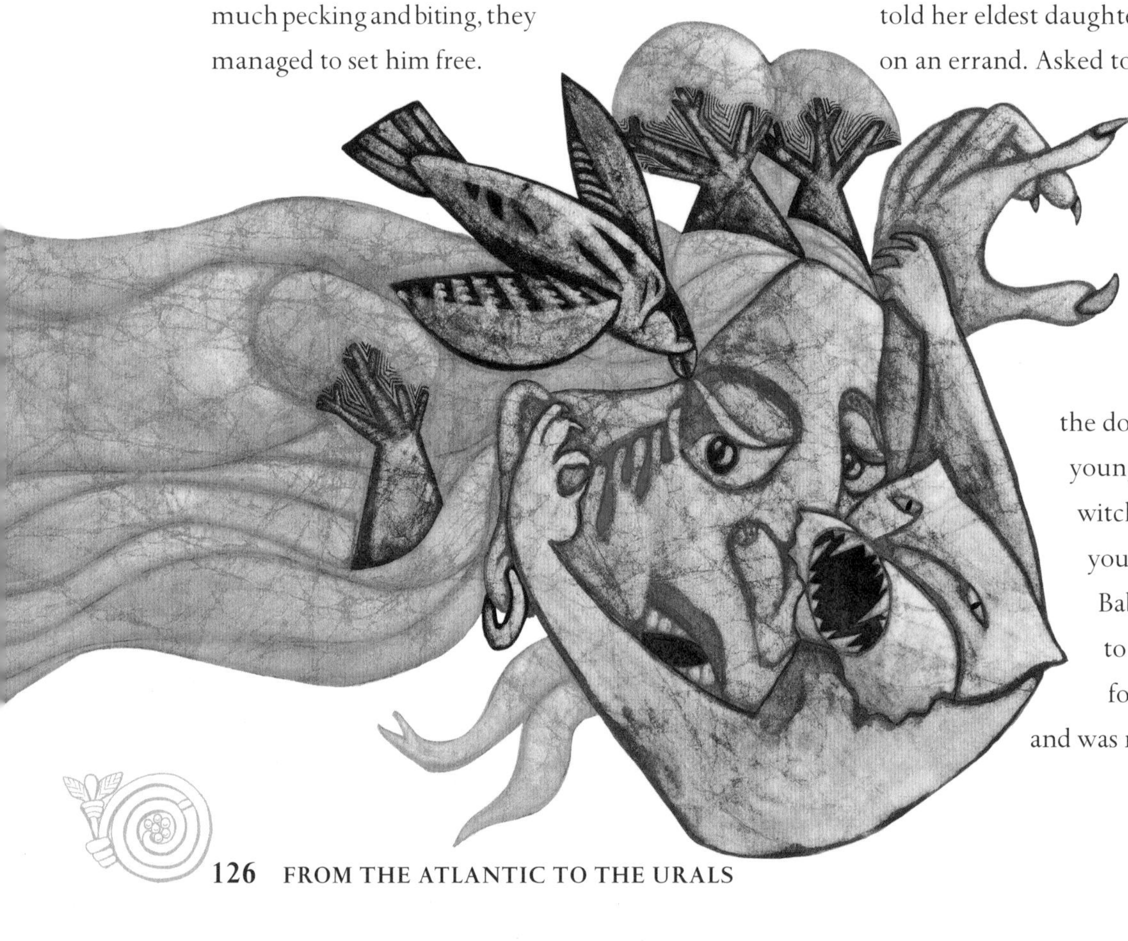

The Reluctant Werewolves

A revered figure in Slav myth, the changeling sorcerer, or *oboroten*, could take on almost any form, be it a stone, a haystack or a ball of string – or even an animal or bird. Yet not all changelings were willing participants in their transformation.

The word *oboroten* was also used to describe those whose appearance was changed against their will, those whom some sorcerer had condemned to inhabit an alien form. These were no malevolent beasts, but tragic victims of evil magic – and the most notorious of these changelings was the *volkodlak* or werewolf.

There are numerous examples in Slavic folklore of these unwilling werewolves. A Polish story tells of a young man who was loved by a witch but who scorned her passion, little guessing the danger he was in. One day, grazing his cattle in the woods, he decided he would cut some wood. As he raised his axe, however, he saw his hands becoming paws before his very eyes. He looked on helplessly while his fingernails turned into curling claws, and great tufts of hair started to sprout all over his body. When he ran to his cows, intending to herd them quickly home, they stampeded in abject terror. He sought to call them back, but could only howl. To his horror, he realized he was now a wild and lonely werewolf.

In Belorussia, it was said, a slighted sorcerer once blighted a whole wedding feast, not allowing anybody to leave in the form in which they had arrived. The groom and other men were changed into werewolves, the women into chattering magpies (the magpie was often associated with witchcraft). The bride herself was left until last; then she became a cuckoo, and searched for her husband far and wide, seeking him endlessly with the same monotonous, melancholy cry.

Tsar Medvyed, King of the Bears

In Slavic folklore the bear was associated with thunder, a link that may have been based on the creature's passion for honey, since that was the food of the Aryan gods. In this strange story Tsar Medvyed, the King of the Bears, vies in turn with a hawk, an eagle and a bull-calf.

Tsar Medvyed was a mighty ruler who governed his dominions with all the force in his power. He once exacted a cruel tribute from a human king, by requiring his son and daughter to live with him as his servants, pandering to his every whim.

The king rebelled at this treatment, and attempted to conceal his beloved children to keep them safe. But the bear-king found them cowering in their underground hiding place and carried them roughly away.

The next day, however, a hawk went out hunting and saw the children unguarded in Tsar Medvyed's lair. The bird swooped down and, taking the prince on his right wing and the princess on his left, flew off to return them to their father.

But the bear looked up and saw the hawk escaping with his precious prisoners: he thundered angrily and dashed his head violently against the ground. The earth shook for miles around and a jagged lightning-bolt shot high into the air: it singed the hawk's wings, and he was forced to drop his human cargo.

The next morning, the bear went out again, and this time an eagle saw him go. He swooped down, set the prince and princess free and was flying them off to safety when he too was brought down by a bolt of lightning hurled by the angry tsar.

On the third day, however, a bull-calf found the children unattended. He took them on his back and galloped off through the forest. Tsar Medvyed heard them go, and stormed and shouted in rage. But the bull-calf ignored him and kept running with the young prince and princess on his back. The bear-king flung his lightning bolts but they bounced harmlessly off the bull-calf's hide; he set the earth trembling but the beast charged on undaunted and carried them to safety.

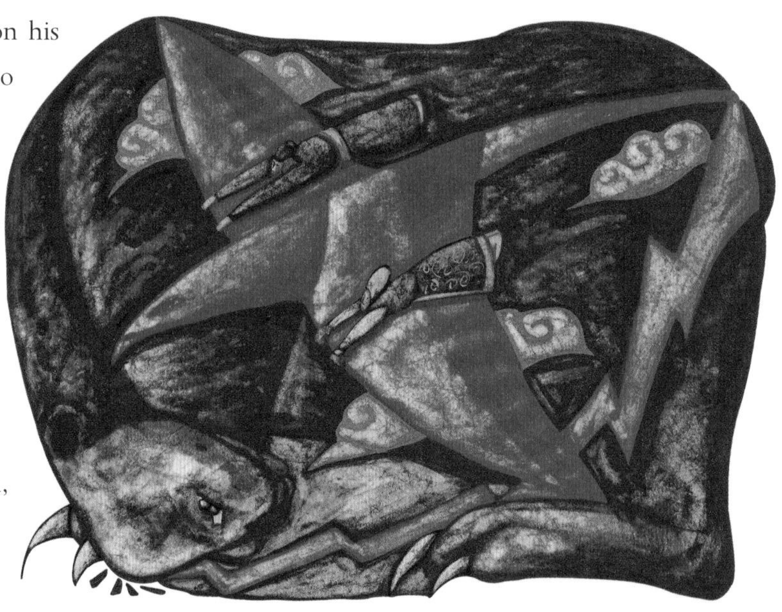

Dobrynya & the Dragon

Dobrynya seemed to personify all the qualities of the Christian hero and his combat with the fearsome dragon Goryinch is often seen as a fight against pagan darkness. He was, however, a far from perfect hero.

One hot summer's day, as Dobrynya was bathing in the River Puchai, the heavens opened to disgorge a huge dragon with three heads and seven claws of copper. The beast, Goryinch, then spoke: it had heard much of Dobrynya, and how he was destined to save his country by slaying it, but Goryinch would now show who the hero really was. Dobrynya replied defiantly that the dragon should win its victory before it began boasting. Grabbing the hat he had left on the shore, he filled it with sand and used its brim as a blade to sever one of the dragon's heads. As he made ready to cut off the other two, the beast begged for mercy, promising never to harm Russia or its people again.

Such was his own honesty that Dobrynya did not doubt for a single moment that Goryinch would keep its word. But only a few days later he heard that the dragon had stolen Zabava Putatishna, the niece of Prince Vladimir of Kiev. The prince was appalled that Dobrynya should have let the dragon off so lightly. He ordered the hero to go to the mountains where Goryinch had its lair; he must kill the dragon this time and not come back without Princess Zabava.

After a long and arduous journey, the warrior finally found Goryinch's home. Man and monster fought fearlessly for three days and nights. Eventually Dobrynya slayed the dragon. He forced his way into the monster's lair and found Princess Zabava, along with forty captive peoples who had been chained there for generations. They followed him forth in their thousands, blinking in the bright sunshine, their freedom finally won thanks to Russia's great hero.

FROM PERSIA TO THE FAR EAST

Persia

Persia was one of the key civilizations of the ancient world, knowing a time of imperial greatness under the Achaemenid kings. Tracing their origins back to horse-riding Indo-European nomads who found their way to the Iranian tableland during the second millennium BCE, the Achaemenids created an empire that threatened the survival of the city-states of ancient Greece until finally humbled by Alexander the Great in 331 BCE.

The nomads had brought with them a cult of pagan gods worshipped at fire altars and through libations of a sacred hallucinogen called *haoma*. The first records of these divinities were only put down in writing in the sixth century CE, when they were collected in the pages of the Zoroastrian holy book, the *Avesta*. The myths, however, almost certainly predated the prophet Zoroaster himself, although his dates too are uncertain; most authorities think that he lived in the sixth or seventh century BCE, although some place him several centuries earlier.

Whatever his birthdate, the prophet grew up in a world of multiple divinities. Zoroaster singled out from the pantheon the creator god Mazda and perceived him as a supreme power for good, locked in perpetual conflict with Angra Mainyu, the primal force of evil. In the Zoroastrian dispensation, other gods were transformed into *yazata*, "worshipful ones", lesser immortals occupying a position analogous to that of angels in the Christian and Muslim traditions.

Zoroastrianism spawned myths of its own, some of them recounting miraculous visions of the prophet's birth (see page 136). The new faith also developed a creation story, telling how the first man, Gayomartan, was slain through the wiles of Angra Mainyu. Yet Mazda's work was not in vain, for Gayomartan's seed magically conceived a couple who went on to become the legendary ancestors of the Iranian tribes and so of the entire human race (see page 137).

The *Avesta* also contained tales of human heroes such as the mighty Keresaspa, fated to save creation in the endtime, when he will be called down from heaven to confront the chaos dragon Azhi Dahaka (see page 135). Yet the great treasure-house of Persian hero legend is another work, Persia's national epic the *Shahnameh*, which was written by the poet Firdowsi at the turn of the tenth and eleventh centuries CE. In some 50,000 couplets this Book of Kings recounts the legendary history of the Iranian people from the creation to the Arab conquest in 642 CE, after which the nation's Zoroastrian heritage gave way to Islam.

The protagonists of the *Shahnameh* included the white-haired warrior-prince Zal (see page 138) and, even more, his son Rustam, greatest of all the champions of ancient Persia (see page 139). Rustam had to contend not just with enemies, both human and supernatural, but also with the rash stupidity of Kay Kavus, the king he was destined to serve, whose pretensions included an ill-fated attempt at powered flight (see page 140). Toward the end of his life Rustam was confronted by a rival in the shape of Isfandiyar, himself a resourceful dragon-slayer (see page 141), although when the two men finally came face to face in battle it was the younger man who fell.

Along with accounts of epic fights, the *Shahnameh* also found space for folktales like that of Barbad the musician and the ruse he employed to win royal patronage (see page 143). Many more such stories found a permanent home in the *1,001 Nights*, a collection postdating the Arab conquest that took its material from across the Middle East, drawing heavily on Persian sources. Even before the first European translations of this work appeared early in the eighteenth century, some of the material had filtered out to the West, ensuring an enduring international audience for its tales of the ingenuity of lovers, such as the story of the goldsmith and the singing girl (see page 142), or of the guile of commoners such as the fisherman who used his native shrewdness to extract a small fortune from the generous-hearted King Khusrow (see page 145).

Mithra's Trusty Guardian

Mithra was the glorious sun god of Persian mythology, later to become the chief deity of Mithraism, a cult that spread across the Roman empire in late classical times. Serving as an escort at his side was a fierce boar – a manifestation of the warrior god Verethragna.

His name meaning "pact" or "covenant", Mithra was the guarantor of the cosmic order in early Persian religion. His association with the daily passage of day and night established the link with the sun, which was hymned in an Avestan text: "He who first of the heavenly gods looks over the Elburz Mountains, before the undying, swift-horsed sun; who, foremost in a golden array, takes hold of the beautiful summits, and from thence looks over the abode of the Iranian people with a beneficent eye". Yet he was also a mighty warrior, famed for his hundred-sided mace and as the guardian of the *khvarnah* or Divine Glory that alone bestowed legitimacy on kings.

In his martial guise he was protected by the fearsome warrior god Verethragna. The *Avesta* lists ten separate forms that this deity could assume, from a strong wind to a wild ram and a swordsman with a golden blade. To protect Mithra he took the shape of a boar, described thus in another Avestan hymn: "a sharp-toothed he-boar, a sharp-jawed boar, that kills at one stroke, pursuing, wrathful, with a dripping face; strong, with iron feet, iron forepaws, iron weapons, an iron tail, and iron jaws".

Keresaspa – Saviour of Creation

Unmistakable in his curly sidelocks, the youthful Keresaspa was in some ways the most human of the Avestan heroes, appealing in his dashing manner and his easy-going ways. Yet these very qualities would one day prove his undoing.

Although he killed many monsters, including the horned dragon Sruvara, and preserved the world from countless attacks by the forces of evil, Keresaspa was not as observant of the ritual pieties as he ought to have been. Once, when preparing a meal, he set light to a pile of vegetation without realizing that a dragon was sleeping beneath it. As it fled the flames the monster spilled the pot, polluting the fire – a sacred element for Zoroastrians. So, when Keresaspa approached the glorious portals of the heavenly sanctuary after his death, Ahura Mazda refused him entry. Only after interventions from the other gods and heroes, who pleaded his cause eloquently and passionately, did the Wise Lord of the Sky finally rule that he might be admitted after all.

And yet, according to the *Avesta*, this spiritual scapegrace is marked down by destiny to save the world in its hour of greatest need. For, at the end of time, Azhi Dahaka, the three-headed monster whose body is made of lizards and scorpions, will break free from the prison in which he is restrained, returning to harrow humanity and threaten creation. With his work of many ages on the point of destruction, Ahura Mazda will have no alternative but to recall from the dead the greatest warrior of all time. Keresaspa will sweep swiftly down from heaven and smite the demon dragon with his mighty club. Only then will the terrible curse of evil be ended once and for all.

Visions of the Great Protector

As Zoroastrianism became established, mythical traditions grew up around the life of its founder, emphasizing the prophet's great holiness. It was held that he had been chosen by the Wise Lord Ahura Mazda himself to spread wisdom throughout creation.

Zoroaster's story began before his incarnation on Earth: it was believed that his birth and the wonderful deeds he would perform in the name of Ahura Mazda were revealed to a chosen few long before the great prophet was actually born.

In the first days, when the evil Angra Mainyu attacked the good and bounteous creation, it slaughtered the first man and bull. The bull's soul flew to the very peak of heaven where Ahura Mazda sat in majesty on an enormous throne that shone and sparkled with brilliant light. The bull complained to the Wise Lord that it was without a protector and was granted a vision: the celestial soul, or *fravashi*, of the great Zoroaster would one day protect cattle and all of creation, instituting a new era at the end of which evil would be entirely destroyed and the universe be restored to the perfectly good form intended by Ahura Mazda. Gladdened, the bull descended to Earth once more. Later, it revealed the secret of Zoroaster's coming to a mythical Iranian prince named Us.

Another tradition held that the divine light of Ahura Mazda was to be found on Earth long before Zoroaster was born, and that it was handed down from a series of holy men to the prophet. It shone most brightly in the breast of the brave and righteous Zoroaster.

The Coming of Mortals

The first human in Iranian myth was Gayomartan, whose name meant "Mortal Life". His stay on Earth was short, but years later bore fruit in a plant from which the primordial couple emerged to populate the world.

Gayomartan was made from the soil, a large, impressive figure as wide as he was tall, described in the *Avesta* as "bright as the sun". His splendour attracted the malicious attention of Angra Mainyu, the spirit of evil, who killed him. As he was slain, though, his semen passed into the earth. For forty years the sun shone on the spot and eventually a seedling, shaped like a rhubarb plant, forced its way from the soil. Over time the plant's stalks grew into the form of the bodies and limbs of a man and woman. The two, named Mashya and Mashyanag, were to be the father and mother of the ten races of humankind.

Fully human at last, the couple broke free of their roots to walk upon the Earth. Ahura Mazda himself sought to enlighten them, instructing them that they should always seek to do good and avoid evil. But the forces of wickedness also worked on Mashya and Mashyanag, and in their delusion the first man and woman came to see the world as a harsh and unwelcoming place, believing it to be the creation of Angra Mainyu. It was the first and greatest of all sins, a sacrilegious denial of Ahura Mazda's handiwork.

Mashya and Mashyanag lost their way and strayed far from the path of *asha* ("truth") that Ahura Mazda had laid out for them. Although they made ritual sacrifices and did not shrink from virtuous labour, they were unable to escape the spell cast over them by Angra Mainyu. They even lost their desire to people the world through sexual union. For fifty sterile years they produced no offspring.

Finally, however, Mashyanag gave birth to twins. But instead of loving and protecting their firstborn, Mashya and Mashyanag butchered and ate them. At that time the flesh of children tasted sweet – so Ahura Mazda took that delicate flavour away. Many years later Mashya and Mashyanag produced another set of twins, and these two grew into strong, healthy adults. They were to become the parents of the tribes of Iran, and through them of the entire human race.

The Triumph of Love

The central section of the *Shahnameh* begins with the story of Zal, father of the supreme Iranian hero, Rustam. Zal's love for the daughter of a neighbouring ruler provided the work with one of its most passionate romantic idylls.

Zal's birth was ill-omened, for he entered the world with snowy white hair. Blaming an evil spirit, his father Sam rejected him, abandoning him in the Elburz Mountains. There the baby was rescued by the Simurgh, a mythical bird of enormous size, who raised him in her own brood. Zal grew up handsome and strong, and eventually word of his survival reached his father, by then ruler of the kingdom of Sistan in eastern Iran. Repenting his folly, Sam welcomed him back and made him his heir.

The princess Rudabeh was as beautiful as Zal was fair, and the two fell in love by report before they ever met. But meeting was not easy. Rudabeh's father, Mehrab, was king of the neighbouring state of Kabulestan, and although he accepted the supreme authority of the Iranian King of Kings as Sam did, he did so unwillingly. Worse, he was of the lineage of serpent-shouldered Zahak, the most hated of Iran's early kings.

So when Zal visited Kabulestan, he decided to pitch his tents across the river from Mehrab's capital rather than accept the king's hospitality. Rudabeh was sequestered in the women's quarters of her father's palace, and etiquette would not allow Zal to request an introduction.

Eventually the princess's maids in waiting found a way to break the deadlock. They went to relax on the riverbank in view of the royal party opposite. Seeing a chance to break the ice, Zal snatched up his bow and brought down a passing bird that fell close to where they were sitting. The prince then sent attendants to retrieve the game. Soon the two groups were singing the praises of their respective employers. Zal sent jewels for the princess, and a secret rendezvous was arranged.

The two fell head over heels in love as soon as they met. At first their parents opposed the match, but their disapproval was swept away by the force of their passion. And so the pair were married among public rejoicing, and all the witnesses agreed that no more beautiful couple had ever graced a throne.

A Strong & Trusted Partner

Rakhsh was a steed fit for a hero, and his partnership with the mighty Rustam was ordained by fate. Together they were to endure many dangerous adventures, and together they finally met an untimely death.

Like his father Zal's before him, Rustam's birth was troubled. Fearing that his wife Rudabeh might die in labour, Zal summoned the Simurgh, who had promised always to help him in his hour of need. Seeing Rudabeh's pain, the great bird advised a Caesarean section, providing one of its own healing feathers with which to soothe the wound.

Rustam grew up strong and sturdy, being as big as a one-year-old after just one day. In his early manhood he was powerful enough to confront and kill a stampeding elephant with only his bull-headed mace. The time had come for him to go out into the world.

When the young hero first embarked on a warrior's career, he set out to find a charger strong enough to bear his mighty weight and brave enough to face any danger. He had a simple test for the former; he would press the palm of his hand on a horse's back and see if its belly sagged to the ground. Even though he criss-crossed Iran looking for a suitable candidate, none of the beasts he examined would do.

It was in neighbouring Turan that he finally found what he was looking for. There he noticed an unusually tall bay mare followed by a two-year-old colt of similar colour, flecked with red patches. He liked the look of the young horse, yet when he expressed an interest to the dealer, he was warned not to covet another man's mount. When Rustam asked who the owner was, the dealer told him that no one knew, but that the colt had always been known as Rustam's Rakhsh.

So the hero realized that he had found the steed predestined for him. His choice was confirmed when he pressed on its back and found it firm as steel. And when the herdsman learned his client's name, he would take no money. Instead he told him that the horse was worth more than all Iran, adding that if he really was Rustam, then the only way to pay for it was by rescuing the nation from the enemies that beset it and bringing justice to the world. Thereafter Rakhsh remained Rustam's loyal companion through many adventures until both eventually met their death together at the hands of Rustam's treacherous half-brother.

The Tricking of King Kavus

Like many rulers before him, the Persian monarch Kay Kavus fell victim through vanity to the wiles of a crafty *div* (demon). The lesson that Kay Kavus learned, however, was not fatal – and can even be seen as comic.

Known as Kavi Usan in the *Avesta*, Kay Kavus was a legendary early ruler of Persia who also played a significant part in the *Shahnameh*. At the time of his reign, the Persian people were engaged in an epic struggle with the neighbouring kingdom of Turan to the northeast, now generally identified as a Turkic state. Under their scheming ruler Afrasiyab, the Turanians threatened Persia's very existence, but Kavus was always able to call on the hero Rustam, who at one point rescued the king from the clutches of a fearsome white demon who had blinded the king along with his entire army.

A rash and impetuous sovereign, Kavus had other problems with *divs* in the course of his reign. One morning a *div* came to him in the form of a flattering courtier, telling him that, as he held sway over the entire Earth, the next logical step must be to extend his rule to the sky. The king fell into the trap, and took to brooding on the means by which he could mount the clouds to assert his sovereignty there also.

At last he came up with an idea. He tethered four eagles to a throne to which he had himself strapped. Above the birds, legs of mutton were hung on tall poles. As the eagles beat their wings to reach the meat, they carried the throne up into the air, and soon the king found himself soaring through the sky.

But the birds were not inexhaustible, and when at last their strength began to flag, Kavus came down to earth with a bump. His experiment in aviation ended ignominiously in a forest somewhere in western China. It took a small army under the direction of Rustam to track him down and bring him back to Persia, crestfallen and – for the time being at least – repentant of his vanity and folly.

Isfandiyar & the Dragon

After Rustam, Isfandiyar was the most valorous hero ancient Persia ever knew, for, according to legend, he had been made invulnerable by the prophet Zoroaster himself. His most ingenious exploit was an inventive feat of dragon-slaying.

Isfandiyar was the son of the legendary Persian monarch Gushtasp, and he led his father's armies to many famous victories over the Turanian foe. Eventually the king came to fear that his own fame was being eclipsed by that of the younger man. So, seizing on a false report that Isfandiyar planned to overthrow him, he had the prince imprisoned.

The decision was a disastrous one; in Isfandiyar's absence the Turanian forces swept the field. Eventually Gushtasp had to admit his mistake and release his prisoner to win another stunning victory. But the retreating Turanians took with them two of Isfandiyar's sisters, imprisoning them in a stronghold known as the Brazen Fortress. The prince set off post-haste to rescue them, choosing the shortest route even though he knew it to be fraught with perils.

The most terrible trial that he had to confront on his way was a vast and venomous dragon that swallowed travellers whole. Forewarned of its presence, the prince had a carriage constructed whose roof and sides were stuck with lances and sword-blades, like a pin-cushion. He then harnessed it to a pair of horses to approach the creature's lair. As soon as he heard the monster's threatening roar, he got inside the vehicle and closed the door tightly.

Furious at the intrusion, the dragon swallowed vehicle and horses in one gulp. But the sharp points stuck in its throat, lacerating it horribly. Eventually it was forced to disgorge the lethal mouthful. In a trice the prince leaped from his hiding-place and dealt the monster a death-blow with his sword. Even so, the poisonous fumes that he inhaled were so powerful that it took all his strength and dedication to enable him to continue on his way and successfully complete his mission.

The Goldsmith & the Singing Girl

Persia had one of the world's great heritages of folk tales, honed by generations of professional story-tellers known as *naqqal*. Many of the narratives that were their stock in trade found their way into the *1,001 Nights*, and so eventually won a global audience.

One such story told of a lover's quest that ended happily thanks to the suitor's ingenuity. It told how a Persian goldsmith once saw the girl of his dreams painted on the wall of a friend's house, and discovered from the painter that the model was a singing girl in the harem of a vizir of the king of Kashmir. Travelling to India, he soon learned where she lived, along with news of a peculiarity of the king – that he lived in fear of sorcery and regularly left suspected witches to starve to death in a pit outside the city walls.

The goldsmith decided to put the knowledge to use. Equipping himself with a rope ladder and grappling irons, he waited for a stormy night to break into the vizir's palace. Once inside, he made his way to the harem where, amid all the assembled beauties, he had little difficulty in identifying his beloved. He made no attempt to abduct her, however, but instead took out a knife and nicked her in the thigh. She woke up terrified and, assuming the intruder to be a thief, urged him to take her jewel casket but spare her life.

The goldsmith duly obliged. The next morning he dressed himself in the robes of a travelling scholar and presented himself at the royal palace to crave an audience with the king. Having made his obeisances to the monarch, he presented him with the gems, claiming he had been attacked by witches outside the city gate the previous night and had fought them off, wounding one on the thigh. Fleeing, the sorceress had left the jewel-box behind her, and he now wished to present it to the sovereign as a gift.

Rummaging through its contents, the king found jewels he had given his vizir, who quickly identified the current owner as the singing girl. Summoned, she was found to have a wound exactly where the scholar had described. The king needed no further proof of her guilt. He sentenced her to be thrown into the punishment pit just as the goldsmith had known he would. It was then an easy matter for the suitor to bribe the pit's guard and head off with his beloved to a happy new life in Persia.

Barbad the "Invisible" Musician

The *Shahnameh* describes the cunning ruse employed by one minstrel to win the coveted post of chief singer to Khusrow II Parviz (the "Victorious"), the last great king in the Sasanian dynasty and a notable patron of the arts.

Word of Khusrow's munificence reached Barbad, a talented musician who was inspired to seek his fortune at court. But when he arrived he discovered that the king already had an official minstrel, named Sarkash.

Having heard Sarkash sing, Barbad knew his own talent was greater, but could think of no way of displaying his abilities to the monarch. Eventually he befriended one of the royal gardeners and devised a plan. Dressed entirely in green he was smuggled into the gardens and climbed up a tree just before Khusrow was due to visit. When the royal party arrived, he played and sang so sweetly from his hiding-place that all the guests stopped stock-still and listened open-mouthed. Ravished, the monarch offered to fill the lap of the unseen songster with gems if only he would step forward and reveal his identity.

Barbad climbed down and paid his humblest respects to the king, telling him that he was his devoted slave and his only wish in life was to sing for him.

The ploy worked and from that day on he duly supplanted Sarkash in the royal favour and in the course of time won lasting fame as the greatest of all court minstrels.

Appointment in Samarra

A folk tale set in Baghdad succinctly expresses the theme of the inevitability of death when it is foreordained. Passed down by story-tellers over the centuries, it won international fame when the American writer John O'Hara chose it as the title of a well-known novel.

A servant running errands for his master was going about his business in a Baghdad marketplace when he felt himself jostled from behind. Turning to protest, he was shocked to find himself gazing at a figure that he quickly recognized as Death himself. His surprise turned to terror when the grim apparition fixed his eyes upon him and made a motion as though beckoning him to approach.

Convinced that Death had come for him, he ran as fast as he could back to the house, where he at once started gathering together his few possessions. When his master found him, he had already finished packing and was ready to leave. Asked to explain himself, he stammered out the story of his sinister encounter in the bazaar. He had to get away at once, he said, and would have to borrow a horse if he was to escape his fate. He told his startled employer that his plan was to head for the city of Samarra, some seventy-five miles away across the desert.

The master readily agreed, and the servant departed in haste. Once the younger man was safely on his way, the merchant came to a bold decision: he would seek out Death and demand to know why he had thus threatened his employee. So he went in his turn to the marketplace, and there he too saw the terrible stranger. But when he put his question, Death looked puzzled.

"Threaten him?" he replied slowly. "No – surely not. But I may have given a start of surprise. You see, I was not expecting to see him in Baghdad, for I have an appointment with him tonight. In Samarra."

Khusrow & the Fisherman

An anecdote from the *1,001 Nights* told how a poor fisherman used his wits to benefit from King Khusrow's fabled generosity, but in doing so drew the ire of the king's quarrelsome wife, Shirin.

The fisherman brought a huge fish he had caught to the palace and, as he had hoped, Khusrow gave him the vast sum of 4,000 drachm for it. Shocked by such largesse, Queen Shirin objected that it was too much since their courtiers would complain if they were less well rewarded than a fisherman. Khusrow saw her point, but insisted that he could not go back on his word, so Shirin urged him to reject the fish outright. "Ask the man if it's male or female," she suggested. "If he says 'male', say you wanted a female, and if he says 'female', say 'We want a male'."

Khusrow put the question to his visitor, but the fisherman judiciously replied "It is neither male nor female." The monarch laughed, and gave him another 4,000 drachm.

As the fisherman was leaving the hall, he dropped one of the coins and fell to his knees to pick it up. "See?" said Shirin. "With all that money, he's still too greedy to leave a single coin behind." So the king called him back to reprimand him. But the fisherman replied that he was only worried that someone might stand on the coin, which bore the king's likeness, and so offend the royal dignity. Delighted by the reply, the king gave him a third bag of coins.

India

The enduring impression that strikes most Western observers of Indian myth is one of fluidity. Gods, sages and heroes metamorphose between a variety of incarnations, sometimes appearing in the same story under three or four different names.

One obvious reason for this constant state of flux lies in the belief in reincarnation. This idea goes back to the earliest epoch of Indian history, the Vedic age initiated by Indo-European warriors who migrated to the subcontinent from about the year 2000 BCE on. Through the workings of karma, each individual formed part of a chain of existence that could pass not just through many separate human embodiments but that could even embrace other animal species.

Another factor adding to the diversity was the sheer reach of Indian culture, which in its recorded form spanned four millennia and a whole subcontinent crowded with many different peoples. This immensity spawned a multitude of local gods, goddesses and nature spirits. Over the centuries figures with shared characteristics were assimilated into the cults of a handful of great gods, notably Brahma, Vishnu and Shiva. The result could be a dizzying multiplication of personalities: Vishnu, for example, had ten major incarnations or avatars, ranging from the hero Rama and the divine shepherd-prince Krishna to the tortoise Kurma and the boar Varaha.

In similar fashion Hindu tradition had a number of different creation myths, most of which came to be associated with Brahma. One form that the god took was as Prajapati, who was said to have willed the universe into being and to have shaped it from his own body (see page

148). Yet despite Brahma's divine powers, he sometimes showed human weaknesses; one myth described how the four-headed deity lost his fifth head while pursuing Shiva's wife (see page 149).

Some Hindu myths seem to perform an obvious explanatory function, like those that dramatized the Earth's need for rain in terms of a battle fought in the sky between the mighty storm god Indra and the demons of drought, who sought to rustle the cloud cattle away into their fortresses. One celebrated story told of the disastrous consequences that befell Indra when he was deprived of the source of his strength, the divine intoxicant *soma*, and of the epic churning of the Ocean of Milk needed to obtain a fresh supply (see page 150). Other legends were linked to the great Hindu festivals like that of Diwali, which was held in honour of Lakshmi. A well-loved folktale described how a clever washerwoman used her good sense to win the favour of the goddess, and with it prosperity for herself and her family for seven generations (see page 157).

Among the most important sources for Hindu myth are the two great epics, the *Ramayana* and the *Mahabharata*. The first tells of Prince Rama's struggle to rescue his wife Sita from the demon king of Sri Lanka, aided by an army of apes commanded by the monkey general Hanuman (see page 152). The *Mahabharata*, although primarily concerned with the struggles of a princely clan in the India of the first millennium BCE, also contains much mythological material, including a long section on the youth of Krishna. One episode describes the slaying of the demon Putana, who came to harm the infant prince in the guise of a wet-nurse (see page 153). Another tale told how the prince's mother Yashoda suddenly realized his divine status as an incarnation of Vishnu in a moment of revelation as the youngster was playing with his brother in the fields (see page 154).

Indian mythology was further enriched by the coexistence of different religious traditions alongside Hinduism within the subcontinent. Buddhism in particular accepted many Hindu beliefs – including the transmigration of souls, as a tale of the Buddha's own reincarnation as a six-tusked elephant shows (see page 158). The two faiths even came to share gods, as revealed in the story of the king and his chaplain (see page 159), in which Siddhartha, the Buddha-to-be, achieves impossible tasks with the aid of Shakra, a Buddhist incarnation of Indra.

Prajapati's Tears

One creation myth from Hinduism's Vedic scriptures tells how the creator god Prajapati used parts of his own body to will the universe into being, producing smoke and fire that condensed into a vast sea.

Prajapati was one of several different gods associated with creation in various different Hindu traditions. In time most of these figures were subsumed within the worship of the great god Brahma, himself the embodiment of *brahman*, the transcendent divine reality underlying all existence.

A feature of these myths was that the original matter from which the world was made tended not so much to be created as rearranged. For example, one tale described how the universe came into being from Prajapati's own body parts.

In the story Prajapati simply emerged, but as soon as he was conscious the Lord of All Creatures wept, for he could see no purpose in his existence. As he cried, his falling tears became the Earth. The tears he wiped away became the air and those he brushed upwards became the overarching sky.

Wanting offspring, he settled down to practise religious austerities. First he gave birth to demons, then put aside his body, which became the night. He then created himself anew to make men and women, then cast this second form aside, which in turn became the Moon.

He then assumed a new self, this time creating the seasons from his armpits and the dusk and dawn from his body. Finally he made the gods from his mouth and when he put aside this third body it became the day.

Other parts of Prajapati's various incarnations went to make the chants and hymns associated with the Vedic sacrifices, for one role of the creation myths was to explain and justify the elaborate sacrificial rituals on which the power of the Brahmin caste of priests depended.

Four-Headed God of Wisdom

Images of Brahma showed him astride a goose or sitting on a lotus. He had four heads, indicating the four directions of the compass, and four arms, representing the four Vedas, the most ancient scriptures. Once, however, a burning desire led him to create a fifth head.

As guardian of the Vedas, Brahma was the god of wisdom. One of his names was "Grandfather", because of his status as creator and source of all. There were several explanations as to why he had four heads. One story told how Brahma created a female consort, Sarasvati, from his own great energy. Her beauty was so delicate that he felt a powerful longing for her although she was his own daughter. He turned his passionate gaze on her, but the goddess's natural modesty made her flee from him.

She skipped away to Brahma's left and then to his right, then ran lithely behind him, but each time the god grew a new head so that he could feast his eyes upon her. Sarasvati leaped into the sky, but Brahma sprouted a fifth head to follow her with his eyes. Then the god caught hold of his daughter and made love to her. She gave birth to the first people.

Brahma lost his fifth head in a quarrel with Shiva. One day Brahma filled with illicit desire for another of his daughters, Sandhya, who was married to Shiva. When he approached Sandhya she sensed his lustful intent and fled in the fleet form of a deer, but Brahma transformed himself into a strong-legged stag and galloped after her. Enraged at this sight, Shiva shot an arrow that cut the stag's head clean off. The animal turned back into Brahma, with four heads, and the god came to his senses, humbly paying his respects to Shiva.

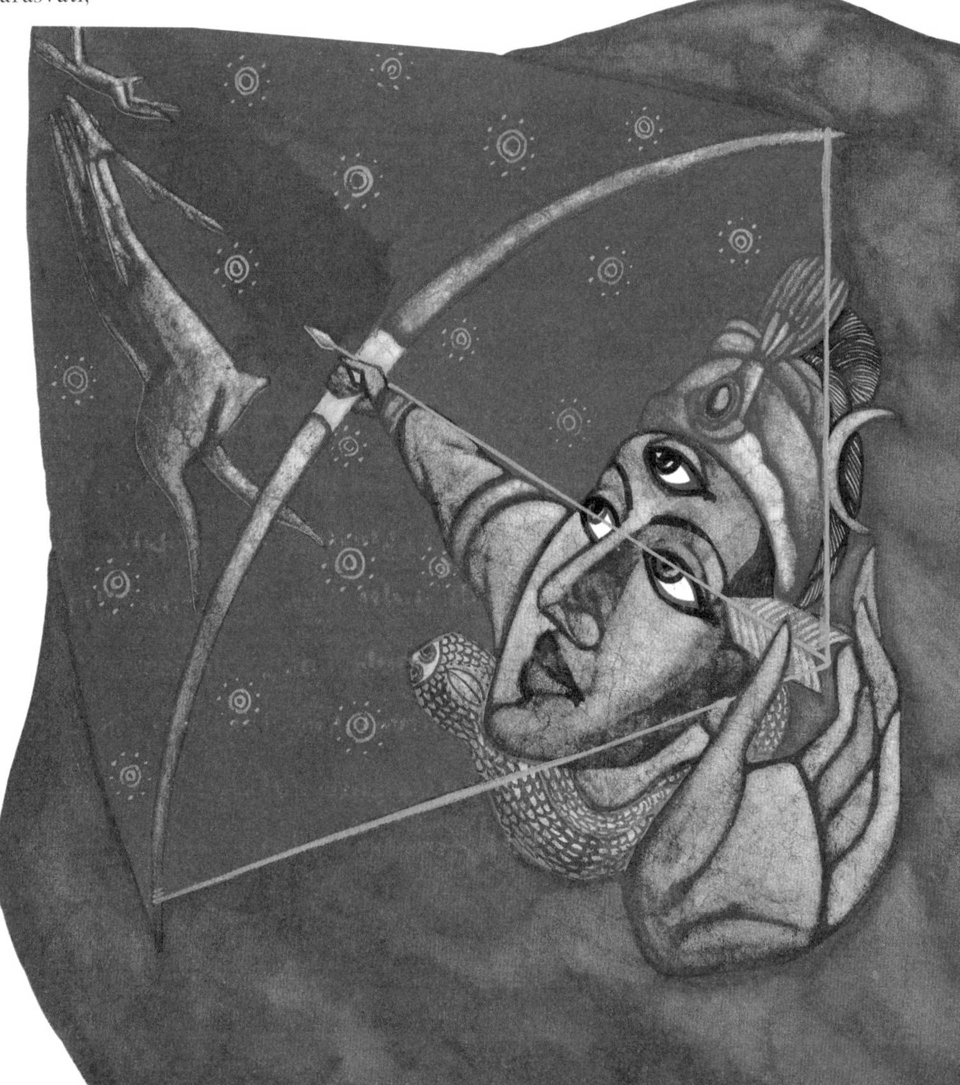

The Churning of the Milk

The great powers of Indra were waning under the curse of a powerful sage. The gods feared that if their leader grew weak they would be overcome by their enemies, the demons. So Vishnu instructed them to churn the Ocean of Milk to create the divine drink *soma*, or *amrita*.

So huge was the undertaking that Vishnu ordered both gods and demons to bring the great Mount Mandara to the ocean's edge to stir the waters with. They balanced it on the back of the king of tortoises, Kurma, one of Vishnu's ten incarnations, and used the great serpent Vasuki as a rope to twist the mountain and so stir up the waters. They soon tired, but lightning burst from Vasuki's mouth and unleashed a refreshing rainstorm. Trees on Mount Mandara were uprooted by the motion and, rubbing against each other, burst into flames. Soon the entire mountain was ablaze and all the animals and plants that lived on it were destroyed. When Indra put the fire out with rain, juices from the trees and plants flowed into the ocean and over the gods, making them immortal.

As the gods and demons churned, the moon arose, followed by the sun; then the goddess Lakshmi, who became Vishnu's wife, appeared. Next came Vishnu's white steed and the white elephant Airavata, which Indra claimed. A flood of blue poison rose up, but before it could devastate the Earth, Shiva gulped it down, keeping it in his throat, which is why he is called Nilakantha ("Blue Throated"). Finally the divine physician Dhanwantari rose up from the ocean, holding a cup full to the brim with *soma*.

The cunning demons turned against the gods and stole the *soma*. Vishnu, dressed as a seductive woman, managed to reclaim it, but the demon Rahu at last got a taste. The sun and moon warned Vishnu and although Rahu was killed, the demon's head and neck were infused with the *soma*, rendering him immortal. He flew up into the sky and to this day wages war on the sun and moon, and sometimes even swallows them, causing an eclipse.

Then the demons and gods fought a tremendous battle. Finally the gods triumphed. They returned Mount Mandara to its proper place, and trooped home, rejoicing loudly. Wondrous Vishnu became guardian of the *soma*.

The Birth of Rama

The great protector Vishnu took the form of Prince Rama to save the Earth from the wicked demon Ravana. Rama combined virtue with courage and beauty with strength, making him one of the most enduring Hindu heroes.

Ravana, the fearsome ten-headed demon, was king of Sri Lanka. One day, filled with energy after great austerities and penances, he asked Brahma to make him so strong that no god or demon could beat him in combat, and Brahma was forced to grant this boon. Once Ravana knew he was invulnerable, he ran riot. Indra and the other gods begged Brahma to help them and he took them to see Vishnu.

The great protector calmed the lesser gods, reminding them that the terms of Ravana's boon did not protect him from men or apes. The gods should descend and take the form of apes, he said; while he would be born in the form of four princes.

Meanwhile, Dasaratha, the king of Kosala, longed for a son and performed a horse sacrifice to propitiate the gods. A fine black stallion was released, accompanied by a priest, and wandered for a full year to fulfil the rules of ritual sacrifice. When it returned priests chanted mantras while Kausalya, the king's principal wife, killed it herself with a sacred sword.

In time, each of Dasaratha's three wives gave birth to sons, and all of them were incarnations of Vishnu. The first to be born was Rama, Kausalya's child, who had half of Vishnu's nature. The second wife, Kaikeyi, was the mother of Bharata, who was filled with one quarter of the great god's spirit. The third wife, Sumitra, then gave birth to twins, called Lakshmana and Satrughna, each of whom had one eighth of Vishnu's being.

Hanuman the Immortal Monkey

Rama's loyal general Hanuman was a golden-bodied monkey with a ruby-red face and a devastating roar. Strong enough to lift a mountain, he also had magical powers to shift shape or become invisible. And he had inherited the gift of flight from his father, the wind god Vayu.

Hanuman was born to help Rama in his battle against Ravana, for Vishnu had told the gods to father a race of monkeys to fight the demons (see page 151).

When King Dasaratha performed his horse sacrifice in the hope of becoming a father, he distributed cakes to his three wives. But the youngest, Kaikeyi, refused hers because she had been handed it last – and a bird carried it away. Deep in the forest the bird dropped it and Vayu with his soft breath blew it into the hand of a monkey named Anjana. She held the cake for a few moments, turning it over and over in wonder, and then Shiva himself appeared to her, ordering her to consume it. As she ate it she became pregnant with Rama's loyal friend.

Hanuman had the great appetite of a god. When one day he caught sight of the sun in the sky, he mistook it for a golden fruit and using his father's power of flight he jumped up to seize it. The sun fled but Hanuman followed. In Swarga, Indra's heaven, Indra attacked the monkey with a thunderbolt and Hanuman fell back to Earth. But Vayu saw what had happened and in a rage for revenge he swept into the bodies of all the gods, torturing them with burning indigestion. Then Indra made peace with Vayu and the wind god persuaded him to grant Hanuman the ultimate boon of immortality.

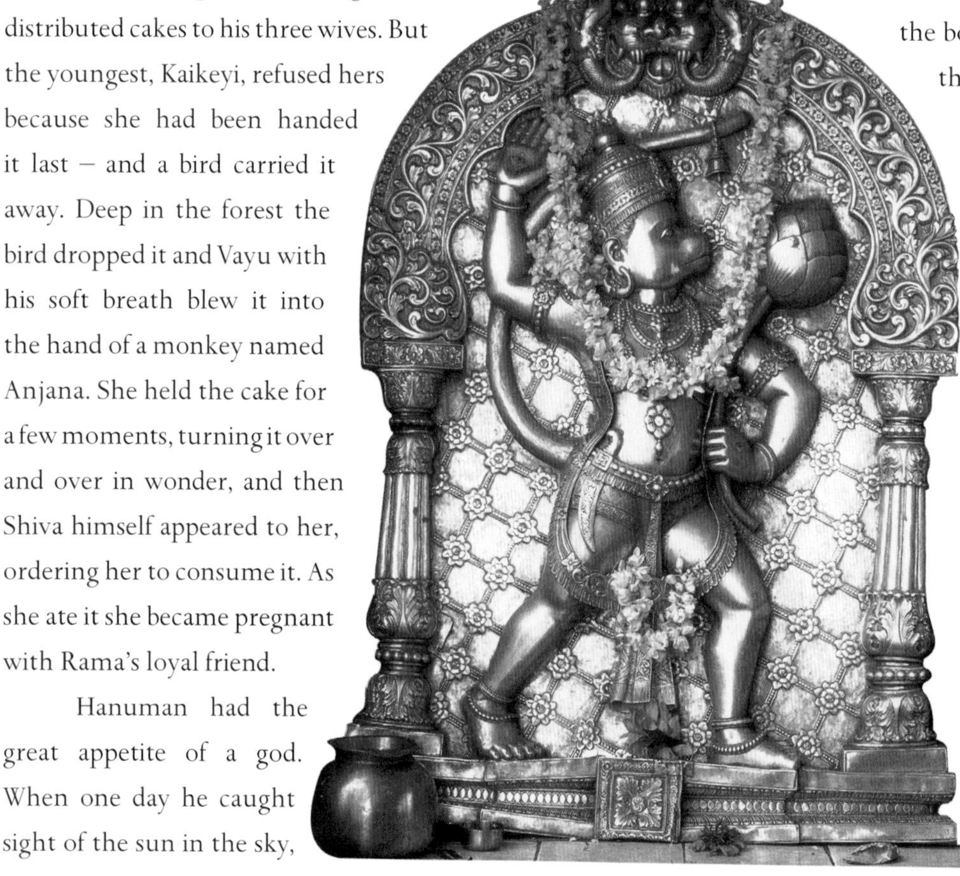

In other versions of the myth, it was Rama who made the monkey general immortal, as a sign of his gratitude for Hanuman's help in defeating Ravana. Rama offered Hanuman anything he wished, and the monkey asked only to live for as long as men talked of Rama – and Rama's fame will live for ever.

The Slaying of Putana

Another of Vishnu's avatars was the princely shepherd boy Krishna. Even as a baby, Krishna had an awesome power that revealed his divine status. On one occasion he defeated the hideous demon Putana who had been sent by King Kamsa to kill him.

Kamsa ruled the Vishni kingdom in northern India. Unknown to him, he was begotten of a demon who, seduced by his mother's beauty, had taken her husband's form to lie with her. Perhaps as a result, Kamsa grew up savagely ambitious – eventually usurping his supposed father's throne.

Warned by an oracle that the eighth son of his sister Devaki would end up killing him, Kamsa ordered that each of her babies be murdered at birth. But Krishna, the eighth-born, was spirited away to the home of a couple of cowherds. Foiled in his plan, the king instructed Putana ("Stinking") to go to their home.

Putana was so ugly that she transformed herself into a beautiful young woman before knocking on the door. When Krishna's foster-mother, Yashoda, enquired what she wanted, Putana replied that she had heard that she was looking for a nurse for her son. It was true, Yashoda said, and the woman seemed so pleasant that she allowed her to stay.

One day Yashoda was unwell and took to her bed. Putana saw her chance. When Krishna woke and began to cry for food, Putana took him on her lap and offered him her breast, which she had rubbed with poison. But as Krishna fed he grew stronger and stronger. Putana began to scream and tried desperately to pull the child away. But he clung on with his gums and did not stop sucking until she lay dead on the floor in her original, terrible form.

Krishna's Mouth

Krishna's awesome power is once again apparent in this resonant story in which his mischievous nature allows his stepmother Yashoda to gain a fleeting understanding of his true status as Vishnu, lord of all.

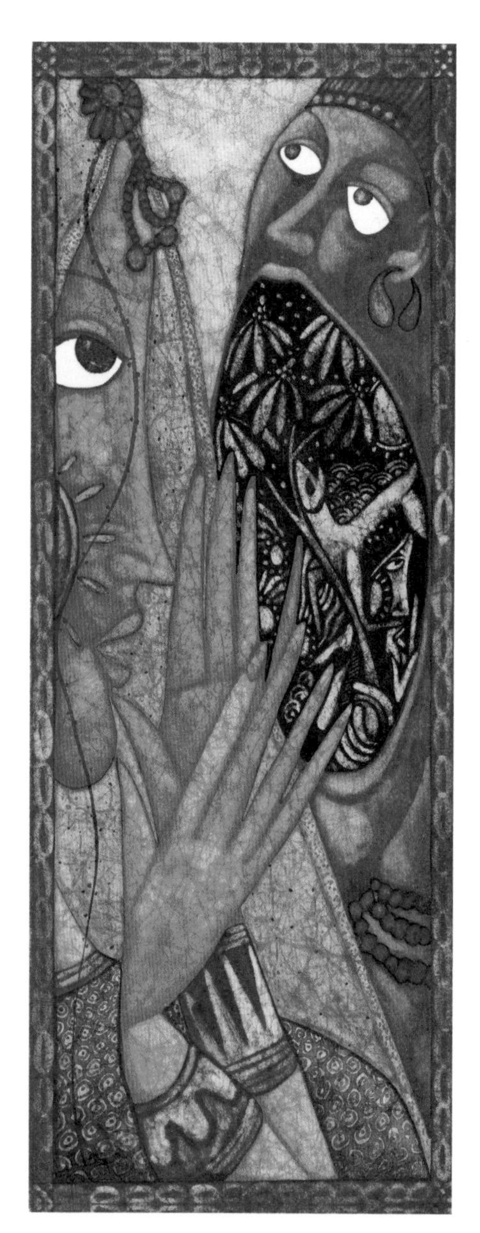

Krishna and his elder brother Balarama were lively, healthy boys. As soon as they had learned to walk they took to running about their home village in northern India, shouting and making mischief. Krishna was particularly impudent – he would knock the milk pails over or steal butter and then lie about what he had done. He would untie the calves and scamper away, his face suffused with glee. But none of the village women could find anything in their hearts but love for him.

One day Balarama and some friends came to Yashoda, saying that Krishna had eaten some dirt from the ground but was refusing to admit it. Yashoda spoke sternly to Krishna, telling him that the dirt would make him sick, but Krishna denied that he had eaten anything. If she did not believe him, he said, she should look in his mouth. So Yashoda, who was used to her stepson's mischievous ways, looked there expecting to see a few pieces of mud – and gasped at what she saw.

There was all time and all space, eternity itself, in the boy's mouth: the great circle of the sky and the sweep of stars, the vast expanse of the Earth and all forms of life, every kind of hope, wish and dream; and she also saw herself and her home. Yashoda was struck dumb for a moment and she wondered what this could mean, for she saw that Krishna was the great eternal god who lies beyond this life and encompasses all things, and she imagined herself bowing down and worshipping him. Then her vision faded, and she promptly forgot everything she had just witnessed. She sat down and took him in her arms and kissed him, and she thought of him as a mother thinks of her son.

A Fateful Game of Dice

One day Nala, handsome ruler of Nishadha, caught a wondrous speaking swan. The bird flew to Damayanti, the beautiful princess of neighbouring Vidarbha, and praised the prince to her. Shortly afterwards Damayanti held a ceremony to pick a husband and chose Nala.

One day the goddess Kali swept into Nala's body and drove him to challenge his brother to a game of dice in which Nala lost everything but his wife. He left the city, but Damayanti followed him.

They wandered in the forests, until Nala—still driven by Kali's evil urgings—abandoned Damayanti while she slept. Having searched for him in vain, she eventually found refuge in a palace at Chedi.

Nala meanwhile freed the serpent Karkotaka from a sage's curse. In return the snake bit him, transforming him into the dwarf Vahuka and causing Kali enough pain that she was driven out. As Vahuka, Nala became chariot driver for Rituparna, king of Ayodhya.

Some time later Damayanti was recognized by a wandering priest and returned to live with her father. He sent priests out to look for Nala with a message from Damayanti, begging him to return. One of them became suspicious when he met Vahuka, so Damayanti held another ceremony, inviting Rituparna so that Vahuka would come too. When, at the feast, Vahuka confessed his true identity to her, he reverted to the handsome Nala and the loving couple were reunited. Rituparna instructed Nala in dice-playing, who then challenged his brother to another game of dice and defeated him. Nala forgave his brother and allowed him to live at peace in his kingdom.

A Matter of Love & Death

Shiva, the great ascetic, had an unremitting rivalry with Kama, the mischievous god of love, which culminated in Shiva destroying him with a blast of flame from his third eye. But, as Kama lay dead, his faithful wife Rati persuaded Shiva's own wife Parvati to help.

Parvati begged Shiva to bring Kama back to life, and he was reborn on Earth as Pradyumna, a son of Krishna and his favourite wife Rukmini. But he was snatched from his cot and thrown into the sea by the demon Shambhara – who had been warned that the child would one day murder him.

Pradyumna was swallowed by a fish. The fish was then caught and Shambhara unwittingly bought it at market. That night his wife, Mayavati, prepared the dinner. And when she gutted the fish she found the child inside.

Now, Mayavati was an incarnation of Rati, and as she stood in the kitchen she had a vision of the sage Narada who told her that the baby was her husband Kama. He then enabled her to make the boy invisible, so she could raise him in secret.

When Pradyumna was young Mayavati tried to seduce him, but he was unwilling for he believed her to be his mother. She then explained to Pradyumna that their souls were those of Rati and Kama. Soon they were lovers and Mayavati became pregnant. When Shambhara began to mistreat her, Pradyumna attacked and killed the demon. Pradyumna and Mayavati then lived as man and wife, but later Pradyumna was killed in a fight. Back in the celestial realm he resumed his form as Kama and ever-faithful Rati soon joined him.

Lakshmi & the Washerwoman

This tale is told about the autumn festival of lights, Diwali, which is held in honour of Lakshmi, the consort of Vishnu. Householders light lamps to attract the benevolent goddess to their home; if she visits, they believe she will bring them prosperity in the coming year.

One year, at Diwali, the king of a northern Indian realm gave his wife the most wonderful necklace of pearls. But when she took it off to go for her morning swim, a crow swooped down and snatched the precious pearls.

To comfort his distraught wife, the king at once dispatched his servants to announce a generous reward for their return.

The crow, meanwhile, had dropped the necklace and it had been found by a washerwoman. When she heard the servants' proclamations, she made her way to the palace and proudly handed the necklace to the king.

He duly offered her a purse heavy with coins as a reward. But the woman refused. Instead she asked the king to grant her a favour. That night, when the Diwali festivities were due to begin, she wanted her hut to be the only lighted house in the kingdom. So the king agreed to forbid the lighting of any other Diwali lamps for this one night.

But Lakshmi was not pleased when she came to the kingdom to inspect the displays of Diwali lamps. At first she thought no one had bothered to light any lamps at all, but then she saw the washerwoman's house and knocked on the door. The washerwoman greeted her, but would let the goddess inside only if she promised to stay for seven generations.

Lakshmi was pleased that the woman was so devoted to her, and she agreed. Blessed with Lakshmi's presence, the washerwoman and seven generations of her offspring enjoyed lasting prosperity and good fortune.

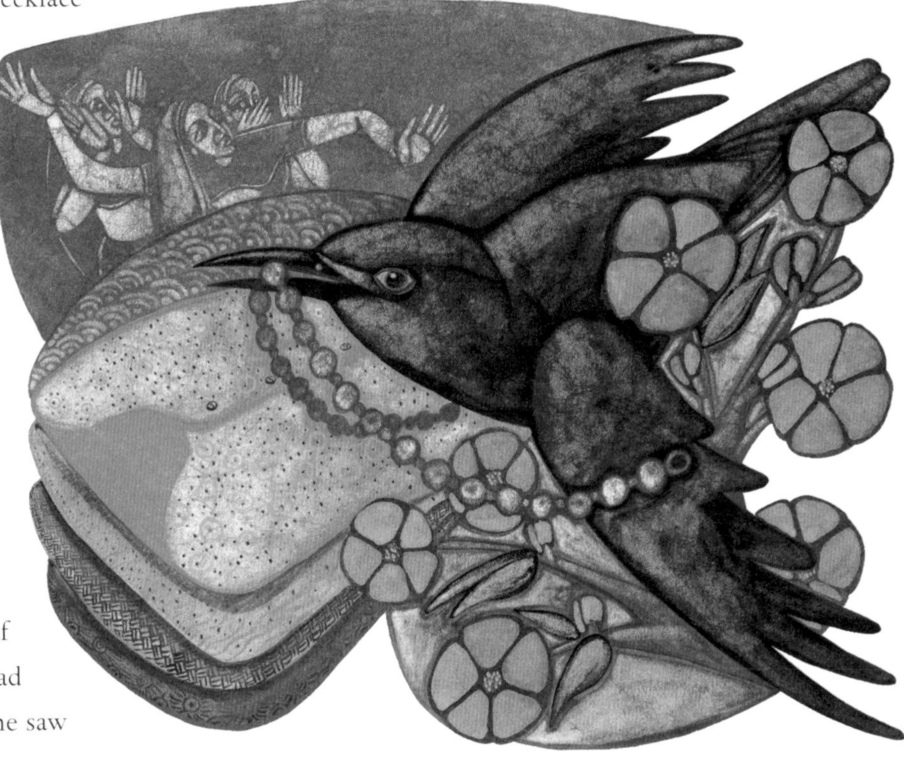

The White Elephant

In the Indian Buddhist tradition, the Buddha was once reborn in the form of a six-tusked elephant Chadanta. He lived happily in the forest, a loving husband to his two beautiful elephant wives. But one wife resented having to share him, however attentive he might be.

Seething with jealousy toward her rival, she prayed to be reborn as a human princess. Her wish was granted and, blessed with great beauty and charm, she grew up to marry the king of Benares. One day she summoned all her husband's huntsmen, and asked them to search in the forest for an elephant with six tusks. They were to kill this prodigious beast, she told them, and bring back his fine tusks. The huntsmen set off, searching vainly for many days, before one of the men, Sonuttara, found what they had sought – a fine bull elephant, with six long and shapely tusks. Quickly, he dug a pit in which to trap it, and soon Chadanta was captured.

As Sonuttara rained down arrows upon him, Chadanta asked why he wanted to kill him. Sonuttara told him of his queen's orders, and the poor elephant immediately understood all. He realized who the queen must be, and the smouldering resentment that must have motivated her malice. Accepting his fate, he even assisted Sonuttara in his deadly work. First he helped the huntsman to climb up his tusks so that he might cut them off at the root; then, when they proved too tough to be cut by human force, he seized the saw with his own trunk and severed them himself, offering his ivory to the awestruck Sonuttara while the lifeblood ebbed away from his mighty body. The huntsman went back to the queen with his astonishing story; when she heard what had happened, she at once collapsed in shock and then died.

The King & his Good Chaplain

Not everyone appreciated the Buddha's holy works. Siddhartha, the Buddha-to-be, once served as a priest to King Yasapani of Benares but fell foul of the king's corrupt adviser.

The royal adviser Kalaka resented the holy presence of the Buddha-to-be, since it highlighted his own corruption. The constant check on his own ambitions was bad enough, but the priest had recently ruled correctly and scrupulously in a case he himself had attempted to pervert. He resolved to get rid of the meddling holy man. So, whispering lies and calumnies to the king, and persuading him to fear his chaplain's growing popularity among the people, Kalaka coaxed his royal master into laying a trap for the priest. He convinced the king to set him a series of impossible tasks and then put him to death when he failed to complete them. For the first test, the king ordered the Buddha-to-be to build him a pleasure garden, but allowed him only a day to complete it. The priest thus spent a sleepless night, wondering what on earth he was going to do, for he knew it would take him hundreds of days and nights to accomplish what he had to do in one. But his answer came from heaven. The god Shakra appeared by his bedside and told him not to worry. He assured the anguished chaplain that the appointed task would be completed with the dawn.

And so it proved, the morning sun rising to reveal a green garden of delectable beauty and exoticism – and the king at once astounded and alarmed. Setting his chaplain a series of ever more challenging tasks, he found him easily accomplishing them all with Shakra's divine assistance – creating a beautiful lake, a pleasure palace and a huge, dazzling jewel. The astonished king was finally forced to recognize that his chaplain enjoyed the support of the gods. It was Kalaka, he realized, who was practising against virtue.

King Yasapani embraced his priest's friendship, and immediately put his scheming counsellor to death.

Tibet and Mongolia

The roots of Tibet's mythology lie in shamanistic pagan traditions of the distant past that gradually codified into the indigenous Bon religion. Bon had a crowded pantheon of gods and spirits, and its own sacred texts, notably the *Klu-'bum* or "100,000 Water Serpents" (see page 169). It also enshrined creation myths featuring a divinity named Sangpo Bumtri (see page 167). Tönpa Shenrap, the legendary founder of the faith, was said to have brought Bon to Tibet from the land of Tazig, far to the west, perhaps in what is now Tajikistan. His life was the subject of two eleventh-century texts, and stories of his doings have also been passed down orally by Bon priests, known as *bonpos*. One legend claimed that Tönpa originally came to Tibet not to proselytize his beliefs but rather to recover horses stolen by demons (see page 162); another described the magic rituals he employed to pacify hostile spirits (see page 169).

Buddhism reached Tibet in the seventh century CE, during the reign of the conquering king Songtsen Gampo. This was a time when the nation was building an empire that for a brief period rivalled that of China, its larger neighbour. Princess brides from China and Nepal brought the new faith with them to the Tibetan royal court, from which it quickly spread outward.

In the following century another strong king, Trisong Detsen, made an ultimately unsuccessful attempt to suppress the rival Bon creed. In his reign the holy man Padmasambhava, known to later Tibetans as Guru Rinpoche, came to Tibet from India, bringing with him the sexual disciplines of Tantric yoga to drive out demons. Legend told of the yogi's miraculous birth in a lotus flower and his rebirth when an angry king sought to have him burned alive (see page 163).

In later centuries the struggle with the demons was taken up by Avalokitesvara. Well known also in China and India, where scholars think he may have taken on some of the attributes of the Hindu god Vishnu, Avalokitesvara was a *bodhisattva*, a Buddhist holy man who had delayed his own attainment of enlightenment to aid other people. In Tibet, he manifested himself with multiple heads and many arms, the better to help the needy (see page 164).

Another Buddhist hero was the sage Milarepa, a historical figure whose life spanned the late eleventh and early twelfth centuries. Known for his writings, the *Songs of Milarepa*, as well as for his holiness, he retired to meditate in a cave near the Nepalese border, where he is said, uniquely, to have achieved complete enlightenment within a single lifetime. One legend described his struggle with a shaman for control of the holy Mount Kailash, a real-life Himalayan peak (see page 165).

Mongolia shared with Tibet a nomadic lifestyle, a commitment to the Mahayana ("Great Vehicle") brand of Buddhism, and an interlocking history that began when Genghis Khan's successor sent troops to conquer the mountainous land in the mid-thirteenth century. Even though Tibet eventually re-established its political independence, the two nations remained closely linked by religion and culture. Mongolia accepted Tibet's own lamaist model of Buddhism in the sixteenth century, and in 1642 the Mongol leader Gushri Khan was instrumental in establishing the fifth Dalai Lama as Tibet's ruler.

Mongolia also had its own pagan faith with a host of *tengri* or gods, who were either overthrown or else converted to new roles after the coming of Buddhism (see page 170). Mongol shamans claimed to be able to foretell the future through scapulomancy; a myth duly expounded the origins of this practice, which involved reading the shoulder-blades of sheep (see page 171).

One distinctive feature of Mongolian myth was its taste for animal fables. Examples include a story explaining why eagles eat snakes (see page 172) and a local version of the widespread legend of swan maidens, best known in the West through Tchaikovsky's *Swan Lake* (see page 173).

The King's Stolen Horses

Tönpa Shenrap was often called "the great teacher", but the first mission he undertook in the mountainous land of Tibet was not to spread the doctrine of Bon, the religion that he had founded, but to hunt down the demons that had stolen his horses.

Shenrap had a great enemy, the demon lord Khyapa Laring – "Penetrating Long Hand" – who blamed the great teacher for cheating him of souls, and for using prayers to dry up the four rivers in his domain, the land of the devils. One day Khyapa decided to take Shenrap's horses – the finest in the world – in the hope that their loss would distract him from his task of saving souls.

Khyapa sent seven of his best demon horsemen into Shenrap's kingdom Wölmo Lungring, in the land of Tazig. There they mounted the animals and, beating them mercilessly, forced them into southeastern Tibet.

Shenrap pursued the rustlers, and although the demons threw a snowstorm, a valley of fire, an ocean, a sandstorm and a mountain in his path, he dismissed all obstacles with a wave of his hand. As he travelled through Tibet, he converted hundreds of demons and humans to Bon, but seeing how many more needed to be saved, and how they were not yet ready to receive the doctrine, he vowed that in future generations his disciples would convert the entire country.

When Shenrap found his horses, they were guarded by Khyapa's mother and a hundred demonesses in the form of beautiful young girls, who tried to entice Shenrap, offering him golden bowls from which to drink that contained poison. Shenrap turned the poison into medicine, and the girls into hags, and reclaimed his horses, although it seems that the animals must have bred in the meantime, because for centuries afterwards that part of Tibet was famous for the quality of its steeds.

The Twice-born Sage

Many stories tell of Buddhist sages who were miraculously born from lotus flowers, but Padmasambhava achieved the feat twice in one lifetime.

When blind King Indrabodhi, of the Indian city of Jatumati, lost his only son, he called together all his priests and had them make offerings to the gods for a new heir. At the time his land was in a state of famine, and the sacrifices not only failed to produce a son from any of the king's 500 wives, but also left the people with nothing to eat except wild flowers.

Indrabodhi decided that religion was a sham, and ordered the priests to destroy their deities, until the Buddha Amitabha sent him a vision foretelling the birth of a miraculous child for him to adopt. Then Amitabha projected a ray of light into a lake, and a full-blown lotus appeared on its surface. At its centre was Padmasambhava, in the form of a beautiful one-year-old boy.

When he had grown into a handsome young man, skilled in magic, Padmasambhava went to Sahor to find the first of five consorts who had been ordained for him. She was the princess Mandarava, and the young sage began visiting her in secret to teach her the yogic arts. As soon as her father the king learned about these visits, he had Mandarava thrown into a pit of thorns, and Padmasambhava burned on a funeral pyre as high as a mountain. When the king returned to the site seven days later, he saw all the wood, still smouldering, cleared into a circle around a rainbow-haloed lake. In the centre of the lake was a lotus blossom containing a glowing eight-year-old boy, attended by eight maidens who all looked like Mandarava.

The boy shouted: "Evil king, who sought to burn to death the great teacher of the past, present and future. Fire cannot burn this inexhaustible body of bliss." Recognizing that the child was Padmasambhava, the king offered him the kingdom, and Mandarava as his wife.

Why the Sage Had Eleven Heads

Avalokitesvara, the Lord of Compassion, knew that Tibet would be the hardest country to subdue, but he knelt before the Buddha and vowed that he would not rest until he had brought all its creatures to the light.

One day Lord Buddha described Tibet as the place all previous buddhas had failed to conquer. When he said this, a white beam shone from his breast and struck Amitabha, the Buddha of Lust, Ideas and Boundless Light. Amitabha recognized this as a signal to manifest the *bodhisattva* called Avalokitesvara and send him to Tibet.

Before even attempting to conquer Tibet, Avalokitesvara travelled through Hell, the realm of hungry ghosts, the worlds of animals and humans, and the domains of the demi-gods and gods, curing all the various sufferings he found there. But when he finally came to the summit of the Red Hill in Lhasa, and looked out over the plain, he saw a place as terrible as the worst hell that he had encountered. Millions of bodiless souls roiled in a lake, endlessly screaming as they suffered the agonies of heat, cold, hunger and thirst. Avalokitesvara gave each soul a healthy body and taught it enlightenment, but even after all his efforts, he realized that he had saved fewer than a hundredth of the beings of Tibet. Beginning to despair and long for rest, Avalokitesvara exploded into fragments. Immediately Amitabha came and bound up the pieces, telling the Lord of Compassion that, since his head had broken into ten, he would have ten faces, with Amitabha's own on top as an eleventh, and since his body had split into a thousand fragments, he would have a thousand hands with which to help the suffering.

The Struggle for Mount Kailash

Mount Kailash, in western Tibet, is sacred not only to Buddhists, but also to Hindus and followers of Bon. When the Buddhist saint Milarepa first went there he encountered a Bon magician who challenged him to a competition for control of the mountain.

Dzutrul Phuk, "the Cave of Miracles", was one of Milarepa's favourite caves in which to meditate, and he performed the magic that gives the place its name. He and the Bon shaman Naro Bonchung were running a race to see who could circle the mountain first. Milarepa was moving clockwise round the peak – the traditional Buddhist way to circumambulate a holy site – while Naro Bonchung was racing anti-clockwise.

They crossed at Dzutrul Phuk, where they were hit by a thunderstorm. The pair agreed to cooperate in building a shelter, but even this turned into a contest. Naro Bonchung split stones with his magic, while Milarepa drilled holes with his gaze. In trying to emulate the Buddhist, Naro Bonchung's eyes fell from their sockets and he was temporarily paralysed, so Milarepa finished the shelter, leaving imprints of his feet and head in the rocks for future generations to worship. The defeated *bonpo* knew he would be thrown off Mount Kailash, but begged to be given a vantage point from which he could worship the peak. Milarepa threw a handful of snow in the air. It fell on Mount Bonri, to the east, and Milarepa gave this site to Naro Bonchung.

To this day, Buddhist pilgrims retrace Milarepa's clockwise circumambulation of Kailash and followers of Bon undertake the route in an anti-clockwise direction.

Child of the Rainbow

Cosmic eggs, divine beings and rays of light are often born out of each other in Tibetan myths. But in the enchanting tale of the Rainbow Child, a mountain cave serves as a symbolic egg, a place of refuge in which a heavenly child grows from a rainbow's light.

The king of Zhangzhung and his wife had wide power and great prosperity but no son. Among their many possessions was a wise elephant that regularly used to climb off into the mountains. One day a *mahout*, or elephant driver, followed the trail of the elephant, and after a laborious trek, came upon it listening in rapture to a clear tune coming from the Sala Bapug cave in the side of Mount Kailash. The *mahout* reported his discovery to the king, who made the long and difficult journey to the mountain with his wife and ministers. None of them could tell whether the beautiful song was a message from the gods or a seductive trick on the part of some evil ghost, so the king ordered the local people to clear a path through the boulders into the mountain.

A child of eight, created from the light of a rainbow, was discovered inside the cave. The king asked the luminous orphan where he came from, and was told: "My father is emptiness and my mother is the dawning of wisdom. I come from the ungenerated and go to the unobstructed. My name is 'the Incorruptible One Invested with Immortality' and I came here for the sake of all living things."

The king was delighted and begged the child to become his adoptive son, upon which the child blessed the king and queen and vanished like a rainbow back up into the sky. But the following year the queen gave birth to a son, Dranpa Namka, who could remember 500 previous lives and was reputed to be the incarnation of an immortal.

Black-headed People

Tibetan myths give human beings a lowly place in the hierarchy of creation. In one well-known Bon story, the making of the Tibetan people is only a small element in an expansive account of the origins of the universe.

The Bon religion had many creation stories, and they featured certain common elements. Most started with a void that brought forth its own unformed matter. The first step in the process was often the appearance of a light to illuminate the primordial darkness. Then the emptiness produced an egg or eggs, which in turn gave birth to creator beings.

One account described how being grew out of nothingness and engendered two separate glows, each embodying a basic facet of life – one was bright and fatherly, the other dull and motherly. Then, as sentience spread, coldness developed, followed by frost and glittering dew. These settled into a mirror-like lake, which rolled itself up until it became an egg.

From this egg two eagles hatched. One was called Rich Brilliance and the other Tormented Darkness. When the birds mated they produced three more eggs – one was white, one black and one speckled. The creator god Sangpo Bumtri emerged from the white egg; from the black egg came an arrogant, dark man, and from the speckled egg a prayer issued forth. Sangpo Bumtri then called the inhabited world into being.

At his right hand he placed gold and turquoise and murmured a prayer. A gold mountain and a turquoise valley grew there that was to become the human world, and within it the race of black-headed people had its beginnings. At his left hand he set a mussel and a gem; when he prayed again, a mussel mountain and a valley of jewels sprang up as the birthplace of the heavenly spirits. Before him he put a crystal and a red light, which turned into a home for the world's animals.

Allies of Convenience

Horses, once the carefree inhabitants of heaven, were met with violence and death when they descended to the Earth beneath. They were forced to make a pact with humans.

One day three colts were driven down from heaven by their hunger; they could find no grass or water in the pastures of the sky. Alighting in Tibet, the three brothers split up to go and search for grazing: the eldest, headed north into the mountains; the second set out along the plateau, while the third descended to the valley, where he found sparkling streams and lush, juicy grass. Returning to their rendezvous to share their discoveries, the second and third brothers waited vainly for the eldest. Eventually, they realized they would have to go and find him for themselves.

Climbing high into the hills, they found a region ruled by yaks – and the body of their brother, gored to death as an alien intruder. Grieved at his loss, the two younger colts mourned him, but while the middle one was resigned to accept his brother's death, the youngest was full of anger, and resolved upon revenge. Without help from his brother, though, he had no obvious course of action, so he went down to the plateau, and entered the world of men. The gods warned him against it – men would capture him and gag him with a bridle – but the colt was determined, and would not be deterred.

At the first community he came to, the colt struck a bargain. If the man would avenge his brother, he would serve him a hundred years. He would carry him on the Earth throughout his mortal life, and then bear him to heaven when his time came to die. Agreeing to these terms, the man rode him into the mountains: he slew the murdering yak, and the horse was avenged. Well pleased with his bargain, he served his master faithfully – as have his descendants to the present day.

Blue Water Snake

In the tale of the king and the blue water snake, only the wisdom of Tönpa Shenrap could rescue the king from the snake's unearthly power.

A man so virtuous and powerful that the gods called him "the Elect of the Created World" became king of his district. One day a blue snake appeared, then vanished, at a water mill in the kingdom. Disturbed by this omen, the king asked a priest and a small child with divine powers of insight what it could mean. The priest was uncertain and declined to make a pronouncement, but the child told the king that he must throw jewels and medicines into the mill as an offering for the snake.

Later, the king and queen were ploughing near the mill when a marmot appeared in front of them. The king tried to kill it, but it vanished before his eyes. The priest declared that the rodent was a god, and soon afterwards, as if in punishment for the king's actions, the royal couple fell ill.

The priest could not identify the god responsible, so the king appealed to the White Lady of the Sky. She consulted the King of the Sky, and when he looked into his magic mirror he saw that the ploughing of the land near the mill had angered the king of the serpent-like *klu* water spirits.

But even the sky king could not suggest a cure for the sickness. It was the small child who finally asked Tönpa Shenrap for help, and the great teacher said that the *klu* must be calmed, and its own health restored, before the king and queen would get better.

Shenrap said that the *klu* could be pacified by offering it cakes in the shape of birds, fish and animals; and desirable things fashioned from wool, feathers, silk, gold and turquoise. The god Garsa Tsanpo should be invoked by beating drums and flat bells. Drink should also be offered to the *klu*. The priest should imitate a dragon to summon the spirit, but use the voice of the cuckoo to persuade it. All was done as he prescribed, and the king and queen recovered.

How the World Will End

One of the divine heroes of Mongol myth was Erlik Khan, who was represented in the firmament by the planet Venus, which, as the Morning Star, killed all the other stars each dawn. Under Buddhist influence, Erlik was relegated to king of the Underworld.

In later times a story arose that combined animist and Buddhist elements to explain Erlik's fall from grace and also to predict his ultimate revenge. It told how, after the creation of the Earth, Qormusta, king of the tengri (as the animist gods were called), destroyed Erlik's territory in the heavens. When Erlik asked for even a tiny plot of land on Earth in exchange, Qormusta turned down his request point blank. Instead, he would only agree to give him the dark domain beneath its surface, a place of punishment where the souls of the dead were confined.

However, according to a prophecy, Erlik will one day have his revenge. When the mountains turn to dust he will emerge with nine iron warriors on nine iron horses from nine stones at the bottom of the sea and destroy everything in his path. Amid the chaos, people will cry for help from Qormusta and from Mongke Tengri, "Eternal Blue Sky", the creator of the visible and invisible worlds. When these two chief gods of Tengriism fail to answer their prayers, they will turn instead to Sagjamuni, the name Mongols gave to the Lord Buddha, and will beg him and his holy men to intercede on their behalf. But they too will be deaf to their pleading. Then the two greatest warriors in Erlik's army, Karan and Kere, will rise from the Underworld and attack Sagjamuni himself; and the Earth will be consumed in the flames that burst from his flowing blood.

The Burning of the Yellow Book

Shamans had many duties, not least of which was to divine the future. In Mongolia one of the most common divination techniques was scapulomancy – reading the shoulder blades of sheep. The origin of the practice was explained in a myth.

In the earliest times, before even the shamans had come among the Mongols, there lived a king who owned a wonderful yellow book. This magic book had the power of divination. Every time a crime was committed, the king had only to open the book to discover the name and whereabouts of the villain.

Inevitably, the king had the most loyal courtiers and soldiers in the world. Even when prospective suitors offered them huge bribes to reveal where their jealous master had hidden his famously beautiful daughter, they refused, knowing that the book would give them away.

One day, however, a cunning young suitor called Tevne devised a way of deceiving the book. He lured an old serving woman from the court to a place where he had dug a deep hole. Then he forced her into the hole, built a fire over the top of it and placed a kettle of water on the fire. Speaking through a long piece of iron pipe, which he laid through the kettle into the hole, he told the terrified old woman that he would not let her go until she had taught him how to find the princess. Armed with the old woman's answers, Tevne went to the palace and courted the princess, whom he was able to identify among a score of identically dressed maidens in the royal entourage.

When the king learned that his daughter's heart had been won by a trickster, he turned to his yellow book, but all that it could tell him was that he had been betrayed by a man who had an iron pipe for vocal cords, lungs filled with water, a body of fire and earthen buttocks. In his fury the king burned the book, and its powers devolved to the sheep that ate its ashes. Forever afterwards the shamans, who could read the signs with the help of the great Fire God, were able to reveal the unknown and foretell the future by burning the shoulder blades of sheep.

A Feast Fit for a King

Few Mongols would dare to kill a snake for fear of offending its master the dragon, who supported the tree of life. The eagle, king of the birds, had no such qualms. The eagle's unlikely preference for snake meat was explained by one of the oldest myths.

Soon after the world had been created, the supreme god, Mongke Tengri, sent the swallow and the wasp to discover which meat was sweetest and most suitable for a king. While the wasp worked busily, sampling with its sting every creature it met, the easy-going swallow soared aimlessly through the clear blue sky admiring the beauties of the newly made world.

Just before sunset, the wasp rejoined the swallow in the sky. When the swallow asked if it had found the sweetest meat, the wasp replied that human flesh tasted best. The swallow was horrified. All day it had watched men and women tending their herds, taking care of their families and hunting in the forests and the steppes. If these creatures were to become the prey of birds, they would never prosper.

As the two turned back toward heaven, the swallow pounced on the wasp and tore out its tongue. When Mongke Tengri asked for their report, the wasp could do nothing but buzz; and when the supreme god turned to the swallow, the little bird thought quickly, remembered the most evil and useless creature it had seen in its day of exploration and answered, "The serpent".

Mongke Tengri nodded, summoned the eagle and sent it to Earth with the mischievous swallow's instructions; and that is why the king of the birds kills snakes whenever it can, even though it is powerful enough to dine every day on the much sweeter meat of hares and goats instead.

The Mongolian Swan Lake

The story of the beautiful creature who turns into a woman and marries an ordinary man is common to most cultures. The Mongolian version of the myth takes place on one of the mysterious lakes that dot the landscape of Central Asia.

Like all Mongols, Khori Tumed the herdsman believed that swans were beautiful young women in disguise. When he saw nine of them swooping down from the northeast to land on the banks of the lake near his home, he crept closer through the reeds to watch. Crouching low in the mud, he saw nine beautiful girls taking off their feathered dresses and diving naked into the sacred water.

Khori crept unseen toward the bank and stole one of the feathered dresses. When the swan maidens returned, only eight of them were able to put on their feathers and fly. Naked and helpless, the ninth could only watch them go. She was a prisoner in her human form. When Khori offered his protection, she had no choice but to accept and marry him. For eleven years they lived together, and in each of those eleven years the beautiful bride bore Khori Tumed a son. Although Khori was a generous and attentive husband, he cruelly refused to tell his wife where he had hidden her feathered dress.

At last, however, after the birth of their eleventh son, Khori relented and brought in the dress, taking care to block the doorway to their tent. But as soon as she was a swan again, his wife flapped her wings and escaped through the smoke hole above the fire. The swan circled in the air three times, bestowing her blessing on her sons and all the generations that were to spring from them. Then she flew away, toward the northeast from where she had come; and Khori stood alone staring helplessly after her with tear-filled eyes, just as she had done eleven years earlier when her sisters flew off without her.

China

China can lay claim to be the world's oldest continuous civilization. Its mythology reflects the richness of its heritage, not least in the extraordinary degree of order that generations of antiquarian-minded scholars have bestowed upon it.

Yet the roots of the tradition go back into a distant shamanistic past. Only traces of the early beliefs can still be glimpsed, mostly through the distorting mirror of Daoism. This movement, which traced its origins to the sage Laozi, began life as a philosophy emphasizing spontaneity and the importance of going with the flow of the natural world. In time, however, it developed the attributes of a religion, embracing mysticism and magic and taking on some of the practices of the earlier *wu* shamans. Daoism also produced a creation myth in the story of Pan Gu, a divine being who unleashed the elements that went on to make the universe and then moulded the first humans out of lumps of clay (see page 176).

Another part of early Chinese religious practice was ancestor worship. The belief that the spirits of the dead could reward or punish the treatment they received after their demise lingered well into the historical era, as a story set at the Tang court makes clear (see page 187).

Respect for the past was a defining characteristic of Confucianism, the other main pillar of the Chinese intellectual tradition. If Daoism stressed the importance of impulsiveness, Confucianism instead promoted the rule of reason, together with a respect for authority. The Confucian approach put a premium on education, and it was unsurprising that, in a society where advancement to high rank depended on academic study, one of the most popular gods was Kui Xing, a poor scholar eventually deified as the god of examinations (see page 185).

The main contribution Confucius's followers made to the Chinese mythological canon was to organize it chronologically into a sequence that eventually segued into the nation's real historical record. Scholars proposed a line of mythical rulers, starting with the serpent-bodied Fu Xi, a culture hero who taught humans to make fire and cook their food. He was able to do so because he was the son of the Thunder God and so had direct access to heaven (see page 177).

Fu Xi's successor, the bird-headed Shen Nong, invented the cart and the plough and taught people to grow crops, but could not prevent his daughter being lost to the sea in a boating accident (see page 178). He was followed by the Yellow Emperor, Huang Di, the legendary ancestor of the Chinese people. Famed for his sagacity, Huang was also a renowned warrior, quite capable of taking on a giant in single combat (see page 179).

Further down the list came the Sage Kings. The first, Yao, had to call on the help of the divine archer Yi when ten suns rose over his kingdom, threatening a devastating drought. Yi shot down nine of the suns, only to be punished for his temerity by his fellow gods, who reduced him to mortal status. A legend described his subsequent murder by a human rival (see page 182).

Yao chose not to pass the throne to his offspring Dan Zhu, whose extravagant behaviour showed him to be unfit for high office (see page 183). In contrast Yu, last of the Sage Kings, started China's tradition of dynastic imperial rule by installing his son as his successor. The line he thus started, the Xia, was followed by the Shang Dynasty, which, although firmly established in the historical record, spawned legends of its own, mostly concerning the misdeeds of its last ruler, Zhou Xin, whose excesses caused its downfall (see page 184) in around 1100 BCE.

A final layer of myth was added by the coming of Buddhism, which established itself in China in the third century CE; by 420 there were reportedly 1,768 monasteries in southern China alone. A Buddhist tale of later times told of a wandering monk's stay in one such establishment – in his case a vanishing monastery inhabited by a community of ghosts (see page 188).

Pan Gu Creates the First People

Many accounts credit the mother goddess Nü Wa with creating the first human beings. However, according to an alternative version of the first days it was the creator Pan Gu himself who made the first people out of clay after he had separated heaven from Earth.

Before the universe came into being, there was a giant egg, at the heart of which Pan Gu, the creator, slowly came to life. When he awoke he split the egg open, which sent the elements of creation flying through space. The lighter, purer parts, or yang, flew upwards and became heaven, while the heavier ones, or yin, sank to take shape as the Earth. In one place heaven and Earth were linked but Pan Gu worked away at the join until they were separated.

Next, Pan Gu brought plants and animals into being. But he felt unhappy with his handiwork, because none of the birds and beasts had the power of reason; he decided there ought to be one creature with the ability to care for and make use of other living beings.

With his strong, skilful hands he began to mould the first people from mud, and as he finished each figure he set it to dry in the sunshine. Some of the creatures he filled with the female qualities of yin and fashioned into women, others he endowed with the male qualities of yang, turning them into men. He worked all day beneath the hot sun, piling up his people against a rock outcrop.

As the sun went down he straightened his aching back and looked up at the sky, where he saw a bank of dark stormclouds. Some of the clay people had not yet dried and he realized that his handiwork would be obliterated if the storm broke over the figures. He hurried to move them into the shelter of a nearby cave, but as he worked a great wind arose, whipping up the clouds until they filled the sky. Pan Gu cried aloud with anguish as the thunder cracked and the rains poured down while he was still moving the figures. Those damaged were the ancestors of people with unusually shaped bodies or disabilities.

Fu Xi Scales the Heavenly Ladder

One account of the life of the culture hero Fu Xi made him the son of a country maiden and the god of thunder. He had a divine nature and could travel between Earth and heaven.

The mythical territory of Huaxu was an earthly paradise where people lived to a very great age. They enjoyed a blessed life without fear of fire or water and could follow the invisible paths of the sky as if they were roaming on the ground. A maiden of this land was one day wandering through the swamp of Leize, when she came across a giant's vast footprints in the soft ground. Curious, she stepped into the indentation, which was the footprint of the god of thunder. She felt strangely warmed in her belly and later discovered she was pregnant. In due course she gave birth to a healthy boy, whom she named Fu Xi.

The child had the nature and attributes of a god, and he could come and go between Earth and the heavenly realm. He went by way of the tree of Jianmu which grew at the very centre of the Duguang plain in southwest China. It had long and tangled roots, but above ground grew straight up without branches for miles into the sky. No mortal could find a grip on the smooth, soft bark. At the very top, far above the Earth, there was a proliferation of branches.

The plain of Duguang where the tree of Jianmu grew was said to be the very centre of the Earth and was itself a paradise – a place where plants and trees never dropped their leaves and a wonderful and diverse menagerie of beasts and birds had assembled.

Fu Xi, traveller between heaven and Earth, taught mortal people many wonderful things. Among other things, he showed them how to make fire by rubbing sticks together, and how to use it for cooking. He made a stringed instrument and showed men and women how to make music. Inspired by the intricacy and effectiveness of the spider's web, Fu Xi also made a net that people could use for hunting and fishing.

How the Sea Defeated Jing Wei

Fu Xi's successor, Shen Nong, had a favourite daughter – the delicate, slender-necked Nü Wa, who shared her name with the great mother goddess. But to his dismay she drowned in a boating accident. After death she vowed to avenge herself on the sea that had killed her.

Shen Nong's daughter loved to row on the deep waters far from land, watching the sea birds swoop through the buffeting winds or skim low over the waves. But one day a squall caught her boat and she was swept overboard and drowned. When she did not return that evening, Shen Nong wailed loudly in the echoing dusk – but for all his divine strength he had no power over death and could not restore his lost one to her former shape.

From Fajiu the bird flew to the Eastern Sea carrying a pebble or twig in its white beak – and dropped it into the water. Then the girl's spirit told the waves that she would fill them up with wood and stones and turn the great ocean into a marsh to prevent it robbing any more young people of their lives. But the sea just laughed, and told her she could never achieve her goal, no matter how hard she might try.

For her part, Nü Wa was filled with anger toward the cruel sea that had ended her life before its time. Her soul took the form of a white-beaked bird with a many-coloured head and red feet. Named Jing Wei, the bird looked like a cross between a crow and an owl. It nested on Fajiu Mountain in modern-day Shaanxi Province.

Jing Wei turned her back contemptuously on the proud water. She flew back to Fajiu Mountain, picked up another twig and returned to drop it into the sea. From that day on the bird known as the *jing wei* has laboured ceaselessly to fill the sea, but despite its efforts the waves still roll and crash upon the shore.

Huang Di & Xing Tian

Huang Di, the Yellow Emperor, faced a number of challenges to his authority. In one instance, an enormous giant named Xing Tian arose in the south, determined to usurp Huang Di, and the two fought a titanic struggle which began in heaven and ended on Changyang Mountain.

As he marched north to face Huang Di in heaven, Xing Tian shook with fury, for he was a long-time enemy of the Yellow Emperor. The giant shrugged off the challenge of one guard after another until he came face-to-face with Huang Di himself. Xing Tian contemptuously challenged him to fight – and the emperor rose at once and seized his best sword. A mighty conflict ensued, in which the two warriors tested their strength to the utmost and the air around them shook with their cries.

Without noticing, they left heaven behind and fought their way across the slopes of Changyang Mountain in western China. Here Huang Di saw his opportunity and with a single stroke sliced off the giant's head. From the top of his vast body it crashed to the ground, making the mountains themselves shudder. But Xing Tian did not fall, for the blow had not killed him: headless, he could not see but still had strength for the fight.

The giant lowered himself onto his haunches and searched for his head. As his huge hands groped here and there, they smashed whole cliffs and entire forests. Huang Di meanwhile had the advantage. He saw where the head had landed and quickly cut open the adjoining mountain so that it rolled into the crevice. Then he resealed the mountain and the giant's head was encased in rock.

The Kingdom of Birds

A beautiful fairy named Huange loved to visit the glorious celestial mulberry tree that stood near the Western Sea. There a young man would wait for her; he was the morning star. They became lovers and in due course a god called Shao Hao was born.

Shao Hao grew into a handsome youth, and was so capable that his great uncle Huang Di named him God of the Western Heavens. In his prime, he travelled to the five mountains of the Eastern Paradise and established a kingdom populated entirely by birds. As its ruler he took the form of a vulture and oversaw a vast feathered bureaucracy, with the phoenix as his Lord Chancellor. He put the hawk in charge of the law, and to the pigeon he gave responsibility for education, while the changing weather across the four seasons he placed in the charge of the pheasant, the quail, the shrike and the swallow. For many years Shao Hao ruled the bird kingdom with wisdom, but eventually he went back to the west, leaving his son Chong in charge of the birds. With another of his sons, Ru Shou, he settled on Changliu Mountain and ruled over the Western Heavens. Father and son together were responsible for the sunset.

The Friendly Fox

A wily fox played a good-natured trick on a farmer who had a fondness for wine. In the farmyard stood a vast pile of straw, part of which had been hollowed out as the stalks were taken and used.

The mischievous beast made its den in the hole and often stopped to talk to the farmer. In order to converse with a human it took the form of a whiskery old man. The farmer knew its true identity, but it did not bother him.

One evening the old man invited the farmer inside the stack of straw, where to his astonishment he found a row of splendidly decorated rooms. The friendly old man served his guest with fragrant tea and exceptional wine.

Over the following weeks the farmer often saw the old man creeping away at dusk and then returning at dawn. Curious, he asked where the trips took him and the old fellow confessed that he went away to taste wines with a friend. Having enjoyed his visit to the straw stack, the farmer asked to go with the old man, who at first refused, but finally agreed. The two set off at once, carried up magically into the night air as if driven before a strong wind.

They landed in a city and went to a crowded restaurant. The old man seated the farmer on a raised gallery and went invisibly among the diners below, bringing back fine wines and foods for his guest. When a waiter appeared with dessert, the farmer asked the fox if he could taste some. The animal replied that he could not approach the waiter, as he was an upright man. The farmer was stricken, realizing his own loss of virtue since he had begun to consort with the animal; and he promised himself that he would improve.

Perhaps the realization brought him to his senses, for in that instant he had the sensation of falling. He awoke on the floor of the eating-salon; instead of the gallery, he saw that he had been sitting on a roof beam. He told his enthralling story to the other diners, and as a sign of appreciation they funded his return journey, for the restaurant was a very long way from his home.

The Death of Yi

The divine archer Yi, who had lost his immortality (see page 175), managed to procure a magic elixir that could restore it. However, his wife unwittingly swallowed the potion, and the great archer finally fell victim to the jealousy of a human rival he had chosen to befriend.

Feng Meng's skill at archery was surpassed only by that of Yi himself. Yi did his best to encourage the young hunter, teaching him the finer points of the bowman's art: how not to blink when aiming, the special skill of learning to see small objects as if they were large.

Soon Feng Meng began to consider himself a rival even for his divine master. One day he challenged Yi to a shooting contest, taking aim at a flight of geese high up in the sky. In an instant he had shot down three of the birds as they flew in line. Before Yi could draw, the rest of the flock scattered across the skies, creating a seemingly impossible target. Even so, Yi brought down another trio, convincing Feng Meng that he would never outdo him.

In his bitterness, the hunter planned to kill Yi, knowing that he was now as mortal as any other man. Taking cover in a forest, he sought to ambush him, but each time that he sent an arrow whistling through the air, Yi countered with another that struck its shaft in mid-flight.

Thwarted at bowmanship, the assassin resorted to cruder methods to achieve his goal. He waited until Yi had set aside his bow to pick up a bird that he had downed. Then he leaped upon him, bludgeoning him to death with the peachwood rod he used to carry home the game.

The Preposterous Dan Zhu

Emperor Yao, the first of China's Sage Kings, chose not to pass on his throne to his son Dan Zhu, who for later generations became the archetype of the irresponsible heir unfit to inherit high office.

Dan Zhu's selfishness and insensitivity knew no bounds. He loved to go on boat trips even when drought gripped the kingdom, forcing sweating minions to carry the craft along the dried-up riverbeds. When his father taught him chess to keep him harmlessly occupied, he chose to play it in the most extravagant way imaginable, planting an entire plain in a chequerboard pattern of groves and open spaces and using live rhinoceroses and elephants to serve as the thirty-two pieces.

His excesses so alienated Yao that the emperor determined to banish him to the far south. There the angry prince stirred up trouble, raising the flag of revolt among disaffected border tribes. But he had no talent as a military leader, and soon he and his supporters were fleeing for their lives from the emperor's armies, halting only when they reached the sea. There, in his despair, Dan Zhu killed himself by leaping into the waters. But it was not the end of him, for his spirit took the form of a bird called the *zhu*, shaped like an owl but with human hands. In later times it showed itself only in lands that were badly governed, its appearance a sure sign that high officials were about to be dismissed.

Zhou Xin the Shang Sadist

In China's moralistic view of history, dynasties collapsed when their rulers misbehaved. Just as the virtues of the Sage Kings promoted their subjects' well-being, so the wicked ways of Zhou Xin ensured that he would be the last emperor of the Shang Dynasty.

Zhou Xin was said to have a lively, inquisitive mind, though he satisfied his curiosity in a highly perverse way. To judge from the stories, he had a particular interest in the workings of the human body, which led him to conduct horrific experiments. On one occasion, he saw some peasants wading through a stream in mid-winter, and had their legs cut off so he could study the effects of the cold on their bone marrow.

When his uncle, Prince Bi Gan, reproved him for his failings, he replied, "You're said to be a sage, and I have heard that sages have seven openings in the heart" – whereupon he ordered that the prince be killed and cut open so that he could check if the claim was true.

The Examination God

One of the most popular deities in the Chinese pantheon was Kui Xing, who supervised success in imperial examinations. Candidates would keep his image in their home, and across China many millions of anxious prayers rose up to him in the tense days before the final assessment.

Before taking his place among the gods, Kui Xing had been the most brilliant scholar of his day, but, unfortunately, he was also physically repulsive. When he took the examinations for entry into the imperial civil service, he got the highest marks. Custom demanded that, as top scholar, he should receive a golden rose from the hand of the emperor himself. But the ruler took one look at Kui Xing's ugly face and refused to present it.

The young man was devastated. In his distress, he attempted to drown himself in the sea. But a strange turtle-like beast rose from beneath the waves and carried him to safety. Subsequently he ascended to heaven and took up residence in the Great Bear constellation.

A Foolish Dragon

Dragons were powerful beasts, capable of mounting the clouds to bring rain or harnessing rivers in time of floods, but the legends also often portrayed them as stupid. One told how a sea creature on a mercy mission was easily outwitted by a monkey.

One day a dragon living in the ocean saw that his wife was unwell. Hoping to restore her health, he asked if there was any particular food that she would like to eat. At first she refused to answer, but when pressed confided that she had a craving for a monkey's heart.

The dutiful husband made his way to the shore, where he spied a monkey in the tree-tops. To tempt it down, he asked if it was not tired of its own forest, offering instead to carry it across the ocean to a land where fruit grew on every branch.

Easily persuaded, the simian climbed onto the dragon's back. It soon had an unpleasant surprise, however, when the dragon dived down into the ocean depths. Panic-stricken, it asked where they were going, at which point the dragon explained apologetically that he needed a monkey's heart for his sick wife. "Then you'll have to go back to land!" shouted the monkey desperately. "I left my heart in the tree-tops!"

Obediently, the foolish dragon did as he was told, swimming back to the shore and letting his prey scamper back to the trees. Scrambling rapidly to the safety of the topmost branches, the monkey thought to itself as it watched its former captor waiting in vain below: "What simpletons dragons must be to fall for a story like that!"

The Demon-Eater

A legend dating from the Tang dynasty (618–907 CE) told how one tormented soul repaid a debt of gratitude to the imperial family by protecting its members from other, more malicious spirits.

Emperor Ming Huang had a fever, and one night a demon assailed him in his troubled sleep. The imp was fantastically dressed in red trousers and a single shoe. Having broken into the palace through a bamboo gate, he was gambolling through the state chambers playing a flute, showing none of the respect due in those sacred precincts.

Angrily, the emperor asked him what he thought he was doing. "My name," he replied, "is Emptiness and Desolation." The ruler was looking round in vain for a guard to remove him when suddenly a fearsome apparition rushed in, wearing a tattered robe and a torn bandana. The newcomer seized the demon, crushed it into a ball and swallowed it.

Startled, the emperor enquired whom he had to thank for his deliverance. The spirit replied that his name was Zhong Kui, that he had lived in Shaanxi Province in the preceding century, and that he had been unjustly deprived of first-class honours in the public examinations. In his anger he had committed suicide on the steps of the imperial palace; but instead of treating his corpse with ignominy, as his behaviour had merited, the reigning emperor had ordered it to be buried ceremoniously in a green robe – an honour normally reserved for members of the imperial family. Out of gratitude, Zhong had vowed to protect his successors for all time against the demons of despair.

At that point the emperor woke up, his fever gone. He subsequently described the apparition to a court artist, who painted a portrait of Zhong Kui that was still hanging in the imperial palace 300 years later.

The Vanishing Monastery

A Buddhist tale told of a wandering monk named Ban Gong, who got lost in the hills. While the sun began to set, he heard the sound of a bell, which led him to a monastery. As he approached, guard dogs barked at him, but a monk beckoned him in.

Inside, the whole place seemed deserted. Ban Gong found a small cell containing a bed, where he decided to stay for the night.

Some time afterwards, he was disturbed by voices from the main hall. Looking out, he was astonished to find that it was filling up with monks entering not through the door but from the ceiling, floating down like feathers from a hole in the roof.

Hearing someone mention a famous Zen master's name, Ban Gong interrupted to say that he had studied under the man. At that moment, the whole spectral host disappeared along with the buildings, and the monk was alone again on the hillside. When he eventually came to a real monastery, he learned that he was not the first to encounter the vanishing cloister, though few ever knew more of its presence than the tolling of an unseen bell.

A Close Shave

Journeying in priestly guise in search of the Buddhist scriptures, Monkey and his strange band of companions faced many dangers. One requiring special ingenuity was the Land that Hated Priests.

The novel *Journey to the West* is one of the world's oddest literary classics. Written in the sixteenth century, it took its title and basic premise from a non-fiction work that first appeared almost 1,000 years earlier, describing the voyage of the monk Xuanzang to India in search of Buddhist scriptures.

The fictionalized account turned Xuanzang's adventures into a wildly comic fantasia. In its pages the monk had an unlikely trio of fellow travellers. One was a monkey endowed with supernatural powers, another a hybrid creature with a man's body and a pig's face, and the third a disgraced official turned brigand. All donned the garb of Buddhist priests, hoping to win redemption for past misdeeds by helping Xuanzang.

On their way the four faced many challenges, including traversing a land whose people were known to kill all priests. The band took off their monks' robes and spent their first night over the border inside a wardrobe in a roadside inn. But robbers stole the cupboard, only to abandon it soon after when stopped by police.

The travellers' plight now seemed desperate, for they knew their priestly tonsures would betray them when they were found the next day. But Monkey, thinking fast, found a solution. Using his magical powers, he created 1,000 monkeys just like himself and gave each one a razor so they could shave the heads of all the land's leading citizens as they slept. In a land of bald-headed men, the pilgrims' own bare scalps went unnoticed.

Japan

The mythology of Japan originated in nature worship centred on *kami*, beings of power inhabiting natural phenomena such as mountains, rivers or oddly shaped boulders. Ancestors too could become *kami*, and were also objects of veneration. Early in the nation's history, this huge and disorderly pantheon was clasped within the embrace of Shinto, Japan's indigenous religion. The term, which means "The Way of the Gods", was first used in the eighth century CE. By that time Buddhism had also reached Japan, and the two faiths quickly came to an understanding that has endured to the present day.

The word "Shinto" was coined in the *Nihongi*, one of two compilations of ancient myth and history that appeared at the time (the other was the *Kojiki*). Both books were commissioned by the Empress Gemmei as a means of presenting the nation's heritage of myth in a way that reinforced the central role of Japan's ruling dynasty. The result was a mythical history that traced the story of Japan from the creation to the birth of the first emperor, Jimmu, traditionally said to have ascended the throne in 660 BCE. It told how the first gods emerged from a primeval egg, among them Izanagi and Izanami, who created the eight largest Japanese islands. The divine siblings then populated the land with a multiplicity of gods and spirits, the greatest of whom were the sun goddess Amaterasu and the moon god Tsukiyomi, together with the disruptive Susano. The most familiar version of their creation had them born of waters used to cleanse Izanagi's face, although a variant myth insisted he generated the three merely by looking into mirrors (see page 192).

Amaterasu and Tsukiyomi initially lived together as man and wife, but they fell out after Tsukiyomi killed the food goddess Ogetsuno (see page 193). Thereafter they avoided one another's company, as the sun and moon do to this day. As for Susano, he proved so unruly that the other gods banned him from the High Plain of Heaven, and he ended up as the deity presiding over Yomi, the shadow land of the dead.

From her heavenly abode Amaterasu extended her control over the human realm below. She established a divine dynasty that descended through her grandson Honinigi, who married an earthly princess, producing three children, Honoakari, Honosusori and Hikohoho. Despite the unpropitious circumstances of their begetting (see page 195), they carried on the dynastic line when Hikohoho fell in love with a daughter of a sea god, who bore him a child before returning forever to her watery realm. This boy would in his turn father many offspring, among them the father of Jimmu, the founder of the dynasty that rules Japan to this day.

Another strand of Japanese myth consisted of hero legends, setting sword-wielding champions against brigands, dragons and monsters. They themselves were not always models of physical perfection – indeed, Issun Boshi (roughly, "Little One Inch") was as small as Tom Thumb (see page 198) – and the tactics they resorted to were at times less than heroic (see page 196). Yet their constant battles with the forces of evil, sometimes in supernatural form like the terrible spider-woman confronted by Yorimitsu (see page 197), made them models for the samurai warriors who rose to fame under the shoguns. Inspiration for some of the stories came from real historical events, notably the twelfth-century struggle for power between the Taira and Minamoto clans, which literally haunted the imagination of succeeding generations (see page 199).

Japan also has a rich legacy of folktales, many of them featuring an exotic bestiary of ghosts and spirits. The nation's distinctive supernatural fauna included the *tengu* (see page 200), a malicious birdman who guarded the forests, and Yuki-onna, the beautiful but destructive spirit of the snows (see page 201). Even living organisms like trees could have spirits (see page 203), giving the nation an abundant stock of stories of ghostly visitations and second comings (see page 202).

Heavenly Illumination

Early sources gave three variant accounts of the birth of the sun goddess Amaterasu and the moon god Tsukiyomi. All credited their creation to the god Izanagi, who with his sister-wife Izanami was earlier responsible for bringing into being the islands of Japan.

One account had Izanami giving birth to the gods in much the same way that she had earlier begotten the eight main islands of the Japanese archipelago. The other two stories, however, both made Izanagi alone responsible for creating the sun and moon.

A version given in the *Kojiki* tells how Izanami, having engendered the eight islands, died giving birth to the fire god Kagutsuchi. The grief-stricken Izanagi followed her to the land of Yomi, the Japanese underworld, but fled polluted back to the upper world from the horrors that he saw there; Amaterasu and Tsukiyomi, along with their sibling Susano, were born of the water he used to wash away the impurities.

The third account had Izanagi standing alone in Onogoro, the original Japanese island, and declaring his intention to create offspring who would rule the world. He took a mirror of white copper in his left hand and, merely by gazing into it, brought forth a deity named Ohohirume ("Great Noon Female", an alternative title for Amaterasu). Then he lifted an identical mirror in his right hand and with his gaze gave form to Tsukiyomi. Finally he looked sideways into the mirror to create Susano.

The first two divinities cast a bright glow all around, so Izanagi set them in the firmament to illuminate the

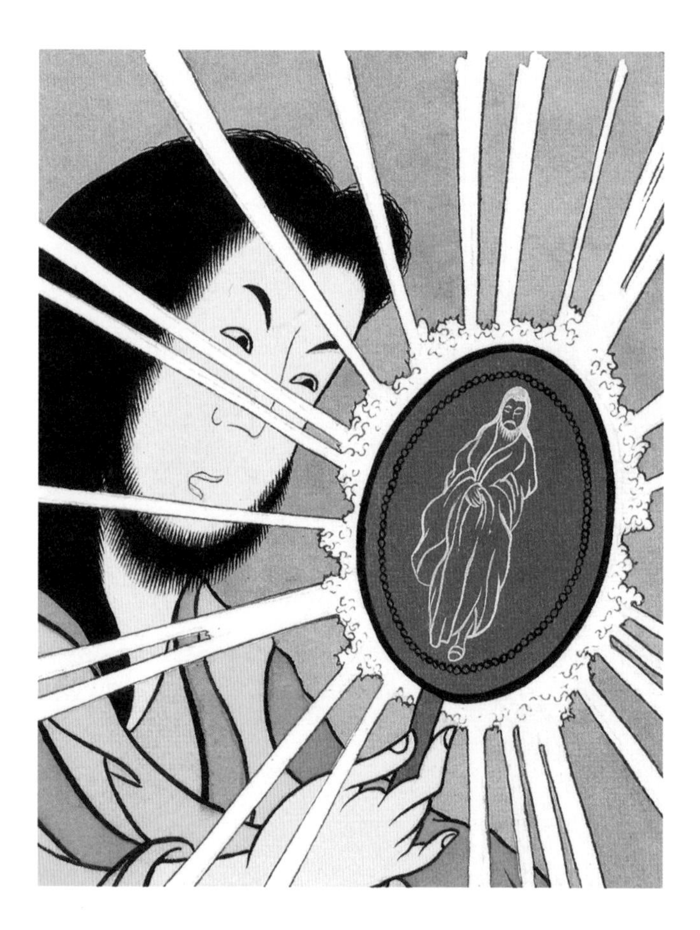

Earth: Tsukiyomi would shine with a pale luminescence by night, while Ohohirume's fierce rays lit up the day. But the third deity, Susano, soon proved to be nothing but trouble, so Izanagi dispatched him to govern Yomi, home to foul hags and demons.

A Wondrous & Fulsome Harvest

Amaterasu, the great goddess of the sun, sent her brother Tsukiyomi, the god of the moon, to pay court to the food goddess Ogetsuno. Their divine encounter led to violence, but was not without a productive outcome.

Ogetsuno lived in the Central Reed Plain, where mortal men and women would one day settle, and Tsukiyomi descended from heaven to visit her. Seeing the approach of so august a visitor, the goddess produced foods with which to welcome and entertain him.

When she looked toward the land she gave issue to rice, while on setting her face toward the waters of the ocean she produced the many fish and other sea creatures. She faced the forbidding, snow-capped mountains and all the many creatures of the land, soft of pelt or covered with hard bristles, issued from her bodily orifices.

Tsukiyomi was disgusted that she was offering him food from her own body, and he drew his sword in anger. With a single stroke of the blade he brought the goddess down and returned to heaven buzzing with satisfied anger. But the great Amaterasu was displeased when he spoke of his adventure, and from that day on the sun and moon were rarely seen together.

Amaterasu then sent another celestial deity, Amekumabito ("Heaven-bear-man"), to see the food goddess; scholars believe he may have been meant to represent a cloud, for clouds were often divine messengers in Japanese tradition. He found that the food goddess was indeed dead, but from her body came a wondrous harvest of good things. On her forehead grew millet; on her stomach, rice; in her genitals wheat and beans; in her eyebrows were silkworms; while circling her head were the ancestors of those hardy animals of the field, the ox and the horse.

Tales of Izumo

A distinct cycle of myths set in the Izumo region of Japan begins with Susano's descent from heaven and continues with the exploits of his descendant Okuninushi. In Izumo tradition, it was Okuninushi – not Izanagi and Izanami (see page 192) – who created the islands of Japan.

Looking out to sea from Cape Mipo in Izumo, Okuninushi saw a diminutive god adrift in a boat made from the pod of a kagami plant. Okuninushi called out to the newcomer, asking his name – but received no reply. Eventually he discovered that the dwarf god was named Sukunabiko and that he and Okuninushi were destined to give form to the islands of the Central Reed Plain.

After the two gods had performed this honourable task, Sukunabiko travelled on in his tiny craft to Tokoyo-no-Kuni, the distant land of eternity beyond the ocean.

Okuninushi spoke aloud in grief demanding to know how he alone could keep order in the land. Then a mysterious deity appeared like a band of heavenly light across the ocean and agreed to help him govern Japan. He declared that he would always be at Okuninushi's side if he would in return establish a shrine for the god's worship on the sacred peak of Mount Mimoro.

A later ruler of Izumo was Omitsunu ("Master Field Beach"), a grandson of Susano. He expanded Izumo territory in a novel way. Omitsunu was troubled that Izumo was so small, and he saw that across the water there was spare land lying untended on the shore of Korea. Therefore he took a rope, tied one end to the Korean shore and the other to a peak in Izumo, Mount Sahime, and ordered his subjects to pull for their lives. A great mass of land tore away and attached itself to Izumo. He later repeated the trick, using ropes to haul in islands from the Sea of Japan and mould them on to Izumo. The remains of the last rope made the beach of Yomi.

The Fiery Birth

Amaterasu's grandson Honinigi fell in love with Princess Konohana the moment he met her while walking by the sea, and asked her to marry him minutes later. On the night of their wedding they joyfully consummated their marriage beneath a gentle moon.

Within hours the princess appeared to be pregnant, throwing Honinigi into a frenzy of doubt and jealousy – for he reasoned that the child could not be his. His restless mind could not leave the subject alone and at length he confronted her. Konohana was furious that Honinigi doubted her fidelity; she stalked away in silence, plotting a way of proving her innocence.

Near the beach where they had first met, she had a straw hut built. She declared loudly that she would prove her offspring to be those of Honinigi. When her time came to give birth she would go into the hut and set fire to it. If the babies emerged unscathed it would prove that they were under the divine protection of Honinigi's bright grandmother, Amaterasu the sun goddess.

Konohana kept her promise. When her labour was advanced she had herself shut inside the cabin. Then, with a flourish, she lit the straw walls of the tiny house. The flames roared and onlookers gave her up for dead.

But Konohana delivered three healthy children. The first, Honoakari, emerged when the fire was first lit. The second, Honosusori ("Fireshine"), was born when the flames were burning most fiercely. The third, Hono-ori-hikohoho, or Hikohoho ("Fireshade"), came forth as Konohana recoiled from the heat of the flames.

Neither the babies nor their mother were harmed by the blaze. She cut their umbilical cords with a knife of bamboo and nursed them. His wife's honesty proven, Honinigi rejoiced at the opportunity to make up for having stained her reputation and lovingly waited on her as she recovered.

An Ignoble Deed

Hero myths describing the mighty deeds of princes and warriors were an essential part of Japan's heritage of story. Yet the tactics employed by some of the protagonists, however effective, fell far short of modern ideas of courageous nobility.

One hero particularly given to subterfuge was Yamato Takeru, a legendary prince said to have been the son of the twelfth emperor of Japan. As the traditional chronicles told the tale, he grew up brave but quarrelsome, always spoiling for a fight. After he killed his elder brother in one such brawl, his father had had enough. Fearing the fresh havoc that the young trouble-maker might cause, he dispatched him to the southern island of Kyushu with the task of subduing the brigands for which the region was then infamous.

From the start Yamato used cunning to achieve his ends. Tracking down two outlaw brothers, he dressed himself up as a young and pretty woman to gain access to their tent, and was duly invited to stay to serve rice wine at a drinking party. When the two were helplessly drunk, he whipped out a knife and stabbed them both to death.

The means that he used to overcome the brigand chief Izumo-takeru were even more devious. Yamato initially contrived to get close to his quarry with protestations of undying friendship. Having duly won the bandit's confidence, he secretly fashioned a wooden sword, carrying it in his own scabbard in place of his usual blade of hardened steel.

One hot afternoon when the sun beat down without respite, Izumo-takeru suggested taking a swim in a nearby river. It was the moment for which the prince had been waiting. As Izumo plunged heedlessly into the water, Yamato – who had lingered behind on the bank – switched swords with his victim. Their dip over, the prince suggested a fencing contest – just for fun. Izumo did not even have time to pull the wooden blade out of its sheath before his supposed friend had cut him to pieces.

The Skull & the Spider-woman

There is more than one story involving the great hero Yorimitsu pitting his courage and cunning against evil monsters. This example by the chronicler Kenko Hoshi is one of the most sinister and disturbing tales in all Japanese mythology.

By Kenko Hoshi's account, Yorimitsu was riding out with Tsuna, his most trusted companion, when they were both amazed to see a skull before them, floating along as if blown by the breeze. Following it across the plain for some considerable distance, they were still more startled to see it disappearing through the open door of a ruined mansion which neither had ever seen or heard of. Within was a wizened, white-haired crone, her eyelids falling back over her head like a hat while her breasts hung below her knees: the very picture of hideous decrepitude. She was 290 years old, she told them, housekeeper to a mansion full of demons – and as the men listened, they could indeed hear the ghostly footsteps of a great host of evil spirits.

Yorimitsu was making for his sword as if to defend himself, but suddenly he froze at the sight before him. Where an ugly hag had been was now the most beautiful maiden. Long seconds he stood there in dumb amazement before he realized that his temptress was busily enveloping him with sticky gossamer. He stabbed her with his sword, but she vanished clean away. With Tsuna's help he went searching through the ruined building until they found a giant spider in a corner of the cellar. It lay sick and wounded, a broken-off swordpoint embedded in its body. Looking down at his own weapon, Yorimitsu saw that the tip was missing: this monster was the maiden who had come so close to catching him in her web of charm. Dragging her out from her lair, the heroes killed her and, cutting her thorax open, they found there the remains of thousands of human victims.

The Miniature Hero

One childless couple, tradition has it, were so desperate for a child that they begged the gods to bless them with a baby – even if it were no bigger than the end of an adult's little finger. Taking them at their word, the gods responded by giving them Issun Boshi, "Little One Inch".

Issun Bochi's parents were delighted, despite his minute size, and brought him up lovingly until at the age of fifteen he announced his intention of going out into the world to do heroic deeds. He used a rice bowl and a pair of chopsticks as a boat and oars to make his way downstream; a needle and hollow straw served as his sword and scabbard.

Arriving at Kyoto, then the capital, Issun Boshi entered the service of a noble family. One day he had to accompany the daughter of the house to the shrine of the goddess Kannon, where she wanted to pray.

When two evil spirits attacked them, Issun Boshi hopped about furiously in an attempt to distract them. Seeing him, one devil reached down scornfully, picked him up and swallowed him whole. Setting about him with his sword, the midget bodyguard caused the demon such unbearable pain from within that he coughed him up and spat him out before doubling up in agony. Issun Boshi then leaped straight at the other demon's eye, where he once again put his sword to work.

Soon both demons were fleeing from the scene of the ambush. Leaping unhurt to the ground, Issun Boshi was receiving the thanks of his grateful mistress when they spotted a magic mallet the evil spirits had left behind them in their flight. It was a lucky mallet indeed: if banged on the ground it granted a wish. Issun Boshi's lady did so, wishing that her retainer be a normal size. All of a sudden, there stood her champion at her side, a full-sized samurai. They married, to live happily – and in his case heroically – ever after.

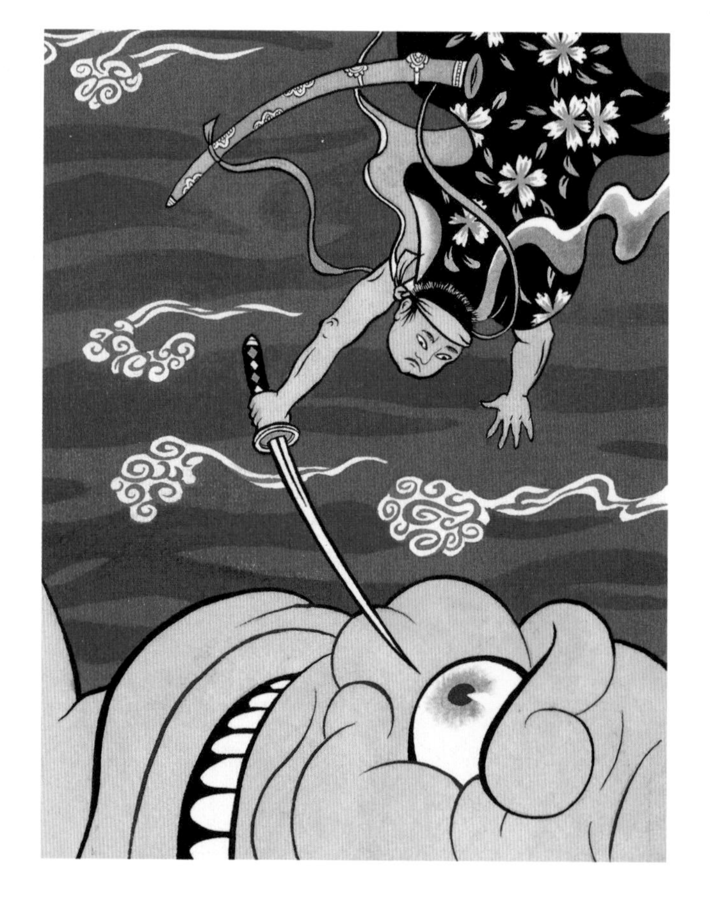

The Ghosts of the Taira

The twelfth-century war between the Taira and Minamoto clans, in which the Minamoto ultimately prevailed, gave rise to many legends. Tales abound of how the ghosts of Taira warriors haunt the battlesites where they were defeated.

Strange lights in the night still, they say, flicker on the waters of the Strait of Shimonoseki where, in 1185, the Taira were finally smashed at the Battle of Dannoura. Certain scuttling crabs frequent the shores here: the spirits of the Taira dead, reluctant, even now, to leave the scene of battle.

A blind lute or *biwa* player, Hoichi, was renowned for his renditions of the Taira story. He lived at the family's memorial temple by the strait. One night, an armed samurai appeared before him and summoned him to come and perform to a party of dignitaries who wished to view the scene of the ancient battle. The warrior led him to a large chamber where an appreciative audience heard his recitation: there were many samurai, and fine ladies accoutred in the antique mode. Time after time thereafter he was called to perform again, until one stormy night a monk missing Hoichi from his room and fearing for his safety, started to search the temple for the old minstrel. He finally found him sitting on a stone monument in the cemetery in the bitter cold, smiting his *biwa* and declaiming his tales to an audience of Taira tombs. When the monk tried to persuade him to come inside, Hoichi reacted furiously: how dared he interrupt him before such a distinguished company?

The Revenge of the Tengu

The bird spirits known as *tengus* were among the best known of the supernatural beings that haunted the traditional Japanese imagination. Guardians of mountains and wild places, they were mischief-makers whose notoriously quick temper could sometimes prove lethal.

Today *tengus* have become figures of fun, having exchanged their original beaks for comic long noses. Even now, though, their tricks can seem rough and ready to modern Western eyes, sometimes recalling the odd behaviour – strange lights and knockings, unexplained breakages – associated with European poltergeists. In their original form, however, they thought nothing of taking the lives of those who mistreated the lands they guarded.

Any fun had at their expense also had to be paid for dearly. On one occasion a wrestler named Tobikawa with a taste for practical jokes set out to mock the superstitions of his rural neighbours. Clad in a feather cloak in impersonation of a *tengu*, he climbed a pine tree and squatted on a branch, laughing as awe-struck peasants bent down to do him homage and placed small offerings at the tree's foot. But the spirit of the mountain was not amused, and Tobikawa's merriment turned to terror when a sudden gust of wind tore him from his perch and dashed him to his death on the path below.

Another individual too smart for his own good tried to get the better of a *tengu* through deception. Having cut a length of bamboo, he made his way to a nearby forest. There he sat down in a glade and put it to his eye, gasping with amazement as he did so. His odd behaviour soon caught the attention of the local *tengu*, who came to ask what he was doing. The youth insisted that the straw was a magic spyglass through which he could see distant places. Intrigued, the *tengu* offered him a straw cloak with the power to make the wearer invisible in exchange for the twig. Accepting the offer, the joker ran off contentedly, but he did not get far. The angry spirit quickly caught him and plunged him into an icy river, from which he barely escaped with his life.

Yuki-onna, the Snow Maiden

His snow coverlet drawn aside by the searchers' shovels, the lost traveller was finally revealed, a smile of fulfilment on his face. Far from being buried in an icy grave, he had the air of one who had spent the wild night in living passion, enveloped in the arms of a beautiful mistress.

The agonies of frostbite forgotten, and his panic-stricken struggles stilled, a feeling of serenity stole over the hypothermia victim preparing him for the most seductive of all deaths. This paradox was personified in the form of Yuki-onna, the Snow Maiden, who lured hapless men to her soft bed and her embrace. Her face a ghostly, ghastly white, she had the most beautiful body and the gentlest caress: no man could resist her advances – nor were many so fortunate as to survive them.

One young man who did survive fell in with Yuki-onna while travelling through the mountains with an older companion. They took refuge from a blizzard in a remote cabin. Waking with a start in the deepest midnight, the youth saw a beautiful woman come into the room. She leaned over his sleeping companion, and breathed on his face. Then she told the young man that she would spare him if he swore never to mention her visit to a living soul.

Next morning he found himself alone, the woman gone and his friend dead. Seized with terror, the young man went on and said nothing to anyone about what had happened. Years later he fell in love with a young woman named Yuki. They married, had children and lived happily.

One night as he saw her pale face reflecting the light of evening, he was reminded of that night in the mountains so many years before. Amused at the thought, he told his young wife the whole strange story. Suddenly her appearance changed; there before him stood the Snow Maiden, her white face a mask of fury. Had he not promised, she demanded, to keep her secret?

If she now spared him a second time, she went on, it was only for the sake of her beloved children; thereupon she melted away into the night, and was never seen by her family again.

The Wife Who Returned

A certain young couple – O-Tei was the woman's name – were betrothed to be married: both longed to be united more than anything. But as is so often the way, the course of true love was crossed by misfortune, in this case by O-Tei's alarming decline in health.

Before their wedding could take place, her condition became critical: she had consumption, and it was clear she could not live for much longer. She summoned her love to her, and told him that she must now leave, but that she would return in a stronger body if he would only wait a while. He gave his word and when next day she died he repeated his pledge in writing, burying the note with his beloved.

The years of mourning went by and in time memories of O-Tei had become a little more faded. The young man's parents insisted that it was time for him to put his old love behind him; he was wasting his life this way.

So when they found him a prospective bride, he went along with the arrangement. He did indeed find happiness of sorts with this new wife, and with the child their love brought into being. His family was fated not to flourish, though. First the young man's father and mother died; then, hardly had they gone than his wife and child were snatched from him. Reeling from this fourfold blow, the young man determined to travel far away.

And so it was that, some time later, he found himself in a remote village in a far-flung province he had never for a moment thought of visiting before. There was an oddly familiar look, he thought, about the young woman who waited at his table in the inn. Even though he could swear that he had not met her before, she reminded him of the woman he had loved years ago.

When he asked her who she was, she told him she was his own O-Tei. The letter he had left in her grave had given her spirit comfort, she told him. Now she had returned to be with him as she had promised. Their love rekindled, they enjoyed a long and blissful marriage – yet from that moment O-Tei lost every recollection of any life previous to the one she was living now.

The Great Chestnut of Kurita

A host of stories testify to the vital part played by flora in Japanese mythology; they have living, feeling souls in this tradition, just as humans and animals do. Even bonds of love and respect were said to have existed between different plants.

While many myths concern particular species and relate to what may well have been real trees, some sound far too outlandish ever to have existed: the truth of these tales can only be symbolic. The story of the oak of Tsukushi, for example, so tall that it cast a shadow across hundreds of kilometres, starts to make sense only in its end, where the tree falls down and measures its length on the ground. As long as a mountain range and wide enough for hundreds of people to walk on it side by side, its story seems to have been dreamed up to explain the existence of a rich seam of coal.

The purpose of another giant tree, the great chestnut of Kurita, in the Omi region, is to teach a moral. So tall was this tree that its shadow darkened the rice fields of many districts, and at last the provincial governor ordered that it should be chopped down.

Try as they might, though, his men could not fell it, for all the cuts they made in its trunk by day were mysteriously mended the next morning, forcing them to start again from scratch.

The other plants of the region honoured the tree as their king and lent their own balm each night to heal it – and by such ecological solidarity they seemed to be winning the war. But a moment of pride proved the tree's undoing: when one night the ivy offered its balm to treat its wounds, it haughtily rejected the help of such a lowly creeper. Deeply offended, the ivy determined to be avenged. It went straight to the woodcutters in a dream and told them why their work was being frustrated. Not only that, but it taught them how to prevent the other plants' healing from taking effect. Within a few days the mighty chestnut had been brought crashing down.

FROM POLE TO POLE:

THE AMERICAS

The Arctic

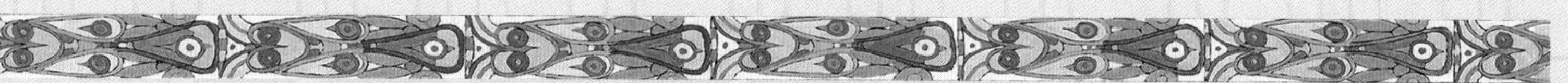

Inhabiting Greenland and the high latitudes of North America, Scandinavia and Siberia, the Arctic peoples were never numerous; even today they number only a few hundred thousand individuals. In terms of population density, these are the loneliest groups on Earth. Perhaps in compensation, though, their communities have always been unusually closely knit, egalitarian in mindset and reliant on co-operation and mutual aid.

From early times the northerners' lives were dominated by the struggle to survive in one of the world's harshest environments, and their myths duly reflected that daily battle. Nature was not seen in the stories as an enemy, but rather as a mechanism working by rules that humans had to respect if they were not to fall foul of forces more powerful than themselves. Specifically, they had to observe taboos and show respect for the animals that they killed so that they themselves might live. The tales they told by firelight in the long winter nights reflected their hopes and fears and passed on to the younger generation the ritual knowledge considered necessary for survival.

So they handed down cautionary stories of the dangers of offending the powerful spirits that lurked all around, even in the home; one such detailed the terrible punishment meted out to a mother who affronted the fearsome Mistress of Fire (see page 210). There were moral fables, too, warning of the dangers of selfishness, gluttony and other vices that threatened the cohesion of the social fabric in the small communities in which they lived (see page 216).

Another genre of tales explained how the world came to be the way it was, accounting for the origins of remarkable phenomena such as fire and death (see page 208) or expounding why ravens are black (see page 214). The Saami people of Lapland had a particularly haunting account of the coming of song, brought to an ungrateful world by a daughter of the sun (see page 217).

A central theme of Arctic legend was the close relationship between the human and animal worlds, reflecting the daily reality of life for people who depended for their survival on the creatures they stalked and killed. In the stories a boy could be taken by wolves to be raised as one of their own (see page 211), and a wolf could be a friend to a man – even in exceptional cases a relative (see page 212). Similarly, a girl who rejected human suitors could find herself married to a dog, bearing litters that mingled babies and puppies (see page 218).

Some of the most disturbing stories involved shamans, people of influence in the northern communities who acted as a conduit between the human and spirit worlds. To venture between the two, they would enter a trance in which their souls would leave their bodies and fly off on fantastic mental voyages, sometimes to the highest heavens to converse with their human-seeming occupants (see page 215). Or, if people were going hungry, they might travel to the seabed domain of Sedna, the Sea Mother, to persuade her to release the seals and other marine creatures on which the community depended for their food. A shaman's soul could also enter a prey animal, making it and its ilk kindly disposed to the hunters who pursued them, always provided that they treated those they killed with proper respect. Such was the case with an Inuit youth from the Tikigaq community in Alaska who spent a winter sporting with the whales (see page 213).

Always, though, the fear of death haunted the imagination of the northern peoples, for whom the threat of starvation was never far away. Over the centuries, many individuals out hunting in the lonely wastes or else visiting isolated coastal communities at the time of the summer thaw must have come across scenes of horror like the one described in a Greenland account of a house of corpses (see page 219). At the best of times the Arctic environment was a demanding master for those who lived in it; at worst it could be lethal.

The Origins of Fire & Death

Once the only flint in the world was owned by the bear, who guarded it jealously. The other animals, however, conspired to steal a piece of it for themselves and enacted a cunning plan hatched by the mouse.

One day, the mouse asked the bear for some fur to make his young a nest. The bear saw nothing wrong in this, so he let the enterprising young father nose about in his fur. Suddenly he realized that the mouse had found the flint in its hiding place beneath his tail, and before he could act the wily rodent had thrown his loot to the waiting fox. Although the bear set off in pursuit he had no chance of catching the fox, who at once began breaking up the flint into fragments and distributing it among the other animals.

Buoyed up by his success, the fox went down to the lake. He broke the surface with a hollow reed and marvelled as water came seeping up through it. How wonderful it would be, he said, if when people were dead and buried they might rise again in this way. But the bear heard this comment, and he was in a dark mood.

He hurled a rock into the water, interrupting the fox's reverie; as far as he was concerned, he roared, the dead could just lie there like lumps of stone. And so it has turned out: our lives have thankfully been transformed by fire, but when we come to die it is for ever.

The Tempest Tamed

The people who lived in the northern lands saw themselves as more than just helpless victims of the elements. The story of an enterprising young Nlaka'pamux boy from the Thompson River lands of British Columbia showed one human taking the initiative against them.

In the subarctic lands of British Columbia they say that the wind once terrorized the world unchecked. No tree was safe from its ravages and no tent could be raised because of its icy blast. In fact, no human activity was possible when the wind did not wish it, and the Indians accepted its tyranny because they had never known any other way.

But one little boy had other ideas, and he resolved to domesticate the wind. Having made up his mind, he carefully considered the best way to fulfil his mission. When the hunters of his tribe wanted to tame a wild beast, they first set traps to catch it. So he decided to lay a series of snares in the wind's favourite stamping grounds, out where the land was most exposed.

Aware of his efforts, the wind screamed derisively for days until, to its astonishment, it found it was well and truly trapped. It bucked and howled in its efforts to escape, but the boy quickly gathered it up into a blanket and carried it off in triumph to show to his people.

When he told them of his success they laughed scornfully, refusing to believe his story. But they gasped in amazement when he loosened a corner of the blanket and a fierce blast of air came rushing out. Bundling the wind back into place, the boy agreed to release it only on condition that it quieten down. The wind had little choice but to accept, yet even so insisted that sometimes it would be obliged to blow up a storm. Seeing the justice of its claim, the boy racked his brains to think up a way of giving it the freedom it needed while also limiting the harm it could do to his people. Eventually the two reached a compromise: whenever a tempest was in the offing, the wind would first turn the dawn sky red to give humans advance warning.

Mistress of Fire

In the icy wastes of the north, fire was an element which needed to be accorded the utmost respect. The Selkups of Siberia tell the tale of a woman who treated her hearth with disdain, and paid a terrible price.

One evening a young mother was rocking her baby by a fire when a spark shot out from the flames and caught the defenceless infant, who screamed in pain. The woman started cursing the fire and, laying her baby down, she took an axe and beat at the burning logs. Then she doused the embers with water until no trace of the fire was left; it served it right, she said, for hurting her child.

But now her tent was dark and cold. Unable to relight her fire, she went to ask her kinsfolk for some, but in each tent she called at the fire flickered and went out. Soon the whole settlement was left in cold and darkness.

Everyone was angry with the young mother but one old woman agreed to come to her tent to find out what she could possibly have done to make the Mistress of Fire so upset. The old woman rubbed sticks together with little success, but from the faint glow she did manage to create, the voice of the Fire Mistress could just be heard. The whole of humankind, she said, would now be deprived of fire because of this young woman's disrespect. She would only change her mind if the woman paid for her sacrilege with her own son. From his dying heart would be kindled the flame that would save humanity. Weeping, the mother handed over her beloved baby. The Mistress of Fire rose up in a towering flame and swept the infant up into the sky – and neither were ever seen again. The young mother wept bitterly for her baby but in the camp and throughout the world beyond, men and women sighed with relief when all their fires came spluttering to life again.

The Boy Taken by Wolves

Dependent on animals for food and clothing, the people of the Arctic developed a close relationship with the beasts that they hunted. Many stories celebrated this harmonious co-existence, but the following tale shows what could happen when the relationship went wrong.

An Inuit couple had a baby boy, the joy of his father and mother. But so fine a boy was he that he was coveted by wolves: they determined not to be denied him. One afternoon, therefore, a he-wolf slipped out of his skin and approached the boy's parents, appearing to them in the form of a naked man. As his wife looked on, the wolf-man suggested that they too should undress. He sang a strange song, and before they knew it they were naked and dancing. They were jerked back to startled consciousness, however, when the wolf abruptly ceased his spell; his wolf-wife had the child and it was time for him to run off and join her.

Seeing the big grey wolf loping away, the horrified couple turned as one to look for their son: they saw his empty cradle, and at once knew what had happened. Resolving to track their child's abductors down, they armed themselves, each with a bow. They would need to bring down both male and female wolf in an instant if they were to ensure the boy's safety. All day they searched, until suddenly they stumbled upon a rocky ravine in which the wolves were playing with their little "boy cub". Waiting till the strange family slept, the man and woman let loose their arrows: both wolves were killed – but so too was the sleeping child. So tightly had the she-wolf been holding him in her love that a single shaft had pierced both bodies right through. Dutifully, the boy's parents bore their dead son off home for burial.

The Relation Who Was a Wolf

Feared hunter of the tundra and kinsman to the domestic dog, the wolf's image among the Inuit was nothing if not ambivalent. Many tribes tell the story of the man out hunting in the first age of the world, who was helped by a wolf who turned out to be his brother-in-law.

Times were hard and the man found he was setting his snares in vain – but traps were all the weapons he had at his disposal in those days before the bow and arrow. Day after day he trudged through the deep snow to check them – his progress painful and slow, since nobody had yet invented snowshoes. The thought of his hungry wife and children, cold and miserable at home, drove him on – but despair was slowly sapping his will to continue.

Suddenly he came to a blazing fire, in whose cheery light he saw a stranger, tending a bubbling stew. He was Wolf, the man said, and he was actually the hunter's brother-in-law. This campfire and food were for him, his valued relative; here were several caribou Wolf had killed to feed and clothe his sister's family. Here too were some snowshoes to make the homeward trek easier. Greatest gift of all, however, was the bow and arrow he gave the man – now he could hunt not just rabbits but bigger game such as elk and caribou.

Joyfully the man thanked Wolf for his generosity, and they laughed and joked together deep into the night. At last, however, the hunter fell asleep exhausted. He awoke just in time to see a dark form slinking off into the morning mist: his benefactor and brother-in-law, a real wolf!

At One with the Animals

When a human took the shape of an animal it sometimes marked a stage in their initiation as a shaman. In a tale from northwest Alaska, the soul of a Tikigaq man named Aquppak lived among the whales for a whole winter and the experience brought him great powers.

One autumn day saw Aquppak walking the deserted strand. It was the time of the whaling ceremonies when wooden carvings of people, whales and other creatures were paraded and burned to ensure a successful hunt. Aquppak met a group of men about to launch a boat. They invited him to join them but when he declined they stole his soul. In truth they were not humans but some of the carvings which had come to life.

They carried Aquppak's soul out to sea, to the land of the whales. There his soul took the form of a whale and lived among the creatures over winter. He learned that the whales kept a close watch on the people of the Alaskan coast; they would wait until they thought the hunters were ready and then swim north to meet them.

The following spring Aquppak's soul swam north with the whales to the region of Tikigaq. When he saw his relatives out in a boat he offered himself to their harpoon. They rejoiced at the catch although they did not know the whale contained Aquppak's soul. When they brought the whale back to land and cut up its flesh, his soul was released and entered his body again.

Aquppak recovered and found that he now had shamanic powers. When he heard that the Utqiagvik people had murdered his sister, he vowed to avenge her.

He changed himself into a snowy owl to bring trouble to the Utqiagvik. The following winter the Utqiagvik saw a great owl haunting their settlement like an angry spirit. Their hunt was unsuccessful and their food supplies spoiled; that winter many Utqiagvik men and women, killers of Aquppak's sister, starved.

Why the Raven is Black

The story of how the raven, sharpwitted trickster of the northern regions, came to be black all over is told in many variant forms throughout the Arctic. This version is from southeast Greenland.

There was a time, so the elders say, when all the birds were white and they could talk just as people do today. Then the raven and the great northern diver alighted on the towering rocks of the Greenland coast and began to talk about their colouring.

The diver complained that its brilliant white plumage made it hard for it to approach its prey without being spotted. The raven suggested that they could solve that problem by painting each other's feathers, and the diver immediately agreed.

The raven went first. While the diver sat perfectly still, with its eyes closed, the raven skilfully stained its companion's plumage black, leaving only a few delicate speckles of the original colour. The raven flew away a few wingbeats to view the pattern from a distance and thought it good work. It told the diver to look – and the bird was very pleased with its new coat. Then the raven stood completely still while the diver eagerly set to work.

The diver was so pleased with the pattern on its own feathers that it copied it exactly in decorating the raven. But when the raven saw the result it was unimpressed, dismissing the diver's handiwork as crude and unattractive. For a moment the diver lost its temper and covered the raven from head to foot in deep glossy black. Then the raven flew away, cawing in rough-voiced anger. It never afterwards consorted with the diver and to the present day the raven has kept its glossy black colouring.

Kukiaq & the Moon

The Arctic shaman was a community's link with the spirit world. One tale from the Netsilik Inuit of northeastern Canada told how a shaman was transported to the celestial realm, where he met the spirits of the sun and the moon.

One evening a shaman named Kukiaq was waiting patiently by a seal's breathing hole for the chance to spear one of the creatures. Land, sea and air were frozen, silent, and he looked with a steady gaze on the vast moon that hung in the sky.

As he stood watching, the moon came nearer, sweeping through the night-sky until it loomed directly above him. It then took the form of a tall, stern-faced man on a sledge made from whale jawbones and pulled by dogs. At Moon-man's command Kukiaq sat on the sledge, closed his eyes and was swept away across the star-sprinkled sky.

Then he heard the sleigh crunch on new ice and opened his eyes to see a village crowded with people. He met two friends from the old days, long dead, and they clapped him on the shoulder in welcome; he knew he was in the celestial country of the dead, far above the Earth.

Moon-man showed the bright windows of his home to Kukiaq and invited him in. For a moment Kukiaq blanched: the walls of the entrance passage and of the house were moving in and out in a terrifying fashion. In the entrance itself lay a fierce dog. But Kukiaq knew that if he showed no fear he would be unharmed.

Inside he encountered a beautiful woman who sat peacefully nursing a child. At her side was a lamp turned so high that it scorched Kukiaq's neckband. This woman, Kukiaq understood, was the sun herself. She welcomed the shaman and made space for him on the bench at her side. Kukiaq longed to stay, but he was wise enough to know that if he sat with her once he would never find his way back to Earth.

He ran from Moon-man's house, and allowed himself to tumble down to Earth. At the end of a long fall he found himself standing on the ice by the very same hole from which he had departed only moments earlier.

The Porcupine-Eater

The Arctic way of life insisted that much was shared, ensuring that everyone remained on fairly equal economic terms. And whenever an individual did become rich, he or she would hold a lavish feast and gift-giving ceremony known as a potlatch.

In a culture in which generosity was such an important virtue, greed was a punishable vice – as one selfish Alaskan husband discovered to his cost. This man, who had two wives, grew tired of sharing the game that he trapped with his partners, and started eating some of the best parts himself before he brought home the day's kill.

In particular he had a fondness for the layer of fat that keeps female porcupines warm in the long winter. But he did not realize that one of his wives had shamanic power that enabled her to know exactly what he got up to on his own in the forest. And it just so happened that her animal spirit helper was a porcupine.

The result was that the next time he settled down to one of his secret snacks, his wife used her magical abilities to make the dead porcupine's jaws fasten onto his lips, preventing him from eating anything. However hard he tried, he could not get the creature off. His wife only relented and made it let go after he had promised, through necessarily gritted teeth, never again to indulge himself so selfishly.

How Song Came to the Saami

According to a legend of the Saami people in Lapland, the gentle gift of music was provided to them by the kind-hearted daughter of the sun. Yet her generosity was wasted on some members of the tribe.

The Saami claim that the art of song came to Earth with Akanidi, the daughter of the sun, who on her daily journeys across the heavens noticed that the people below her seemed listless and sad. So she won her father's permission to visit them. She fetched up in the house of an old and childless couple who lived on a lake island. They treated her as their own daughter, but would only allow her out to mix with other people once she had come of age.

When she was old enough, she wandered off into the world and achieved great things. She introduced all the people she met to the joys of singing and dancing, and also taught them how to make the colourful costumes for which Laplanders have ever since been famous.

Yet not everyone was happy with her innovations. The elders of the tribe wanted nothing to do with the new ways. All that interested them were the gemstones she magically produced to adorn jackets and skirts – and then only so that they could exchange them for valuable trade goods.

When Akanidi, sensing their greed, refused to give them any more, the elders plotted to kill her. Knowing that she was protected by the sun, they sought the advice of a cunning old witch named Oadz. The hag came up with the suggestion of blocking the smoke-hole of Akanidi's tent so the sun could not see them battering her to death.

But the murderers in their haste failed to block the hole entirely. So, when they struck Akanidi down, she did not die. Instead she faded into translucence; then, singing a final song, she floated up like firesmoke and disappeared for ever from human sight.

Yet she still looks down on the world from the heavens. And every time she spots people singing, she smiles, for it reminds her that she did not make her journey in vain.

The Girl Who Married a Dog

There was once a young woman who would not take a husband. Angered by her stubbornness, her father one day shouted at her, "If there is no man good enough for you, why don't you marry a dog instead?"

The next day a new suitor came to their camp, and the girl noticed that he wore an unusual amulet of dog-claws. This time her father would brook no refusal, so she agreed to go and live with the stranger on an island off the coast nearby. But she soon realized that her husband was actually a dog who could take on human form. Her suspicions were confirmed when, having become pregnant, she bore a litter of five human babies and five puppies.

Being a dog, her husband could not go hunting to provide for her and her offspring. Instead, he would swim across the sound to pick up packs of meat provided by the girl's father. But eventually the old man tired of the chore and put in boulders with the meat that so weighed down the dog that it sank and drowned.

Now the girl had no one to support her. Blaming her father for her predicament, she set her dog-children on him next time he paddled across to see her, and they mauled him so badly that he died. Left with ten hungry mouths to feed, and no easy way to gather food, she eventually decided that she would have to send her children out into the world to fend for themselves. So by magic she transformed her boots into boats and dispatched all ten – and they became the ancestors of both the native North American peoples and of white men.

The House of Corpses

Starvation and exposure were ever-present threats for the peoples who dwelled in the far north. A story passed down from the old days in Greenland captured the fear that the constant threat of unexpected death could generate in those living in isolated communities.

Living as they did on the edge of the inhabitable world, most Inuit grew up from childhood familiar with tales of tragedy. Many of these related to real-life disasters that had afflicted their communities in the past or that had befallen long-dead ancestors, for the folk memory of such events stretched down the centuries. Yet, as if to steel themselves for the very worst that could happen, many also had a taste for horror stories pure and simple – chilling tales that drew on the imagination as well as on the harsh realities of lives at continual risk from hunger and cold.

One such told of a shaman on Qeqertarsuaq, an island opposite what is now the Thule airbase, who set off one day on his sledge to visit his married sister. He had almost reached her house when his dogs suddenly stopped, refusing to go any closer. Approaching the apparently deserted building on foot, he looked in through the window and saw to his horror the entire family frozen in death.

Only one occupant showed any sign of life, and that was his sister. When she saw him, she gave no sign of recognition but crept toward him, her mouth opening and closing hungrily. He fled in terror back to his sledge, but the dogs still refused to budge. Only when the spectre was quite close, jaws agape to devour man or dogs, did they suddenly jerk into action, not stopping again until they reached the safety of home.

Subsequently the shaman went on a soul-flight to find out the cause of the tragedy. He discovered that the entire household had been frightened to death by a premonitory apparition: the vision of a discarded kayak-skin used to carry a corpse to its final resting-place.

North America

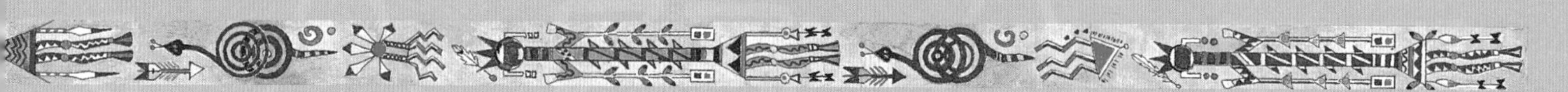

America was the last continent to be settled, possibly no more than 15,000 years ago. Most scholars believe that the first settlers crossed a land bridge over the Bering Strait in the course of the last Ice Age. If so, they probably brought with them memories of Siberian shamanism and a belief in a world peopled by spirits.

Native North American myths certainly accepted the idea of a spirit-filled cosmos. They portrayed a world of infinite possibilities, where a boy could talk to a star only for it to come visiting, taking him back with it to the sky (see page 229). One consequence of the universality of spirit was the need always to respect the natural world. The Tuscaroras of the Atlantic coast made the point with a story that explained bad harvests in terms of human neglect of the spirit of the corn, who became old and bedraggled as a result of the tribespeoples' thoughtlessness (see page 231).

There was no overarching ideology behind the myths, more a set of oft-recurring themes. Like their counterparts elsewhere in the world, early North Americans sought to understand how the universe came into being, offering almost as many explanations as there were tribes. The Blackfeet credited Napi, "Old Man", as their creator spirit. Other peoples preferred twin beings: a mysterious pair called the Giver and the Watcher in one Tututni myth from southern Oregon (see page 224); spirits named Nagaitcho and Thunder in a Californian Kato story (see page 226); the sun god Tawa and Spider Woman for the Hopi (see page 242). Most agreed in making the creators ultimately happy with their work.

One motif that cropped up in several regions was that of earthdivers: creatures, most often birds, that plunged into the primeval ocean in search of mud from the seabed that could then be used to create the land. The Crow people credited two ducks with the deed, sent at the behest of a figure named Old Man Coyote (see page 241).

Coyote turned up in the tales of other peoples too, although more often as a disruptive figure responsible for marring the harmony of the original creation. Two tales placed the responsibility for bringing death into the world firmly on his shoulders. In one he prevented the dead from coming back to life as originally intended, so making death final (see page 227); in the other, related by California's Wintu people, he frustrated the creator spirit's wish to build a stairway to heaven, allowing those nearing the end of life to renew their youth (see page 243).

Other common genres drew on tribes' oral history as passed down by the elders to the younger generation. Often the stories stretched back beyond living memory deep into the realm of myth. For example, the Tewa people of northern New Mexico had a legend to explain the origin of their various clans, incidentally disclosing why one, the Snake, lived in the desert, away from the other clans (see page 222). The Lakota Sioux told of an emissary from the Great Spirit who brought the essential rites of their religion before taking the form of a white buffalo calf to return to the heavens (see page 240). There were hero myths too, telling of the great deeds of people of supernatural power, and tales of monsters to frighten youngsters around the campfire at night. One tale from Oregon mitigated the terror by allowing a pair of resourceful children to repeatedly outwit the protagonist of the story, a cannibalistic ogress called the Atatalia (see page 236).

Perhaps the most striking feature of the myths, though, was the extraordinarily close relationship between the human and animal worlds that they portrayed. A boy might go to stay with snakes able to take human form (see page 222), or else choose to live among bears (see page 238). Hunters might even marry a caribou girl or a female buffalo, learning from their spouses the secrets of success in the chase (see page 239). Here again, though, the crucial factor was respect; those who failed to show it could never expect to go unpunished (see page 237).

Why the Snake Clan Lives Apart

Stories such as the migration myth of the Tewa Snake Clan of northern New Mexico explain how groups of people came to revere certain animals – in this case the snake – and to live in particular regions of North America.

Once, a boy of the Tewa lived by a river. Every day he sat by it, saying to himself, "I wonder where this water is running." So one day he cut down a tree to make a box and told his parents that he wanted to go downriver. His uncle made prayer sticks. "If you meet any holy being," said the uncle, "give them prayer sticks." Next morning, the boy sat in the box with his bundle of prayer sticks, and boated down the river.

He travelled until he came to a place with a mountain. As he walked around the mountain a girl came toward him. "I am the one who made you come downriver," she said.

She led him up the mountain, where he found a house with people inside who gave him food. His hosts looked human, though their skin was yellow and scaly. But when they went outside, they became snakes. The boy thanked the headman and gave him prayer sticks.

The snake folk showed the boy their dances; they sang their songs and invited him to join them, asking him to marry the girl. Years later, after marrying her and siring several children, the boy was told by his father-in-law: "It is time for you to return to your parents. Take your family with you."

When they reached the boy's home they were welcomed. All was well until the snake family's children began to bite other children. The family decided to move away to the south.

Soon they met other people. "Who are you?" said the snakes. "We are the Sand Clan," said the strangers. "Well, you are my people," said the snake-woman. So they travelled together and met other clans: the Antelope and Tobacco clans, the Lizards, the Bears and the Coyote. That is how the clans of the Tewa met, and some of them joined each other. However, the snakes could not live with other clans, so they settled in the desert.

A Spider's Quest for the Sun

A Cherokee story from the Southeast begins in the shadowy gloom of primordial myth time. Frustrated at bumping into each other in the darkness, the people and the animals convened a meeting to decide how to bring light into their world.

At the meeting the red-headed woodpecker was the first to speak: "People on the other side of the world have light," he observed, "so perhaps if we go over there, they will give us some."

Possum volunteered to make the journey. When he reached the other side of the world, he found the sun, grabbed a piece of it and hid it in his fur. But the sun was so hot it burned his tail to a crisp, and when he came home, he had lost the light.

Next, Buzzard went on the quest. He dived out of the sky and snatched a piece of the sun in his claws. He set it on his head, but the sun burned off his head feathers and was gone. When Buzzard came home bald, everyone despaired.

Suddenly they heard the tiny voice of Grandmother Spider from the grass. "You have done the best a man can do, but perhaps a woman can do better." She rolled some clay into a bowl and started toward the sun, leaving a trail of thread behind her. When she was near the sun, Spider reached out gently and took a tiny piece of the sun. Placing it in her bowl, and following the thread she had spun, she returned from east to west. And as she travelled, the sun's rays grew and spread before her, across the world.

To this day, spiders spin webs each morning in the shape of the sun, as if to remind people of their divine ancestor.

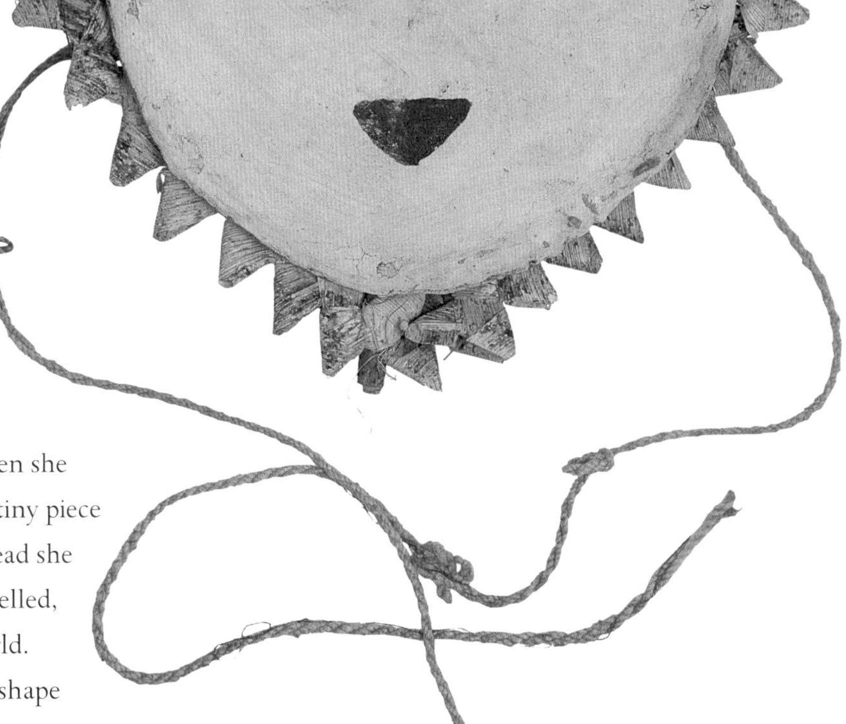

The Giver & the Watcher

According to this Tututni myth from southwest Oregon, two creative beings, the Giver and the Watcher, emerged from the purifying steam of their sweat lodge to collaborate in the formation of the world and the making of humanity.

Having created the land and put trees and grass on it, the Giver and the Watcher decided it was time to make the first people. The Giver rubbed together some grass and mud to make two figures. After four days two dogs, one male and one female, appeared, and the dogs bore a litter. Then the Giver fashioned two figures out of sand. This time he had made snakes.

Soon the Giver thought, "How can I make people? I've failed twice!" The Watcher spoke, "Let me smoke tobacco tonight, and see if people emerge from smoke." For three days he smoked, and from the smoke a house appeared. After a while, a beautiful woman emerged. The Giver was glad, and said: "Now we'll have no trouble making people."

One day the Giver said to his companion: "Stay here and take this woman to wife. I'm leaving this world. Everything on it shall belong to you." The woman became pregnant, but she couldn't see her husband. When her son was born, she still did not know his father. So she wrapped up her child and went on a journey.

The woman and her son travelled for ten years. At last the boy asked, "Mother, where is your husband?" She replied: "I've dreamed of my husband." When the Giver heard her say this, he turned to his companion and told him: "The woman is home now."

At dusk the next day the Watcher, now a man, came in and the boy exclaimed: "My father has come!" The Watcher duly told them all that had happened. Meanwhile, the Giver brought order to the world and made the animals. He told the Watcher to have many children: "You, your wife and children shall be the parents of all the tribes."

Old Man Arranges the World

Some myths describe how the Earth's sacred identity derives from the fact that the creator was once physically present. The mountainous landscape of northwestern Montana, home of the Blackfeet, bears the imprint of Napi, "Old Man", the mythical creator of the Earth.

The Blackfeet origin story tells of Old Man moving through primal territory, creating the features and inhabitants of the rugged mountainous land that was to become the cherished homeland of the Blackfeet nation.

All animals of the region at one time knew Old Man. He made the mountains, prairies, timber and brush. Everywhere that Old Man went, he made new things. And all these things were connected to each other and were mutually useful. Old Man covered the ground with grass for the animals. And when things were not quite right, he was prepared to adjust them. The prairies, for example, didn't suit the ways of the bighorn. So Old Man took those animals by the horns and led them to the mountains. "This is the place that suits you," he said. He did the same when he made the antelope, leading them down from their first home in the mountains to the prairie. In this way, particular terrains and the creatures living upon them became suited to one another.

As he went about his primal, earth-moving and animal-arranging labours, the Old Man of the Blackfeet was often challenged by other great spirits, such as those of the sun and thunder, but his engaging and agreeable personality won through. He liked to rest every now and then, and had a keen sense of humour. A lighthearted episode in the Blackfeet origin story describes how the creator sat on the top of a steep hill and surveyed with satisfaction the country he had made. "Well, this is a fine place for sliding," he mused, "I'll have some fun." He promptly began to slide down the hill; the marks he made while doing so can still be seen today at Old Man's Sliding Ground in Montana.

Tireless Nagaitcho

The Kato people of northern California believed that the creator named Nagaitcho did not rest from his labours until he was sure that the Earth had resources enough to sustain the first people.

Two creative spirits, Nagaitcho and Thunder, presided over an ageing cosmos that was devoid of life. Even the sandstone rock which formed the sky was old. Thunder raged in the four directions. "The rock is old," Nagaitcho said to him, "we will fix it."

They stretched out the sky and walked on it. Then they made the clouds so that the heads of the people to come wouldn't ache from the bright sun.

Nagaitcho made a man out of earth. He made a left leg and a right leg, and then a left arm and a right arm. Then he pulled up some grass and, forming it into a wad, he made the belly. Then he slapped some grass together and made the heart. He moulded a round piece of clay into a liver. With more clay he made lungs and kidneys. He pushed in a reed for the trachea. "What will the blood be?" he then asked himself. He pounded some ochre and mixed it with water. Next he made the mouth, nose and eyes. "Now the genitals," he said. And having made the male genitals, he took one of the legs, split it and made a woman from it.

Then Nagaitcho created all the things that the new people needed for existence. For example, he put edible seaweeds and mussels in the sea. "What will be salt?" Nagaitcho wondered. The ocean foam was turned into salt. The Indians tried it and decided to use it on their food in future.

Next, Nagaitcho began a tour of the land accompanied by his dog. They surveyed the beautiful landscape of redwood, oak and chestnut trees, springs, creeks, hills and valleys. Animals, large and small, quenched their thirst in the waters that they shared with people. "I have made a good earth, my dog," said the creator. The nuts and berries and grasses were ripe. Fish for people swam in the streams. All kinds of edible things had grown in abundance. Nagaitcho's first people had found their home and lived there in harmony.

Coyote & the Origin of Death

According to this tale, which is told by the Caddo people of Arkansas, death would have been only a temporary interlude if the trickster Coyote had not decided that it should be final. He came to this decision in order to protect those living from scarcity.

In the beginning there was no death, which meant that the Earth became too crowded. So the chiefs held a council, and one man said that people should die, but just for a while, and then they should come back again. But Coyote declared that people should die for ever. If these people came back to life, there would not be sufficient food to sustain everyone.

It was decided that the village medicine men should build a grass house facing east and place a black and white eagle feather on top of it. When anyone died, the feather would become bloody and fall over. Then the medicine men would sit in the house and sing: this would call the spirit of the dead person, so that he or she would live again.

After a time, the first feather grew bloody and fell over. The medicine men gathered, and after some days a whirlwind blew in from the west, circled the house and entered it from the east. Once the wind was in the house a fine young man who had recently been killed emerged. Everyone was happy, except Coyote. So next time the feather grew bloody and fell from the roof, and the whirlwind circled the house of grass, Coyote closed the door. The spirit in the whirlwind, finding the door closed, swept on by. From that moment on, death became final.

The Sun Snarer

In a story told by the Menomini people of Wisconsin, an unsympathetic sun is humbled by a resourceful young hunter. As he struggles to free himself from a magical, hair-spun snare, the mighty sun relies on the services of a puny mouse.

Two men went out to hunt in the forest, but refused to take their younger brother with them. Upset and angry to be left alone, the young boy wrapped himself in his beaver-skin robe and lay down to weep. The morning sun rose, and at midday sent down a ray which shrank his robe and exposed the boy. "You have treated me cruelly and burned my robe," he shouted at the sun. "Why have you punished me? I do not deserve it!" The sun merely smiled and held its peace.

The boy gathered his burned robe and his bow and arrows and returned to the camp site. When his sister came into the tent and asked him why he was crying so bitterly, he told her of the sun's cruel treatment.

The next morning when the boy woke up, he said to his sister, "My sister, give me a thread!" She plucked a hair from her head, and as the boy took the ends between his fingers, the hair began to lengthen. Then the boy returned to the place where he had first lain and, making a noose from his sister's hair, stretched it across the path. At the moment the sun touched it, the snare caught the sun around the neck and choked him. The cord was hot and became embedded in his neck. The sky grew dark and the sun cried out for his spirits to help him. He implored a mouse to gnaw the thread, and after much labour, the mouse succeeded.

The boy then said to the sun: "For your cruelty I've punished you. You may go now." He returned to his sister, delighted with what he had done. And the sun rose once again and daylight returned.

The Boy Abducted by a Star

Many Native myths present celestial bodies as benevolent forces that come to the aid of human beings. However, the Tsimshian people of the Northwest Coast have a story that shows how the sky spirits can on occasion be cruel.

One night a boy innocently said to a star, "Poor fellow, you must be cold!" The star heard the boy's words, and came down to take him up to the sky. The boy's parents searched everywhere for him. At last his father had news of his son. A woman who lived alone up a mountain said: "Your boy is tied to the smokehole of the star man's house. He cries all the time. The sparks of the fire are burning him." Then she told the man to shoot arrows into the sky until one stuck at the edge of the hole of the sky. The man did as she advised, and continued shooting until all of his arrows had stuck together, forming a line down to Earth from the skyhole for him to climb up.

Once in the sky, the father fetched wood and carved some figures resembling his child. Then he made a fire and scorched the images to test them; eventually he found one made of yellow cedar that cried like a child. The man then travelled further in the sky until he came to the star man's house. The boy was, indeed, tied up near the edge of the smokehole, and when the people inside stirred the fire in the house, the sparks made him cry. The father urged his son to be brave and bided his time.

When the father knew that the people in the house were sleeping, he untied the boy and put the yellow cedar image in his place. Then they ran off. In the morning, when the fire was going, the cedar image cried, but after a while it stopped. The star people realized what had happened and gave chase. But the father and son had reached the skyhole in time. They descended to Earth on the chain of arrows, then pulled the arrows down after them to thwart their pursuers.

Spirits of the Seasons

In this Inuit story the eternal cycle of the seasons that is repeated every year is described as a partnership between two spirits. The spirit Nipinouke brings spring and summer, while Pipounouke brings autumn and winter.

The spirits of the seasons are two powerful beings who are called Nipinouke and Pipounouke. These spirits divide the world between them, each keeping to his own side for as long as he possibly can. But eventually the time comes when Nipinouke and Pipounouke each cross over to the other's side of the world.

When Nipinouke comes, he brings with him warmth, birds, green leaves and fresh grass. But as summer wanes, Nipinouke must give up his place.

Pipounouke then arrives, bringing autumnal decay and the winds, ice and snow of winter. He destroys all that Nipinouke created. In this way there is *achitescatoueth*: succession in nature and balance in the world.

The Corn Spirit

For a continuation of their blessings on hunting grounds and gardens, the spirits of nature had to be honoured. The Tuscarora people, from the Northeastern region, acknowledged the spirit of corn as they harvested and stored their staple crop.

In a village where the corn harvest had always been rich, people became lazy and careless. They forgot to weed and left corn to be trampled. They let the dogs eat the surplus and stored their seed in poorly dug holes and damaged baskets. Worst of all, they neglected to give proper thanks to the spirit of the corn.

Assuming that they could continue to get more food by hunting, the men roamed the forest for game. But the animals had vanished. The hungry people dug up their baskets. But their stores had rotted or been eaten by mice. Only one man, Dayohagwenda, had given thanks for his harvest and stored his corn securely.

Walking in the forest one day, Dayohagwenda came upon an elm-bark lodge surrounded by weeds. Seated there was an old man. Dirty and ragged, the old man was weeping. "Grandfather, why do you weep?" asked Dayohagwenda. "Because your people have forgotten me," replied the elder. As Dayohagwenda pursued his questions, he realized that the old man was the spirit of the corn, and that he was dirty and ragged because the people had become careless and ungrateful. He was weeping because he thought that he had been forgotten.

Dayohagwenda returned to the village and found the people on the verge of starvation. Recounting what he had seen, he warned that the spirit of the corn might leave them for ever. If, however, the people began honouring him again, the spirit would help them. Then Dayohagwenda dug up his own supplies and found that the spirit had increased them.

From that time on, the people carefully planted, weeded, harvested and stored. And they always gave thanks to the spirit who blessed them.

A Foolish Dive

Stories of the trickster tricked are told around the world, but they are nowhere more common than in North America. In this tale from the Plains, a figure called Nihansan goes diving for fruit that in reality are only mirrored reflections.

Like many Native American tricksters, Nihansan was an ambiguous figure. For the Arapaho, a Plains people closely allied to the Cheyenne, he was on the one hand a creator deity, credited with fashioning the Earth and people from mud brought up from the seabed by an earthdiver working to his instructions. On the other he was a vainglorious buffoon and a favourite butt of comic tales. One told how he managed to lose his own eyes and eventually had to borrow those of the mole, which has been blind ever since; in another he unsuccessfully tried to court the elemental Whirlwind-Woman, who unceremoniously dumped him on his head for his pains.

A third tale described how he was walking by a stream one day when he spotted some juicy red plums under the water's surface. The very sight made him hungry, so he took off his clothes, dived into the water and groped about on the stream bed, vainly trying to collect the fruit.

Frustrated, he burst from the stream empty-handed and gasping for air, but he was no less hungry so he resolved to try again. Taking some stones, he tied them to his wrists and ankles to weigh himself down under water. He plunged in for a second time, but once more searched the bottom in vain. Eventually, when he could hold his breath no longer, he freed the stones and floated up to the surface.

Looking up, he suddenly noticed plums hanging on a tree above him. "You fool!" he said to himself, and climbed out of the water. Sheepishly he made his way to the tree, where he ate some of the plums and picked some more for his onward journey.

The Mohawk Rabbit Dance

The animals of Native American myths often lived in clan-like groups, under the guidance of a wise chief, or "master". This Mohawk tale describes how a master rabbit initiated a ritual that was observed by the tribe for many years after.

Many Native American peoples performed ceremonial dances that imitated the movements of animals; the Cherokee alone had rites inspired by eagles, chickens, quails, bears, horses, raccoons, snakes and groundhogs, among others. Over the course of time stories grew up describing the origins of the rituals that sought to explain their significance for the tribe.

A typical example of this kind of tale came from the Mohawk people of the Northeast region. It told how a group of hunters was once travelling through the forest when they came to a clearing among the trees. As the leader approached the glade, he observed a creature whose like he had never seen before. The animal was the size of a small black bear, but it was not a bear. In fact it was an enormous rabbit.

As the men watched, the rabbit raised its head. But instead of fleeing, it nodded toward the hunters and thumped the earth with one of its back feet. At this signal, crowds of other rabbits joined their master. Now the big rabbit started thumping rhythmically, as though beating a drum. The others formed a circle and danced around the drummer. Then, when the activity was at its height, the drum suddenly fell silent. The master rabbit leaped into the air, then vanished into the forest.

When the hunters returned to the village, they went to the longhouse and described what they had seen. "Beat the rhythm of the rabbit chief," said one of the elders. The men took their drums, and the people began dancing to the rhythm set by the master rabbit. From that time on people throughout the Mohawk lands continued to perform the rabbit dance, viewing it as a mark of respect to the animals whose meat and skins they made so much use of.

The Boy & the Horse

A story told by the Pawnee people of the Plains region concerns a destitute boy whose compassion is ultimately rewarded with renown as a warrior. The rise of a person from humble origins to great prowess is a common theme of Native myths.

A boy lived with his grandmother on the edge of a village. The two were so impoverished that they were reduced to eating the soles of old moccasins and the remains of other people's food. On one occasion, near a campsite, the boy was dismayed to see people shooting at a nest of eagles.

Later, as the boy was scavenging, an eagle came up to him. "Because you pitied us, we will help you," it declared. The eagle led the boy to a hill, where an old, unkempt horse was tethered. Despite the animal's woeful state, it had once belonged to a chief, and had been chosen by the eagles as a magical gift to the boy.

When the tribe went to war, the mangy horse transformed itself into a vigorous young bay by rolling in the dust. Riding the magic horse into battle, the boy attacked and killed the enemy chief. He and the horse then promptly vanished.

When the boy reappeared, proclaiming his exploits, the villagers mocked him, as his horse had reverted to its decrepit state. Another battle ensued, with the same outcome. Finally, the boy went out for a third time to engage the enemy, and fought so fiercely that he put them to flight.

As the boy turned to leave the battlefield, his mount was joined first by a solitary grey steed and then by a multitude of horses. The people saw this as a sign of his glory, and hailed him as a great chief.

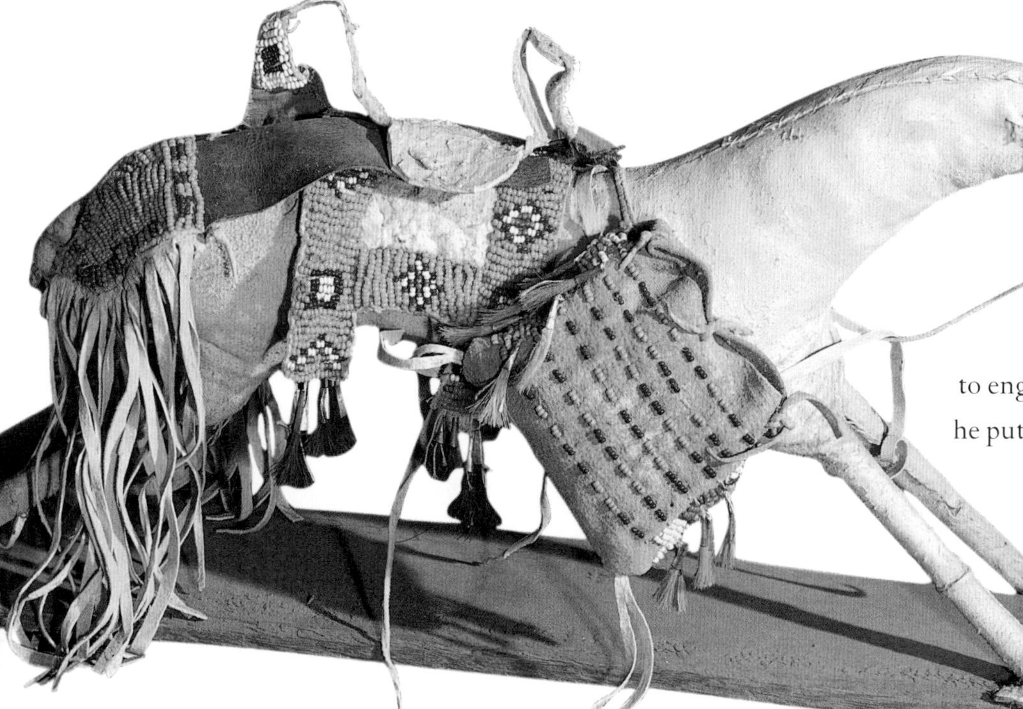

A Hero's Attack on a Giant Elk

A characteristic role for many hero figures was as a guardian of the first humans. They attained this status by vanquishing threatening spirits and monsters. In a legend of the Jicarilla Apache, the hero Jonayaiyin slays a monstrous beast that has been spreading terror among the people.

When the Earth was still young, monstrous animals preyed upon its human inhabitants. One of these monsters was a giant elk, which devoured people whole. The gods resolved to send a hero to kill the monster and restore order.

This hero was Jonayaiyin, the son of an old woman who was the second wife of the sun. Jonayaiyin's supernatural origins allowed him to grow to maturity in just four days. The hero's mother, who knew her son's destiny, directed him to the desert home of his foe the great elk, giving him a bow and arrows to accomplish his task. Jonayaiyin set out, reaching the elk's domain in four huge strides.

As Jonayaiyin lay in wait for the monster, the creatures of the desert came to ask him what he was doing there. When he told them, they offered him their help. Since the elk was lying in open grassland with no trees or bushes to cover Jonayaiyin's approach, the lizard gave him a lizard-skin disguise. The gopher then dug a tunnel, so that Jonayaiyin could attack the elk from below the ground. Jonayaiyin made his way through the tunnel and shot the elk straight through the heart. But the elk stuck its antlers into the tunnel and ploughed up vast amounts of earth, which are still visible to this day as mountains and mesas. As it pursued Jonayaiyin through the burrow, the desert spiders came to his aid. Wherever the elk chased him, the spiders put up webs to impede its progress. At last the elk collapsed with exhaustion, and the hero killed it. In doing so, he freed people from their fear and misery.

The Ogress of Oregon

A story about a child-eating monster is told by the Wasco people from the Columbia river region in Oregon. While evoking childhood terrors of the unseen and the unknown, it also presents the object of fear, a hideous ogress known as the Atatalia, as stupid and clumsy.

A brother and sister were out gathering flints when they spied the Atatalia. The children ran as fast as they could, but the ogress caught them and secured them in her basket. She then set off home to feed her own children on these two tasty morsels.

In the basket, the boy's foot began to itch from where the girl was sitting on it. "Sister," he said, "you're hurting my foot where I have an itch." The Atatalia misheard this for something that sounded very similar in the Wasco language, and asked, alarmed, "What is the matter? Are my children burning up?" Seeing a way to frighten the monster, the girl responded: "Your children are burning up, for sure!" The ogress dropped her basket and ran home. The children took a flint, cut the strings of the basket cover and clambered out. Filling the basket with stones, they ran to the river.

When the Atatalia came back, she took the basket without checking inside, and returned home once more, where she discovered that the children had escaped. She immediately set out again to recapture them.

The boy, who had magical powers, placed five rivers in the monster's path. The Atatalia jumped the first river with ease, but enjoyed it so much that she repeated her leap five times, and did the same at the next four. Finally, she saw the children ahead of her, and breathed in to drag them back. But as soon as she breathed out again, the children flew off ahead of her.

When they came to the Columbia river, the children implored the fish to eat the Atatalia and the cliffs to crush her. As soon as the monster entered the river, the fish began to nibble her body and the rocks came crashing down on her. At length, the stupid ogress gave up and waded off to nurse her wounds, leaving the children to make good their escape.

The Elk Guardian Spirit

Native American hunters were guided by a rigid code of ethics. Lying or boasting about hunting prowess was forbidden, as was killing more animals than the individual or community required. As this Wasco story illustrates, transgressors would be punished severely.

Once a boy who hunted squirrels and birds was upbraided by his boastful father: "When I was your age, I didn't waste my time chasing after squirrels and birds; I hunted elks." Pointing to a scar on his forehead, he lied to his son: "An elk did this." In fact, he had gashed it stumbling into a tree.

The young man soon became a proficient hunter. He had gained the protection of a she-elk, who told him: "If you serve me, I will be your guardian spirit. But you must not kill too many animals."

Nevertheless, his father continued to mock his son's meagre tally of kills. At this, the elk lost patience and had her protégé slaughter five elk herds. But his bloodlust was so great that he turned on his guardian. She ran into a lake and, feigning death, sank below the water as he clung to her.

At the bottom of the lake, the man came to his senses, and saw countless elk in the guise of people. A voice called, "Draw him in." The hunter was drawn to the side of his guardian, who said: "Why did you exceed my command? Do you see all the elk-people that you have killed? Your father lied. Tree bark cut him, not an elk's horn. I can no longer be your guardian."

Then another voice cried: "Cast him out!" and the young man was sent back to his village. He lay in bed five days and nights and then called for water. "Heat water and wash me. Call my friends so that I may talk to them. And bring five elk hides."

When the people had assembled, the hunter told them: "My father was dissatisfied because I did not do as he had done. His wishes grieved the guardian spirit that helped me. My father said that he had been scarred by an elk. He wanted me to kill more than was needed. The spirit has left me." With that, he died.

The Man who Lived with Bears

A story told by the Skidi Pawnee people of the Plains shows that an intense feeling of kinship could exist between humans and other species. Such relationships were thought to be reciprocal: in this tale, the kindness shown by a person to a vulnerable bear is later rewarded.

A man out hunting in the woods near his home once came upon an abandoned bear cub. Instead of killing the defenceless animal, he tied an offering of tobacco round its neck and blessed it, saying: "May Tirawa (the Supreme Deity) protect you!" After returning to his camp, he described to his pregnant wife what had happened, and when she gave birth soon after, their son grew up feeling a powerful sense of kinship with bears. So strongly did he identify with them that often, while alone, he would pray to bears' souls.

When the boy reached manhood, he was caught one day in an enemy ambush. In the ensuing skirmish he was killed and his body dismembered. A male and a female bear found his remains and revived him with the help of supernatural powers. The man was completely restored and lived for a long while with his benefactors. During this time, he came to revere bears as the greatest and wisest of all beings, with the most powerful souls. The bears, however, reminded him of their place in the order of things. Their wisdom, they said, was a gift from Tirawa.

Eventually, the time came for the man to return to his people. As he took his leave, the male bear embraced him warmly, pressed its mouth to the man's lips, and rubbed him with its paws and fur. The touch of the fur gave the man power, while the kiss gave him wisdom. When he returned to human society, he became a great warrior and established the Bear Dance among his people.

Hunters who Married Animal Girls

The union of a mythical hunter with the daughter of the spirit "master" of an animal species is the subject of many Native American myths. Two stories show how such marriages are the ultimate confirmation of a harmonious relationship between a hunting people and its prey.

In a myth of the Mistassini Cree of Quebec, a hunter married a caribou girl and learned to see reality from the caribous' perspective. Whereas other hunters, when shooting a caribou, simply saw the animal fall down and die, he could see its spirit still running, while its carcass remained behind in the form of a white cape.

A Pawnee myth tells how a hunter was about to kill a female buffalo at a watering hole when she suddenly revealed herself as a beautiful woman. He instantly fell in love with her and gave her a necklace of blue and white beads. They married and set up camp together.

One day the hunter returned to find his wife and camp gone. He searched in vain, finally returning in great sorrow to his tribe. Later, he met a small boy wearing the same necklace of blue and white beads. The boy, whom he recognized as his son by his buffalo wife, led him back to the land of the buffalo. The bulls were wary and challenged him to perform several difficult tasks, including picking out his own wife among the cows.

Once the hunter had passed all the tests, the buffaloes accepted him. He took his wife back to meet his own people, but found them starving. The buffaloes agreed to help by allowing the Pawnees to hunt them. The hunter's son joined them in the form of a yellow calf, which the hunter warned the humans never to harm, or

there would be nobody to guide the herd to them each year. But the son said, "No, sacrifice me to the Great Spirit Tirawa. A new calf will take my place each year. Tan my hide and use it to wrap a sacred bundle containing an ear of corn and a piece of meat. Every hungry season, call upon the calf to lead the herd back to the people, and add a piece of the new season's meat to the bundle."

White Buffalo Woman

Plains peoples looked upon the buffalo as an intermediary between the creator and the human world. According to the Lakota Sioux, it was a buffalo in human form that brought them many important rites, including the Sun Dance.

A myth of the Sioux told how the supreme spirit, known as Wakan Tanka ("Great Mystery"), once sent an emissary to the tribes. Two hunters were keeping watch on a hilltop when they saw a beautiful woman approaching, clad in a white buffalo-skin dress. White buffalo were so rare that the hunters at once suspected that the woman came from the spirit world, a hunch that her stately gait quickly confirmed. Yet she was so lovely that one of the young men instinctively reached out to touch her. As he did so a mist shrouded the two men, and when it rose only one was left. The man polluted by desire had been reduced to a pile of bones.

Terror-struck, the other hunter returned to camp bearing instructions from the visitor that a special tipi should be prepared for her reception. There the woman produced the stem and bowl of a pipe. As she put the two parts of the sacred object together, she explained to the assembled elders that they must always venerate it, for its circular stone bowl signified the Earth and all its creatures while the wooden stem rising from its centre provided a direct link between the human realm and the sky. Its smoke also performed a dual function, carrying prayers to the spirit ancestors as it drifted upward while also imparting strength on the smokers. After entrusting her gift to the tribe, the woman left the camp. Her hosts gazed after her open-mouthed, and their astonishment only grew when they saw her suddenly give up her human guise to take the form of a white buffalo calf before finally disappearing from their sight.

Along with the sacred pipe, White Buffalo Woman also imparted to the Sioux seven rites that remained central to their religion. These included the vision quest, ceremonies of purification in the sweat lodge, funeral rituals that ensured that the soul of the deceased returned to the Great Spirit instead of wandering the Earth as a ghost, puberty rites for girls, and the Sun Dance – a grand celebration of the Earth's renewal held in early summer.

Old Man Coyote & the Ducks

A key figure in Native American creation stories was the earthdiver, a creature who plunged into the depths of Earth's primal waters to bring up grains of sand or mud, which then grew into the terrestrial world. In the version told by the Crow, a duck featured as the intrepid hero.

Before the world, there was water; only the Creator, Old Man Coyote, was alive – and he was lonely. So strong was his desire for company that, when he looked on the water, he saw two red-eyed ducks. He spoke to them, suggesting they dive deep to see what they could find.

The first duck dived and for a long time did not return; finally, it resurfaced to say it had reached the bottom, but it brought nothing back. Then it went down again, and came back with a root in its beak. A third time it swam down, and returned with some mud.

Now Old Man Coyote was mighty pleased with what he saw, and he announced he would use the raw materials to create somewhere to live. He took the earth and blew his quickening breath across it. The lump of mud grew and grew until it formed the great expanse of the North American continent and all the other lands beyond. Then he planted the root, and plants and trees spread across the terrain as far as Old Man Coyote could see. Pleased with what he had done, he asked both ducks what they thought.

They agreed that the land was fair, but suggested that it needed variety – perhaps mountains and beaches, together with valleys and lakes. With his quick touch Old Man Coyote made the landscape beautiful. Afterwards, he made the animals and the first people, teaching the humans all the skills they needed to survive.

The Gifts of Spider Woman

The Hopi claimed that the world was created by two deities who resided in the Underworld: Tawa, the sun god, and Spider Woman, the earth goddess. The latter led the Hopi's ancestors to their home in the American Southwest and then taught them all they would need to prosper.

Both Tawa and Spider Woman wished for company and from Tawa emerged Muiyinwuh, the god who controlled the life force, while from Spider Woman came the goddess Huzruiwuhti, keeper of the forms of life. She and Tawa made love, and from their union came the quarters of the world and the expanses of Above and Below.

Tawa and Spider Woman then shared a thought – to make the Earth and creatures for it. Tawa expressed the thought of fishes and running animals; Spider Woman said the thought should have life, so she made the creatures from clay and then sang them to life.

The first man and woman followed. To give them life Spider Woman rocked them gently while Tawa bathed them with his light until breath entered their lungs.

In the world above, the first land had not yet appeared from the primal waters. Tawa climbed into the sky, and his magnificent light brought land into being.

The first Indians had become many and in her underworld realm Spider Woman gave them their place and tribal names. Then she took them through the four caverns of her world to a hole that led into the new land above. Following Spider Woman, the first generation of people climbed through and emerged alongside the Colorado River. On her instructions, each clan followed an animal to its appointed territory. Then, before leaving, Spider Woman taught the Hopi their way of life. and how to perform dances to summon the storms.

Stairway to Heaven

According to the Wintu people of California, the creator spirit Olelbis determined to link the human world to heaven by a stone staircase. At its top he planned to set two fountains, which would restore youth to those people who climbed the stairs and drank the waters.

Olelbis entrusted the task of building the great ramp to two sibling spirits who took the form of buzzards. They got started immediately. But then along came Coyote – an impish trickster who loved to cause trouble. Seeing the pair hard at work, he decided to plant doubts in their mind about the worth of what they were doing.

What was the staircase for, he asked. Would people really want to be forever going up and down, restarting their lives over and over? Would it not be better for them simply to be born, live and then die? "Joy at birth and grief at death are better," he claimed, "for these mean love."

Swayed by Coyote's argument, the brothers gave up the task, and even pulled down what they had already built. Coyote was now alarmed, for he had secretly hoped to skip up to heaven himself before the link was cut. In terror at the prospect of his own death, he made himself wings from flower petals. But when he tried to fly he fell to Earth. And Olelbis decreed that he must die, just as all men and women would from that time on.

Mesoamerica

Mesoamerica – literally "Middle America" – has both a chronological and a geographical meaning. Historically it refers to the civilization that flourished in Mexico and Central America from the earliest times to the arrival of Spanish conquistadors in the sixteenth century CE. Geographically it stretched from the deserts of northern Mexico south to Costa Rica, beyond which a band of virgin forest 2,000 km (1,250 miles) across separated it from the pre-Columbian Andean civilizations to the south.

Many different cultures flourished in the Mesoamerican embrace, starting with the Olmecs of southern Mexico and continuing through the Zapotecs, Toltecs, and the unnamed people who built the great city of Teotihuacan. The only ones to have left a substantial body of myth, however, were the Mayans, who lived in the southern rainforests, and the Aztecs, who came to dominate the Valley of Mexico. Even in their cases, only fragments survive, for much was destroyed in the wake of the Spanish conquest and the forced imposition of Christianity.

By far the best source of material for the Mayans is the *Popol Vuh* ("Council Book"), a sacred manuscript of the Quiché people. Originally preserved in a codex employing the complex Mayan writing system, it survived the book-burnings of the early Christian era and was eventually translated into Spanish by a sympathetic priest.

The *Popol Vuh* recounts the mythical history of the Quiché, from the creation of the universe on. It describes how, having imposed order on a formless primeval void, the creator gods set out to people the world they had brought into being. First they spirited up the animals, only to find that they had no words to pay the gods the respect that was their due. So they decided next to create people, blessed with the power of speech. Their first two attempts failed, when they initially tried to shape humans from clay, which proved too viscous, and then from wood, which was too rigid. Worse still, the wooden people were empty-headed, lacking the intelligence needed to venerate their creators. So the gods swept them from the Earth in a devastating flood, picking off the few survivors in a variety of gory ways (see page 246).

In the twilight era that followed the flood, the bird deity Seven Macaw set himself up as the principal figure in the Mayan pantheon. His arrogance proved his undoing, however, and the creator gods sent twin deities, Hunahpuh and Xbalanque, to destroy both him (see page 247) and his two monstrous offspring (see page 248). After also detailing the doings of the Hero Twins' elder brothers, the Monkey Twins (see page 249), the *Popol Vuh* goes on to describe the creation of the present race of humans from maize and the emergence of the Quiché people.

The Aztecs of central Mexico left no source as comprehensive as the *Popol Vuh*. What is known of their beliefs has had to be pieced together from Spanish accounts and from a handful of surviving codices. Understandably, much remains incompletely understood.

What is clear, though, is that they viewed the universe as inherently unstable. They believed that the present era was that of the Fifth Sun, the four previous ones all having been destroyed by the gods; one myth told how life had been recreated after the fourth such cataclysm (see page 250). One of the gods credited with that achievement was Tezcatlipoca, literally "Smoking Mirror", a fearsome warrior deity also associated with sorcery (see page 251), like the Norse Odin. To sustain the Fifth Sun in the sky and so avoid a fresh annihilation, the gods had to be constantly placated by sacrificial victims, whose torments were seen as echoing the sacrifices the gods themselves had made to install the new creation (see page 252). The most important offering of all, though, was a still-beating human heart, for only thus could the ravening thirst of the Earth Monster be assuaged, ensuring the continuation of the vital crop cycle (see page 253).

The First Genocide

The *Popol Vuh* contains graphic portrayals of how the creator gods, Hurricane and Gucumatz, exterminated the race of wooden people that they had made. After a flood had accounted for most of the people, the gods visited a series of gruesome fates upon the survivors.

To rid himself of the last of his failed creations, Hurricane first called on the services of two fearsome monsters: one, called Gouger of Faces, plucked out the wooden people's eyes, while the other – Sudden Bloodletter – ripped off their heads.

Then the gods rained molten pitch down from the sky onto the wooden people, and sent wild animals into their homes. Even the houses themselves rebelled: cooking pots scalded their owners and hearth stones flew out of the fireplace and landed on their heads.

In the face of this fearsome attack, the wooden people fled in all directions. Some climbed on to the roofs of their houses, but these structures collapsed. Those who clambered up into the trees were shaken down to the ground by the branches themselves. Others hid in caves, only to see huge boulders roll into the cave entrances behind them, entombing them forever.

The Arrogant Impostor

Prior to the dawning of the present era, a monstrous bird known as Seven Macaw set himself up as the ruler of the gloomy twilight world that was left behind after the universal flood. This presumptuous despot had to be destroyed before the human race could be created.

Seven Macaw was characterized above all by his boastfulness. An admittedly splendid creature, with plumage made of precious metals and gleaming blue sapphires for his teeth, he claimed to be both the sun and the moon. Yet in his very arrogance lay the seeds of his downfall, for such a bold declaration was a direct challenge to the authority of the founder gods.

Accordingly, the so-called Hero Twins Hunahpu and Xbalanque were sent to overthrow Seven Macaw. They decided to ambush him, with mixed results: Seven Macaw did suffer a dislocated jaw, which left him with a terrible toothache, but he managed to wrench off Hunahpu's arm and carry it away with him.

Seven Macaw hung Hunahpu's arm over his fire and dared the boys to come and retrieve it. The Hero Twins enlisted the help of two venerable white-haired elders. The four contrived a deception that involved the elderly pair approaching Seven Macaw in the guise of travelling shamans who specialized in dentistry.

Taken in by the ruse, Seven Macaw begged the elders to cure his toothache. "Very well," they replied, "our diagnosis is that a worm is eating your jaw." They told him that in order to get the worm out they would have to extract his teeth, but that they would replace

them with false teeth in "ground bone" of the finest quality. The bogus shamans set to work, removing the monster's teeth of exquisite blue gemstones. However, they did not substitute them with ground bone teeth, but only with kernels of white corn, and then also went on to strip the area around his eyes of its precious metal.

The supposed "cure" applied by the elders simply robbed Seven Macaw of all the signs of his prestige. And since his status rested entirely on outward show, he was nothing once divested of his gold and jewels. He promptly wasted away before their very eyes. The Twins' victory was complete when the elders (who really were gifted doctors when they wanted to be) fitted Hunahpu's arm back into its socket and made it as good as new.

Earthquake's Downfall

Having destroyed Seven Macaw, the Hero Twins still had to deal with his two sons, who had inherited their father's insufferable arrogance. The elder son, Zipacna, called himself "the maker of mountains", while his brother Earthquake styled himself "breaker of mountains".

First the Twins set about luring the gluttonous Zipacna to his death. They constructed a fake crab, placed it in a deep canyon and told Zipacna about the juicy meal awaiting him. The story leaves it unclear whether he fell into the canyon and broke his neck or choked to death on the "crab", but in any event the incident spelled the end of him.

Once again, Hunahpu and Xbalanque used guile to approach Earthquake. They excited his curiosity by telling him about a new mountain they had seen rising in the east. Earthquake told them to take him there, boasting that he would destroy it.

On their way to the mountain, the Twins shot birds with their blowpipes. Their hunting prowess impressed Earthquake, as did their skilful preparation of the wildfowl. Before cooking the birds, the boys smeared them with plaster ground from rocks dug from the soil. What Earthquake did not realize, however, was that they were practising magic: in smothering the birds thus, the Twins were anticipating Earthquake's own enclosure in the soil after his death.

Earthquake ate greedily and they went on their way. But before long the monster's strength left him; the magic coating on the birds had taken effect. He fell down dead. The Twins bound his wrists and ankles and buried him. Thus the world was finally rid of the last of the monsters.

The Monkey Twins

The *Popol Vuh* took an irreverent, even satirical view of the Mayan gods. Just as Seven Macaw was transformed from a creator deity into a preening parrot (see page 247), so the Monkey Twins – usually shown as industrious patrons of the arts – became lazy good-for-nothings.

Shown either in human or in animal form, the Monkey Twins were venerated throughout Mesoamerica as patrons of artists, musicians and dancers. The Aztecs believed that those lucky enough to be born under the day-sign One Monkey would become singers, dancers or scribes.

The *Popol Vuh*, however, painted a very different picture. Naming the two as Hun-Batz (One-Howler Monkey) and Hun-Chowen (One-Spider Monkey), it described them as the first set of twin sons born to One Hunahpu, who later went on to father the Hero Twins Hunahpu and Xbalanque (see pages 247 and 248). While Hunahpu and Xbalanque were warriors prepared to brave the horrors of the Mayan underworld to avenge the murder of their father, the Monkey Twins were portrayed as indecisive stay-at-homes with an evil streak in their characters. Resenting their half-brothers from the start, they unsuccessfully tried to kill them in their infancy, abandoning them first on an anthill and then in a bramble thicket.

Yet the younger pair had the last laugh. Grown to manhood, they persuaded the other two to climb a tree to retrieve a bird stunned with a blowpipe. As they clambered up the trunk, however, the Hero Twins used magic powers to make it soar heavenward, sprouting so high that the pair could not get down. Soon they began growing fur, and when they untied their loincloths hoping to use them as ropes, they found them transformed into tails. In effect, their younger siblings had quite literally made monkeys of them.

The Birth of a New Age

The Aztecs believed that they were living in the Age of the Fifth Sun. Although no single source encompassed the way in which life had been recreated after the destruction of the preceding fourth world, a number of myths described successive stages of the process.

The Fourth Sun was destroyed in an apocalyptic cataclysm in which the waters under the Earth rose to drown the world at the same time that the sky collapsed in upon it. Everything was drowned and washed away. Afterwards chaos reigned until the great creator Ometeotl's four sons, the chief gods of the Mesoamerican pantheon, transformed themselves into trees to lift up the firmament, thereby clearing a space in which creation could once more begin.

A separate myth told how one of Ometeotl's sons, Quetzalcoatl, the "Plumed Serpent", was responsible for restoring humans to the Earth. To do so, he had to travel to the Underworld in search of some bone – all that was left of the fish people, their predecessors of the Fourth Sun: it was in the possession of the sly and possessive Mictlantecuhtli, the skull-faced central Mexican death god. Succeeding in his quest, Quetzalcoatl took the trophy to a mythical spot called Tamoanchan, literally "Land of the Misty Sky". There, Quetzalcoatl's fellow gods decided to cooperate, and ground the bone up like maize and moistened the bone flour with their own blood. Then they fashioned people from the sticky dough. In Tamoanchan, the gods nurtured the infant humans until they were big enough to be sent down to the surface of the Earth by themselves.

However, the Aztecs believed that the present age was destined to end in a huge earthquake. This event was inescapable, but could be postponed by satisfying the gods through the performance of ritual human sacrifices.

Lord of the Smoking Mirror

Among the first four gods created by Ometeotl was Black Tezcatlipoca. This restless, dark deity was described as "all-powerful and unequalled". Capricious in the extreme, he could bestow wealth, long life and happiness and then casually take them all away.

Among the most evocative and inscrutable aspects of Tezcatlipoca was his name, which meant "Smoking Mirror". The god carried one mirror at the back of his head and sometimes a second mirror replaced one of his feet, torn off when he was hurled out of heaven for seducing a virgin goddess. The history of Tezcatlipoca's mirror is as obscure as the images in its smoking surface. Toltec legend talks of a mirror, whose surface was like smoke, that could predict the end of droughts. Tezcatlipoca is said to have stolen this mirror and hidden it, thus prolonging the famine. The mirror "smoked" because it was made of obsidian, a black volcanic glass that reflects darkly and often with distortions. Tezcatlipoca could see into the future with his mirror and into people's hearts. This magical clairvoyance made him patron of shamans.

Although Tezcatlipoca was an unpredictable god who could bring misfortune and humble the successful, he also had his protective side. In one story, it was he who led the Aztecs in their search for a homeland. The dark god spurred them on by recounting the visions he could see in his supernatural mirror. Thus when the Aztecs arrived at Texcoco, across the water from their future capital of Tenochtitlan, the priests set up a mirror in Tezcatlipoca's temple, in which they saw the shadowy and beautiful visage of the deity himself.

The Creation of the Sun & Moon

After the destruction of the Fourth Sun, the gods agreed that the self-sacrifice of a god was required to bring a new sun into being. The vain and handsome Tecuciztecatl volunteered. But the gods decided to make him vie for the honour with the far humbler Nanahuatzin.

While the gods built a vast sacrificial bonfire, Tecuciztecatl and Nanahuatzin did penance on two mounds. When the fire had become searingly hot, Tecuciztecatl ran toward the flames, but four times recoiled from the intolerable heat. So the gods called on Nanahuatzin, who, without faltering, hurled himself into the fire. Spurred on by Nanahuatzin's immense bravery, Tecuciztecatl too ran into the pyre. The gods now waited for the birth of the new sun. But instead Tecuciztecatl rose as the moon, casting a blinding light. To subdue his brilliance, one of the gods threw a rabbit up into his face. This rabbit can still be seen on the face of the full moon.

Nanahuatzin now rose in the heavens as the new sun, but refused to move across the sky until he had been fed with the hearts and blood of all the other deities. Incensed at this demand, the Morning Star attacked the sun with his darts and spear, only to be defeated and hurled down into the Underworld. The sun god was acknowledged as supreme, and all 1,600 gods now allowed themselves to be sacrificed.

Rending the Earth Monster

Because the Aztecs were the dominant group in Central America when the Spanish arrived, most of what we know about Mesoamerican myth comes from them. But they borrowed their gods from the succession of civilizations that had held sway for a thousand years before them.

Part of the Aztecs' legacy of myth was an ancient story that told how the world and the sky were created from the body of the Earth Monster Tlaltecuhtli, a fearsome ogress who would eat anything that came near her.

Tlaltecuhtli's taste for flesh was so great that a single gaping maw toothed with flint knives was not enough to satisfy her bestial appetites; she had subsidiary mouths at her elbows, knees and other joints that also gnashed hungrily. She looked so terrifying that even the other gods were in awe of her. Eventually Tezcatlipoca and Quetzalcoatl, whose relations veer between enmity and alliance throughout the Aztec myth cycle, decided to rid the world of her so as to permit the process of creation to get under way.

Transforming themselves into giant serpents, they grappled with Tlaltecuhtli, finally managing to tear her huge body in two. (In another version of the story, Tezcatlipoca fought in his own guise and lost a foot in the struggle.) Then they threw one half of the corpse up into the sky, where it was transformed into the vault of the heavens.

Meanwhile other gods, shocked by the violence done to Tlaltecuhtli despite all the havoc she had wreaked, determined to form the Earth from the other half of her body. They made trees, flowers and herbs from her hair; wells and springs were fashioned from her eyes; her mouth served for rivers and caverns; and from her nose rose mountain ranges and valleys.

So life returned to the recumbent goddess, and with it much of her old ferocity. For sometimes in the night she could be heard screaming for human blood and hearts – the only diet that could persuade her to continue to bring forth nature's bounty.

South America

For more than two millennia up to the Spanish conquest, the lands between the Andes mountain range and South America's Pacific coast were home to a rich indigenous civilization. This is a region of fertile river valleys cut off from one another by bands of coastal desert, encouraging separatism and the growth of local traditions. A succession of cultures – Chavín, Moche, Nazca, Huari, Chimú – made their appearance in pockets of this terrain and spread their influence out over some parts of the surrounding territory. Only in the last century or so of native rule would a great empire develop that stretched its dominion all along the mountain spine as well as down the rivers that drained it. This was the realm of the Inca.

The Inca empire subsumed the cultures of the peoples it conquered, so many of the legends of earlier times found their way into its own mythology. One strand came from the Chibcha, inhabiting parts of what is now Colombia, who told stories of their great god Chibchachum (see page 256); the Huarochirí of central Peru preserved memories of a time when they lived in more fertile lands (see page 257). Particularly intriguing early legends came from the great city of Tiahuanaco on the shores of Lake Titicaca. These included one story explaining how people came to chew the leaves of the coca plant, a mild stimulant still popular today (see page 258).

The Inca themselves threw most of their energies into warfare and administration, bringing relatively little with them in the way of new myths. They shared their creator god, Viracocha, with other southern Andean peoples; perhaps to explain his universality, one story told how he had given all the different groups their own separate styles of dress, dialects and customs (see page 261). Otherwise, most Inca lore addressed local features like the presence of a monolith outside the capital, Cuzco (see page 260), or preserved legends of their rulers, eponymously known as Incas. Of these, none was greater than the empire-builder Pachacuti, who was honoured in folk memory for his great works and his concern for the common people (see page 263).

Inca civilization was swept away by the arrival of the Spanish conquistadors, who in 1532 captured the ruler Atahualpa and subsequently imposed their will on the entire empire. By forcibly converting the indigenous population to Christianity, they drove most of the earlier mythology underground. One tale that they did help to spread specifically set out to discredit the Incas' claim to descent from the sun god, tracing it back to a conscious act of deception by the first ruler, Manco Capac, who had taken power in Cuzco 300 years before (see page 262).

The conquest soon spawned legends of its own, the most persistent of which was the belief in El Dorado, a mythical land of gold that lured many conquistadors to their doom. Similar obsessions underpinned a supposedly true account of a never-discovered Inca treasure hidden high in the mountains of Ecuador (see page 266). Another enduring folk tale from the Age of Exploration spoke of giants inhabiting the shores of Patagonia, at the continent's southernmost tip; Antonio Pigafetta, the chronicler of Magellan's pioneering voyage round the world, claimed to have seen them with his own eyes (see page 264).

There was of course much more to the continent than the Andean lands where the pre-Columbian cultures grew up. To the east of the mountains lay a vast hinterland of rainforest, inhabited by peoples who had learned to live off the land in small, isolated groups. These forest peoples had their own rich mythology, explaining such matters of general concern as how foreigners came to be created (see page 268) or how the staple root crop manioc entered the world (see page 271). One particularly haunting theme that recurs in many of their narratives recounts the origins or activities of the stars – familiar presences that shone down on the encampments where story-tellers whiled away the long hours of the night (see pages 270 and 272).

The Anger of Chibchachum

The people of the Bogotá plain provoked the god Chibchachum to a fury with their complaints and disobedience. He sent a great flood to wipe out the region, but the people asked the sun god Bochica for help.

Bochica appeared astride a rainbow that arched majestically over the town of Soacha. He brought out the sun to dry up the waters, then took his gold staff and hurled it at Mount Teguendama, creating a chasm in the rocks through which most of the flood flowed away. The magnificent waterfall that Bochica made still exists today, spilling into the sacred Lake Guatavita.

Bochica banished Chibchachum to the Underworld and gave him the task of supporting the world on his shoulders for eternity. From time to time, the weight becomes too much for him and he shifts it from one shoulder to the other – causing the Earth to shudder and grind in an earthquake.

The rainbow had marked the Chibcha people's deliverance from the flood, and ever afterwards they worshipped it as the goddess Chuchaviva. They prayed to be saved from the curse of Chibchachum, who from his Underworld exile decreed that the rainbow's every appearance would also bring death. Bochica's subversive wife Chia may have lent her magic to Chibchachum to create the great deluge, for in other myths she is responsible for floods.

Distant Shores of Paradise

The Huarochirí told tales of a time when their home was a fertile paradise before the god Pariacaca forced them out into drier lands. Scholars believe that the Indians may once have lived in lush valleys nearer the coast but were driven by invaders to the harsher highlands.

The Huarochirí occupied the region around what is now Peru's capital, Lima. Most of what we know of their myths comes from a Spanish priest, Francisco de Ávila, who collected knowledge of traditional Huarochirí beliefs, the better to extirpate all traces of the old religion. Ironically, his writings served to preserve the very stories he set out to destroy.

The myths Ávila collected claimed that the Huarochirí were ruled in ancient times by two gods, Yana Namca and Tuta Namca, until a third being, Huallallo Caruincho, defeated them and took control. He imposed strict rules. Each woman was allowed to bear just two children and was forced to choose between them, keeping one to raise and giving up the other to be consumed by the god, who took the form of a fireball.

In those days the lands were rich and filled with brightly coloured parrots and toucans. Every seed that was planted ripened in five days. Similarly, when men or women died they returned to life after five days. But the people lived evil lives. Their easy existence came to an end when a new god, Pariacaca, emerged from five eggs laid on Mount Condor Coto and defeated Huallallo Caruincho, driving the people inland.

According to Ávila's informants, the lush lands were named Yunca or Ande, the former term referring to the fertile valleys lying toward the coast. In other versions they were called "anti lands", which scholars believe may have been a general term used to refer to warm lowland landscapes.

Food of the Gods

Some say Indians from Tiahuanaco were responsible for discovering the coca plant, the leaves of which the peoples of the Andes have chewed for centuries. The coca's properties of pain and fatigue suppression help alleviate the debilitating effects of living at high altitude.

Coca was revered. The leaves were sacrificed to gods and used for divination. It is said that the plant was found by the Indians of the great city of Tiahuanaco, which lies near the southern end of Lake Titicaca, on the Callao plateau of Peru and Bolivia. One day the people of Tiahuanaco journeyed beyond the mountains. When they discovered lush valleys they settled there, burning the vegetation to clear the land so they could plant crops. But the smoke annoyed Khuno, god of snows, who whipped up a storm that forced the travellers to seek the shelter of mountain caves.

The storm destroyed all they had. But when hunger drove one man to taste the leaves of a green bush that seemed to grow all around, he felt new energy. He shared the leaves with the others and, invigorated, they returned to Tiahuanaco where they planted coca bushes in abundance.

One story tells how the coca bush grew from the body of a woman who had been killed for breaking the hearts of her many lovers. Another involves a mother who lost her child and wandered the land in grief. She came across a coca bush and found its leaves could ease her terrible pain.

Dark Menagerie

The Araucanian Indians of Chile were fierce warriors and their colourful mythology is similarly intimidating. Stories abound of grotesque hybrid creatures and monsters that preyed on innocent souls.

Living close to the ocean, particularly in the southern parts of their lands, the Araucanians told many tales of sea and river beasts. The *camahueto* was a vast seahorse which would cause shipwrecks, while the *cuero*, a clawed octopus, would feast on any man or animal foolish enough to enter the water. Sometimes it would come ashore to enjoy the sun's warmth, and then create storms to blow itself back out to sea.

The *neguruvilu*, or *guirivilo*, was a fox crossed with a snake which emerged from its riverbed lair to catch its prey and dine on its blood. Then there was the *huallepen*, a sheep with a calf's head that lived in streams; if it appeared to a pregnant woman, she would bear a deformed child. The *colocolo* was a small creature with poisonous saliva that lived in underground caverns. The *alicanto* was a bird that ate gold which made it shine brilliantly. When hunted, it could hide this light and in the dark it would lead people to their deaths in the mountains.

Perhaps most terrifying of all, however, was the hideous *chon-chon*. This fearsome creature was a bodiless human head that used its ears as wings and came by night to houses where people were sick. The legends told how it would fight sick people's souls, and, if it won, suck their blood.

The Stone that Wept

A legend of Cuzco told of a massive boulder outside the city walls that wept tears of blood. Behind the tale lay memories of a real-life tragedy that marred the construction of one of the Incas' greatest architectural achievements.

Even today people marvel at the Incas' extraordinary feats of construction, and the tourists' sense of wonder is as nothing compared with that felt by the Spanish soldiers who conquered the empire in the sixteenth century. No building impressed them more than the fortress of Sacsahuaman overlooking the imperial capital of Cuzco. Made of massive blocks of stone, many of them weighing more than a hundred tonnes, it startled the conquistadors with its Cyclopean bulk, leading some to call it the eighth wonder of the world. Yet one of the largest boulders intended for its construction never reached the site. Instead it remained on the plateau in front of the fortress, so exhausted by its long journey from the mines, the Cuzcans claimed, that it had come to rest and wept blood.

The truth, according to the chronicler Garcilaso de la Vega, was more tragic. In fact the stone was deliberately left on the plain by the labourers who pulled it there. They abandoned it following a disaster that occurred during the journey, when the huge stone broke loose on a mountain road, crushing many of those who were dragging it. In the historian's words, it was these victims – he put their number at an improbable 3,000 – who wept tears of blood, and the stone remained isolated and unused outside the capital as their monument.

Why People Dress Differently

According to one Inca myth, all the diverse Andean races could trace their origins back to the repopulation of the Earth after a great flood, when the creator god fashioned them just as they were in imperial times.

The lands ruled by the Inca had a long history of cultural diversity, encouraged by the rugged geography of the Andes region, which limited contacts even between neighbouring valleys. As a result, the various Andean races each had strong local traditions, marked off from one another by distinctive customs and styles of dress.

Over time a myth grew up to explain how the situation came about. The Spanish chronicler Cristobal de Molina was told that the creator god Viracocha made the different peoples out of clay, and then painted on the garments that they were to wear. Each group was also given its own language, songs and favourite foodstuffs – even a preferred hairstyle, long or short. Then the creator dispatched them underground to make their way through subterranean passages to the various regions to which he had assigned them. In later times the caves, lakes and mountains from which they were thought to have re-emerged were venerated as holy places. Legend also claimed that the first generation of humans were turned to stone, and these rocks too subsequently became objects of reverence.

Some of the region's cultural heterogeneity survived the Spanish conquest. Even today adjoining Andean valleys have different traditional costumes, and local people continue to show profound respect for distinctive rocks and boulders.

Manco's Shining Mantle

The Spanish chroniclers liked to tell a story suggesting that the Incas' supposed status as sons of the sun resulted from a deception. According to the Spanish propaganda, the first Inca's clothing fooled the Indians, showing them to be credulous and their rulers to be cynical.

To make his first entry into his future capital of Cuzco, the first Inca, Manco Capac, wore a cape of gold, so the tale goes – or, in an alternative version, two thin plaques of the metal on his chest and back.

He had sent messengers ahead to spread the news that the son of the sun himself was coming to town. When the citizens saw him bathed in his supposed father's reflected glory, they fell down and praised him as a god.

Before his execution in 1572, the last Inca, Tupac Amaru, revealed in a speech that the claims he and his forefathers had made of conversing with the sun were not true. He explained that his predecessor on the throne, Titu Cusi, had told him what to do when he needed to influence his people. He was to go alone to the Punchao – the golden solar disc that was the Incas' holiest emblem. "Afterwards I was to come out and say that it had spoken to me, and that it said whatever I wished. But it did not speak, we alone did; for it is an object of gold and cannot speak."

It seems likely that he made the speech under duress. But it is possible that Tupac Amaru was warning his people not to put too much faith in the old ways, which were already beginning to fail them.

Pachacuti & the Girl from Ica

Pachacuti was the greatest Inca ruler and the man responsible above all others for creating their Andean empire. A folktale commemorating his love for the people told how he showed generosity to one of his subjects even when she rejected his advances.

As a young prince, Pachacuti was not first in line to the throne. He came to power when an army of the neighbouring Chanca people attacked the Inca capital, Cuzco. While the appointed heir fled, Pachacuti led the resistance, decisively defeating the invaders. From that time on he never relinquished power.

Although ruthlessly successful as an empire-builder, Pachacuti also won a reputation as a caring ruler. One story told how, as he was travelling through the province of Ica, he was struck by the beauty of a girl he saw working in the fields. Courtiers ran to tell her that she had the honour of winning the ruler's favour, but in spite of all their offers of costly gifts she turned down the prospect of a dalliance, saying that she loved another man.

The ruler's attendants expected him to punish her, but instead he praised the girl's constancy and offered to reward her with the gift of her choice. Instead of demanding gold or jewels, she said only that she would like water for her village, which lay in an arid desert region. Pleased by her unselfishness, Pachacuti ordered 40,000 soldiers to dig irrigation canals to provide the community with a year-round supply – or so the story claimed, although actually the channels in the area predated the Incas by several hundred years.

The Patagonian Giants

A popular belief in the gigantic stature of Patagonians survived in Europe for centuries after Antonio Pigafetta, who accompanied Magellan on the first voyage round the world, wrote a highly coloured account of his adventures.

Nearing the southern tip of South America, Magellan's fleet put into a cove to see out the winter. There the sailors were one day startled to see a naked giant appear on the shore, dancing, singing and leaping, throwing sand and dust on his head as he pranced. Bemused by the sight, Magellan ordered one of his men to approach the stranger, instructing him to imitate his behaviour in order to reassure him and show friendship.

The seaman did as he was told and was able to lead the giant to an islet where the other crewmembers were waiting. He cut a remarkable figure, almost twice their size and with a huge face that was painted red all over except around the eyes, where the skin was yellow. The Patagonian was equally surprised by the appearance of the visitors, pointing with his finger up to the sky to indicate that he thought they must have come from heaven. Shown his own face in a steel mirror, he was so terrified that he jumped back, knocking over four crewmen.

More giant visitors arrived later. By that time Magellan had determined to take some back to Europe to serve as living proof of the wonders he had encountered on the voyage. Accordingly, he enticed two of the younger ones on board, where they were clapped in chains. Magellan duly set sail with his captives, but his treacherous behaviour did him little good; both were dead before the year was out, unable to survive the cramped and squalid conditions in which they were imprisoned.

Magellan himself died on the voyage, but Pigafetta survived and so did news of the strange encounter. Travellers on subsequent voyages of exploration confirmed his account of a gigantic race inhabiting America's southernmost lands. Over the years stories of their vast stature became magnified, with later accounts making them as much as four times the size of normal humans. Today, researchers think that the tales may have reflected exaggerated accounts of the Tehuelche, a tall race inhabiting the grasslands of the region. Sadly, their numbers were greatly reduced by government troops in the 1870s, and Argentina's most recent national census recorded fewer than 6,000 survivors.

The Brave Women

A Shavante myth from the upper reaches of the Xingu River, in Brazil, tells of a time when women took on the responsibility of attacking other tribes that dared to cross them.

Long ago, before there were any jaguars, the bravest men of the Shavante had all died while taking part in their regular raids to kill people who were not part of the tribe. So the women decided to take the place of these men, and went off to attack some white people. Although Europeans lived very far away in those days, distances were much shorter and it took the women only a few days to reach the houses that they thought belonged to the white people. But when they got there they found only spirits with flat, white faces, and bodies covered with feathers. The women were not sure if these were white people, because they had never seen any before. But they suspected they might be something more dangerous. Neither the spirits nor the women knew who should be more afraid, but finally the spirits ran off and the women looted their village. They took all the mats, baskets and weapons, just as they still do today in the Way'a Festival, which wards off evil. But on their way home they became ill with colds and boils. They all thought they were going to die, and were being punished because they had not planned the attack carefully as men do when they go into battle. However, by tending each other and singing songs to give themselves strength, they made it back to the Shavante village, where they were honoured by the men, and forgiven for their mistake in not planning the attack properly.

The Golden Condor

The *Derrotero de Valverde* (Account of Valverde) contains detailed instructions on how to find a great Inca treasure in the mountains of Ecuador. But although exact copies of the original document still exist, nobody has ever been able to find the gold.

In 1584 the young soldier Juan Valverde fell in love with a native girl and together they ran away to her home village, high in the Andes. There they lived until a Spanish patrol arrived three years later. Valverde was terrified that he would be caught and executed as a deserter, and decided that he and his wife should return to Spain. To help pay for the journey, the village elders told him that the Inca general Ruminahui had hidden a store of gold in the mountains.

Valverde returned with treasures that included a golden condor with emerald eyes and outstretched silver wings. But the village headman declared that the condor had to remain hidden until the Europeans had been driven from the Andes. The bird was returned, but even without it Valverde had enough gold to make him rich.

When the semi-literate conquistador returned to Spain laden with dozens of gold bars, King Charles V ordered him to reveal the source of his wealth, or have it confiscated. The *Account of Valverde* reveals that the great golden condor lies in an artificial lake in the Llanganuti mountains. The route to the lake is described in detail, but it has never been found.

Shapeshifters

Spirits condemned to roam the Earth for eternity after committing a mortal sin, *condenados* fooled human beings by changing shape and voice to imitate anyone they pleased. They could be male, but it was the females who were the more feared.

South America's *condenados* belonged to a category of ghosts found in many different cultures: those trapped between the lands of the living and the dead. Homeless, they roamed the world eternally, bereft of companionship and robbed of all hope of salvation. Unsurprisingly, they were embittered, seeking revenge for their sufferings on those more fortunate than themselves.

The classic *condenado* story opens with a young man travelling alone along a lonely mountain road. He is surprised to come across a beautiful woman – and even more so when she throws herself at him, offering him her body for the night. He succumbs to her blandishments without hesitation, and the couple make passionate love until dawn. But as the sun rises in the sky, the woman informs him that she is a *condenada* (the feminine version of the term). Then she disappears, and within weeks the youth has wasted away and died.

Sometimes *condenados* were cannibals rather than seducers. One gruesome tale described how a young mother waiting for the return of her husband saw a woman in a white jacket hurrying along the road outside her home as dusk was falling one night. The stranger looked so cold that the mother invited her in. Once inside the house, the housewife asked the stranger to hold her two-year-old baby while she knelt down to light a fire. But when she rose to her feet again and turned round, she saw that the woman's mouth was smeared with blood and that her baby had been eaten down to the waist. The housewife herself only escaped by taking flight and hiding among a herd of cows, whose panicked lowing frightened the hungry spirit.

How Outsiders Were Made

Even the most isolated groups have some contact with outsiders, and although a tribe's main concern is generally with its own origins, many myths explain how other races came into existence.

Foreigners are usually described as late-comers. According to the Bororo of Brazil and Bolivia, their own ancestor was the survivor of a great flood, whereas the first whites, blacks and other forest peoples were created much later, by a bored monkey banging a stick into the ground. The Yanomami of Brazil and Venezuela say that there was once a terrible fight in one of their villages near the headwaters of a river. A certain adolescent, who was supposed to be secluded in a sacred hut, joined in, and because the seclusion taboo was broken, the river burst its banks and washed all the brawlers downstream, where they were eaten by giant otters and black caymans. Their blood formed a froth on the river surface, and a supernatural being called Remori gathered this into his cupped hands and spoke to it, creating foreigners and giving them their languages. This is why the Yanomami describe the tongues of others as "ghostlike". Unusually, the Chamacoco of Paraguay say that the supreme being made all the other races first, and by the time he came to make them he was in such a hurry he made them flawed, which is why the Chamacoco consider themselves stupid and slow to learn.

Traffic Between the Worlds

Many South American peoples believed that a world tree linked Earth and heaven. Yet even when the layers of the universe had been separated and the tree or connecting vines had been cut down, it was still sometimes possible to travel between the two realms.

The land where the Canelos Quichua live now lies within Ecuador, east of the Andes in the lowland terrain of the Amazon headwaters. Like other rainforest peoples, the Canelos traditionally believed that weather beings acted as intermediaries between the Earth and sky. Fog transported life upward, while rain brought spirits and other celestial creatures down. Birds were also messengers, carrying songs between heaven, Earth and the Underworld. They also held that the giant anaconda, which lives in rivers, could connect the watery regions with the sky by turning itself into a rainbow.

For the Canelos, even ordinary people could travel between the two worlds. Husbands and wives sometimes made dream voyages together, waking in the hours before dawn to compare and interpret their experiences. In most Amazonian cultures, however, the realms had to be linked by a shaman, who usually journeyed between them while in a trance induced by some hallucinogenic drug.

The Waiwai shaman, for example, drank *kaahi*, which he prepared from a vine said to originate on the banks of Lake Akuena in the centre of heaven. (Modern medicine identifies the potion as a form of *ayahuasca*, a hallucinogenic concoction brewed from giant tropical lianas native to the Amazon rainforest and known by the botanical name of *Banisteriopsis*.) He was then able to embark on a soul journey to the layer of heaven that held his spirit helpers or to the dark, swampy underworld realm of the anaconda people.

A third option was to travel to the mountain where the Father of Peccaries lived, a Lord of the Animals figure responsible for the pig-like creatures on which the tribe depended for much of their game. Once there, he could negotiate with the spirit world on behalf of his terrestrial people. He may have been sent to rescue the kidnapped souls of the sick, or to bargain for a rich supply of animals to be sent to Earth for his people to hunt.

The Birth of the Stars

The movements of the constellations provided a calendar that allowed people to calibrate the seasonal round. As a result, the birth of the stars was linked to that of time itself – a terrible event that destroyed the first beings and brought mortality into the world.

All across the world, people have read patterns and stories into the stars they saw scattered across the night sky. The Amazonian peoples were no exception to the general rule, and the long hours they spent in hammocks or around campfires gazing up at the heavens helped spur their imaginations. Different groups came up with their own stories, which were duly passed down from generation to generation as part of the tribal heritage of myth.

The Toba of the Gran Chaco region of Argentina and Paraguay had origin myths for more than thirty heavenly bodies. Most of them told tales of cosmic disaster involving devastating fires or a universal deluge. One, however, was unusual in seeing celestial evidence of the first hunt. It described the dark Coalsack nebula as the head of a rhea, a flightless bird resembling a small ostrich, whose body was made up of the constellation Ophiuchus, and whose leg was that part of the Milky Way extending down from Scorpio. Storytellers explained that the rhea was chased into the sky by a boy and his dog, who themselves turned into two of the Centauri stars. An alternative version saw both the Centauri stars as dogs, the ancestors of all today's hounds, created from the breasts of two old women.

Some constellations were widely viewed as game or water animals because their appearance in the sky was taken as a sign that life was about to be renewed at the end of the dry season. The Karina people of Venezuela claimed that the tapir, a small, pig-like creature that searches for sustenance by night, was the master of food, because at one time only he knew the whereabouts of the all-providing *allepantepo* tree. When he was destroyed by the divine twins Pia and Makunaima, he entered the sky as the Hyades, while his killers joined him among the stars as Orion and the Pleiades.

How Manioc Came into the World

Many stories told how manioc, or cassava, was first brought to the world by a supernatural being. Through human foolishness, however, the provider was sacrificed, forcing people to learn the secrets of the crop themselves and to develop a true respect for their staple foodstuff.

The Jivaro-speaking tribes of the Amazon Basin believed that manioc was introduced to the world by a short, fat woman called Nunghui who possessed supernatural powers. Despite her strangeness, she was revered because her son could make manioc just by uttering its name.

One day Nunghui was called away on an errand. Before leaving, she asked some of the village women to look after her son in her absence. While he was in their care, however, a group of children, jealous of the talent that made him so special, broke into the hut where he was staying and threw ash in his eyes, killing him instantly.

The community soon had reason to rue their action, for manioc was an essential part of their diet. Not knowing how to grow it for themselves, the people first grew hungry and then desperate. In their misery they looked for a scapegoat to blame for the disaster, and settled on the hapless Nunghui. As punishment for letting her son out of her sight, she was condemned to live underground.

Fortuitously, the penalty proved to be the tribe's salvation, for from that day on Nunghui has pushed the manioc up from under the soil, dancing with the roots to make them grow. Gardeners still perform rites to attract her to their plots of land to ensure a fruitful crop.

Other peoples, especially in the northwest Amazon, give different accounts of the origins of the crop. They claim that manioc grew from the corpse of a white child born to a virgin, or from a maiden who asked to be buried alive.

Fearsome Star Maidens

Some of the most popular horror stories from the Amazon region tell of love affairs between mortal men and irresistible maidens who descend from the stars. In this tale a young man pays a heavy price for succumbing to the attractions of a beautiful supernatural woman.

A young man of the Cherentes people of Brazil once gazed up at the sky and became fascinated by the beauty of the Pleiades constellation. One star in particular caught his attention, one that he wished to carry with him in his gourd wherever he went. When he finally went to sleep that night, he dreamed of the star, and woke suddenly to find a beautiful young woman with glowing eyes standing beside him. She told him that she was the star of his dreams, and insisted that he put her in his gourd. During the days that followed he would peek inside and see her burning eyes, while at night she would emerge and let him admire her beauty. One night she enticed him into climbing a magic tree which took them both to a desolate field in the middle of heaven. There she told him to wait while she went off to gather food. Standing alone in that austere place, he suddenly heard music. He became intrigued and followed it until at last he stumbled on a festival of corpses, dancing around so that their rotten, stinking flesh swung and fell from their skeletons. He fled in terror, with the star-maiden pursuing him, telling him to come back and accusing him of disobeying her. But the man was sick of the sky world, and clambered down the tree to the ground. As he fled he heard the star's voice telling him he would return soon. And when he got back to his village he barely had time to tell his story before falling down dead.

The Taking of Fire

In a number of myths, fire marks the birth of civilization. It may come as a blaze that destroys dangerous creatures, or a gift that allows people to eat cooked food and frighten off animals.

The Opaye of the upper reaches of the River Paraguay claim that the jaguar's mother was the first keeper of fire. One by one the animals tried to take it from her.

First came the armadillo, who tickled the jaguar's feet with a feather until she fell asleep, and then stole a burning brand. But as soon as the tickling stopped the jaguar woke up and called to her son, who chased the armadillo and took back the smouldering ember.

The tapir tried next, by boring the mother to sleep with his conversation, but as he tiptoed out with a burning twig he tripped over a root and crashed to the ground, waking the jaguar's mother who at once reclaimed the prize.

One by one all the animals tried, and while most of them succeeded in getting the jaguar mother to fall asleep, none of them managed to escape with the secret of fire.

Eventually only the *prea*, a kind of guinea-pig, was left to try his luck. Instead of sending the jaguar mother to sleep, he simply walked in and told her he wanted some fire. Then he trotted off with it. For a few moments the jaguar mother was too astonished to shout, and so the *prea* managed to escape. On his way home he met some humans who were fascinated by his new possession. So he gave the fire to them.

Although the jaguar no longer has fire, and is now condemned to eat his food raw, the memory of the flame can still be seen burning in his eyes.

THE SOUTHERN WORLD

Africa

Unsurprisingly, a region as large as Africa had a mythology to match its vast extent and limitless diversity. Even leaving aside the lands north of the Sahara, which had separate traditions of their own, the sub-Saharan bulk of the continent was home to a mass of contrasting ethnic groups pursuing very different lifestyles. The hunter-gatherer Khoi and Kung bushmen, for example, had little in common with Fulani or Somali pastoralists or with the Swahili traders of the East African coast. Each group had its own way of looking at the world, and each evolved a heritage of story to expound and preserve it.

Even so, there were common themes that stretched across tribal boundaries. In largely oral cultures that remained in close contact with the natural world, the storytelling tradition proved particularly rich in animal fables. A myth of the San bushmen could transform a humble mantis into a creator divinity, held responsible for bringing into being the antelopes on which the hunters depended for food (see page 278). Between them, a sparrowhawk and a fly could release the sun from the grasp of Yemekonji, supreme god of the Mongo-Nkundo hunters of the Congolese rainforest, thereby bringing daylight to the world (see page 284). Some animal stories were less cosmic in their reach; the Mbundu people of Angola had a simple tale to explain how the dog became domesticated while its fellow canid, the jackal, remained in the wild (see page 289).

As in most of the world's mythologies, explanation was one major function of the African corpus. Another was to address the innermost fears of people living in difficult environments where life at its worst could be nasty, brutish and short. So the Hausa told tales of witches, figures of evil blamed for bringing sickness and death (see page 280). That final mystery was an especial source of fascination, inspiring accounts of underwater realms of the spirits where deserving visitors might be rewarded and the wicked punished (see pages 279 and 288).

The lack of written records meant that tribal history had to be passed down from mouth to mouth. This role was particularly important in the lands immediately south of the Sahara where great kingdoms had grown up from as early as the eighth century CE on. The first known was that of Ghana (not to be confused with the present-day state of that name), which at its height stretched across parts of what are now Mali, Mauritania and Senegal. This realm was created by the Soninke people, who kept its memory alive in later times through stories of its capital, Wagadu, and of legendary rulers like Dinga and Djabe Sisse. One tale relating how the latter usurped his elder brother's claim to the throne bore a surprising resemblance to the biblical story of Jacob stealing the inheritance of his sibling Esau (see page 287).

Whatever other purposes the accounts may have served, they also often revelled in the pleasure of storytelling for the story's own sake. Generations of youngsters must have sat spellbound in the hot African nights, lost in a world of magic in which bowls of broth could talk (see page 280) and tortoises had powers of divination (see page 282). The land of story was also one in which expected roles might be satisfyingly reversed, so that a lumbering chameleon could accomplish an epic quest that an eagle had earlier failed to perform (see page 281).

More than anything else, though, African audiences seem to have enjoyed stories of people succeeding against the odds. Sometimes the protagonists were heroes in the conventional mode: the Mandinka related legends of the empire-builder Sunjata, while the Swahili venerated the poet-warrior Liongo. More often, though, they achieved their ends through cunning, for the trickster was a favourite figure across many African cultures, whether anthropomorphized as Anansi the spider or as Hare (the origin of the US children's favourite Brer Rabbit) or else in the shape of divine pranksters like the Yoruba trouble-maker Eshu (see page 286).

How Things Got Their Colours

According to the San bushmen, the sacred mantis brought honey to all the various species of antelope, and the animals took their colours from the specific type they were offered. The insect gave its own yellow hue to the rainbow's upper rim.

The San bushmen of the Kalahari Desert told several stories of the beginnings of things, but many featured the praying mantis as the creator. In the first times, they claimed, the insect was married to the hyrax, a small mammal. Their daughter was the porcupine, who became the wife of Kwammang-a, the Sans' primeval ancestor.

The mantis subsequently used Kwammang-a's discarded sandal to fashion the first eland, feeding the giant antelope on honey, which also served as a refreshing balm. When he visited the eland in the evening, the mantis would mix honey with water and use the concoction to rub down the great beasts' quivering sides. The eland has a dark fawn colouring because the mantis gave it dark-coloured wasps' honey.

The mantis brought light-coloured liquid honey to the gemsbok, and the animal is therefore white. The hartebeest was fed on the reddish comb of young bees; although the hartebeests of central and western Africa are brown, those further south are red. Brownish honey also accounted for the dark skin of the now extinct quagga, once a member of the zebra family. Springboks typically have a red-fawn coat because like the hartebeest they ate the honey of young bees.

Meanwhile, according to the San, yellow appears to arch over red in the rainbow because the yellow mantis lies above the red-brown of their ancestor Kwammang-a. In this instance the mantis is ascribed a yellow colour, although most of the insects are in fact green or brown in order to blend in with the foliage on which they perch, invisibly waiting for prey. However, there is one exotic species of African mantis with green-yellow wing markings that appear like eyes when it spreads its wings. The rainbow itself was sometimes called Kwammang-a.

Tales of Other Worlds

Many African peoples tell tales of a traveller's voyage to the lands of the dead. For some cultures, including the Ashanti of Ghana, the spirit world exists alongside that of the everyday; for others, such as the Wacaga of southern Africa, the spirits inhabit an underworld.

Young Ashanti Kwasi Benefo lost four wives, one after the other, to the cold ogre Death. Each time grief stunned him but he dutifully prepared his wife for burial, dressing her in beads and an *amoasie* or silk loincloth.

One day he decided he wanted to follow them all to Asamando, the land of the dead. Setting off from their burial place, he eventually came to a deep river and saw an old woman with a brass pot full of *amoasies*. At first she refused to let Kwasi cross, but finally she took pity on him and made a ford in the river. He walked on and came to a village. He heard his four wives welcome him, and felt them bathe his feet, but he could not see them, for they were as invisible as the air. They told him to return home and marry once more; when his time came to die, they would be waiting for him. When Kwasi awoke he was lying near his village. He married a fifth time and lived to a ripe age.

In a Wacaga tale, a girl called Marwe entered the land of the dead through a hole in the bottom of a pond. There she worked for an old woman. In time she told the woman she wanted to return home. The old woman ordered her to plunge her hands into a pot and, when Marwe did so, her arms were covered with precious bangles. She did the same with her legs and pretty copper chains covered her ankles. Then the woman dressed Marwe in a beaded petticoat and told her that her husband on Earth would be a young man named Sawoye.

The old woman guided Marwe back to the pond and left her there. The local people came to see their newly returned neighbour and the chieftain, enchanted by her beauty and finery, asked her to be his bride. But she refused. Then came a young man named Sawoye, whose face was badly marked by a skin disease. At once Marwe announced that he was to be her husband.

The Talking Bowl of Broth

Fear of the power of sorcery was a very real force in many traditional African societies. Witches were thought to use poison both to kill their victims and to steal their souls. In one Hausa tale, though, the potion itself spoke up to thwart its maker.

Belief in witchcraft was common in traditional African societies, just as it was in Europe and the USA in the sixteenth and seventeenth centuries. In each case the root cause was the same: the conviction that people's misfortunes were somehow due to the malice of unpopular and distrusted neighbours. Also as in the Western tradition, witches were usually thought to be female.

One difference between the two approaches was the emphasis that traditional African societies put on witchcraft as a cause of physical illness. Cases that in Europe would have routinely been referred to doctors for treatment were often placed in the hands of witchfinders in the sub-Saharan lands. These individuals were often powerful and influential members of the community, owing their prestige partly to fears stirred up by stories like one told by the Hausa people of northern Nigeria.

It told of a wicked sorceress who had nine separate mouths on her body, all invisible to ordinary people, and a ravening appetite for evil that led her to seek to kill her own husband and father-in-law. With murder in mind, she gathered noxious herbs from the forest and boiled them up in a broth. But when the two men sat down to eat and uncovered their bowls, a voice from the first warned them, "Cover me up or else you will die." When the same thing happened a second time, the husband suspected witchcraft. Picking up the bowl, he emptied it over his wife's head. Suddenly the nine mouths became visible, and she was revealed as a witch. She ran away from the village and was never seen again.

The Power of Rain

In this Fon tale the regulation of life-giving rains was affected by a power struggle between the Earth god Sagbata and his androgynous brother-sister the thunder god Hevioso.

According to one tale, Sagbata had been sold into slavery. He eventually escaped and returned home, only to discover that Hevioso had been made leader of the tribe. The siblings quarrelled and Sagbata seized power from Hevioso, who took himself off to the sky.

Sagbata ordered his people to raise great crops of corn, but Hevioso looked down from the sky and resolved to withhold the rains. When the wet season was due and no waters fell, famine spread and many died.

Sagbata called together all the peoples and animals of his kingdom. They watched as he created a ladder between Earth and heaven from threads of cotton. Then he asked for volunteers to climb up to Hevioso and demand that the rains be restored. The eagle was the first to go: it soared halfway up the sky but then was struck down by Hevioso. Next the cat tried, but fared no better.

At last it was the turn of the slow, sure chameleon. The chameleon climbed so slowly that Hevioso grew bored and went away to deal with other matters. From time to time, Hevioso returned to fling a thunderbolt down at the poor creature, but the chameleon hid behind the thread to which it clung. Finally the chameleon reached Hevioso's dwelling. He passed on Sagbata's message begging for rain – and Hevioso, seeing that Sagbata was accepting his authority in heaven, relented. Rain fell, and the corn grew tall. Some say that Sagbata had to submit entirely to Hevioso because the thunder god had possession of the two things essential to life on Earth: the water of the rains and the fire of celestial lightning.

The Tortoise's Revenge

According to the mythology of the Fon people, divination was a gift not restricted to humans. Tortoise served as the diviner for the animal race – and he could prove a bitter enemy to anyone who failed to show him due respect.

There was no love lost between Monkey and Tortoise, the one so agile and the other so slow. So when, during a famine, Monkey found a field of grain ready for harvesting, the last thing he would normally have done was go to Tortoise for assistance. But each time he tried to get at the crop, he was driven away by the angry farmer. Eventually he concluded that he would never succeed without the Tortoise's magic, and so went to consult the diviner.

At first Tortoise was unwilling to help, saying that Monkey would run off and give him nothing in return. And when he was finally persuaded, his fears proved well founded. He starved while Monkey stuffed himself. But then Leopard came along, seeking a cure for a sick cub.

It was just the break Tortoise needed to get his revenge. When Leopard described the cub's symptoms, Tortoise told him that there was only one cure for the ailment in question: a monkey's head and tail. Then he pointed out that the ingredients were to hand, gesturing to Monkey in the nearby field.

Thus Monkey came to an untimely end. Leopard got the head and tail he needed, leaving the torso to feed the hungry Tortoise. And, said the Fon with their own diviners no doubt in mind, Tortoise also made sure he received the large fee he always charged for his services.

The Crest & the Hide

Animal fables are among the most popular of all African stories. The tales may be comic or solemn, but the picture of life that they paint is usually remarkably unsentimental. A Lega story from Congo points an uncompromising moral about the limits of friendship.

A lizard and a guinea-fowl lived in a village where the inhabitants took it in turns to be chief. When it was time for the lizard to serve its term, it did everything it could possibly think of to ensure that its investiture was suitably magnificent. It got a ceremonial drum, a sumptuous outfit, a hide to sit on and plenty of beer to refresh the onlookers.

Wanting a plume to top its headdress, the lizard sent word to its friend the guinea-fowl. The bird presented it with feathers of every shape and size, but none would do, for the lizard had set its heart on the guinea-fowl's own splendid crest. Eventually the bird unwillingly had it cut off – leaving guinea-fowl looking shorn ever since.

In time the lizard's rule ended and the guinea-fowl's own turn arrived. It too sought to do everything grandly, gathering the necessary drum, drink and finery. But again something was missing – this time a hide. So the bird demanded one from the lizard – and, on a quid pro quo basis, insisted that none would do but the lizard's own. Public opinion sided with the fowl over the request, so the lizard eventually had to agree to be skinned, with fatal results. A Lega proverb spells out the moral: Don't ask a friend for more than he can give.

How the Sun Rises & Falls

In this tale of the Mongo-Nkundo from the Congo basin, a sparrowhawk was sent up to the great god Yemekonji high in heaven to find the sun's divinely ordained position. Luckily, the brave bird was preceded by a humble fly.

The fly volunteered to accompany the sparrowhawk on its perilous mission. It proposed that it would go on ahead of the bird and eavesdrop in heaven in case Yemekonji's councillors were preparing a surprise.

The fly learned of a plan to hide the sun in one of three parcels. Two colourful ones would be filled with leaves and earth respectively; the third, in plain wrapping, would hold the sun. Thus the fly forewarned the bird.

When the sparrowhawk approached Yemekonji, the great god complained that two previous deputations had come from Earth seeking the sun: the first man had chosen the evening star, while the second had taken the moon. Yemekonji asked the sparrowhawk whether he was hiding a spy and the bird insisted it came alone; Yemekonji in any case knew about the fly.

Then the sparrowhawk was offered the choice of the three parcels and duly chose the plain one that contained the sun. Yemekonji was not upset and instructed the bird how to ease the sun into its orbit in the realm of the windkissed clouds. He went on to explain that from that time the sun would disappear and reappear in a regular pattern.

The sparrowhawk followed the great god's directions to the letter, and then, upon reaching Earth, explained that Yemekonji had plotted the sun's movements so it would set after twelve hours, then twelve hours later rise once more. Forever after it has followed this divine cycle.

Walukaga's Impossible Task

The genre of story in which a powerful ruler sets one of his subordinates an impossible task is familiar from many cultures. Once a king of the Baganda people, in what is now Uganda, tested the skill of his blacksmith Walukaga by asking him to go beyond the limits of his craft.

The king wanted to come up with something out of the ordinary that would make all men regard his territory with awe. He summoned his smith Walukaga and ordered him to make a man of flesh and blood out of iron. Now it was well known that the king would fly into a fury when crossed, so the renowned Walukaga did not demur. But he was troubled, for he saw that he was in an unenviable position: the task was beyond him, but the king would be angry if he did not achieve it.

When he asked his friends for advice, none could help him – save one, a man to whom he had been close but who had since been dismissed as mad. This fellow suggested that Walukaga should agree to take on the task – but only if certain preconditions were met. The king should command his subjects to shave their heads and burn their hair to create a thousand loads of charcoal with which to fire the furnace. He should also order them to collect their tears to make a hundred pots of water to pour on the fire and prevent the forge overheating.

Walukaga laid down his terms and the king issued the orders. But the tribesmen could not do as they had been commanded – their burnt hair provided only a single load of charcoal, and their tears just two pots of water. Then the king summoned Walukaga and announced that he was to be freed from his onerous task because the charcoal and water could not be found. Walukaga thanked his monarch and said that he had set impossible preconditions to the job because the king had asked him to perform an impossible task. The king exploded, not into fury but laughter, and Walukaga's wisdom was praised far and wide.

Eshu the Divine Trouble-maker

Eshu was an important figure for the Yoruba people of Nigeria and Benin, a divine go-between who also protected travellers. Yet the stories told of him painted a picture of a malicious trickster, someone who delighted in making mischief for mischief's sake.

One story told how Eshu had been the slave of Orisha, the Divine Spirit. Rebelling at his humiliation, he climbed a cliff behind his master's house and pushed a boulder over to flatten it. Orisha himself was crushed, but because he was a god his spirit could not die. Instead it scattered to the winds, which is why there have since been so many separate divinities, known collectively as *orishas*.

A more typical tale told how the divine trouble-maker once set out to stir up discord between two neighbours who had been friends from childhood. He made his way along the path that divided the two men's fields wearing a hat that was red on one side but white on the other. More confusingly still, he carried his pipe in such a way that it seemed to be coming out of the back of his head. The farmers were bent over the work as he passed by, but when they straightened up for a rest one commented on the odd-looking passer-by. Before long the two were quarreling bitterly about the colour of the stranger's hat and the direction in which he had been walking. At length words failed them and they began to trade blows. Finally they were dragged before the king.

Eshu came into the royal presence just as the two were explaining themselves, and he duly confessed that he had set up the quarrel. The king ordered his arrest but the trickster took flight and could not be caught. He ran through the town spreading panic by setting fire to the buildings he passed. As the people ran out of their houses trying to save their possessions, Eshu offered to look after the precious bundles. But he deliberately muddled up the parcels that were thrown at him, with the result that a fresh dispute soon began. At this point Eshu took his leave laughing.

Tricking Trikhinye

The Soninke people of Mali and Mauretania looked back to a time of past greatness more than a millennium ago when they built the empire of Ghana. They told the story of how its second ruler won preferment over his elder brother thanks to the guile of a mistreated servant.

Ghana was the greatest of the pre-Islamic kingdoms of West Africa. Rising to prominence in the first millennium CE, it owed its prosperity to the trans-Sahara trade in gold and ivory, exchanged for salt with Arab and Berber merchants from the north. According to legend its founder was a warrior chief named Dinga, who first united the Soninke tribes under his rule.

Inevitably, Dinga at last grew old. Under normal circumstances his eldest son Trikhinye would have inherited the kingship on his death. But, as the bards told the tale, he was cheated of his inheritance by a trick reminiscent of the one used by Jacob against his brother Esau in the Bible story.

In the Soninke version, the scheme was hatched by an old slave named Sitoure who had served Dinga faithfully for many years. Yet for all his loyalty, he had known nothing but abuse from Trikhinye, while the second son, Djabe Sisse, had always treated him kindly. So when the blind chief, close to death, asked for his eldest son to be brought to him for his blessing, Sitoure determined to fetch Djabe Sisse instead. But there was a problem – the younger son was smooth-skinned while the elder was rough and hairy.

Sitoure went to Djabe Sisse and explained the situation. He persuaded the young man to borrow his brother's jewelry – an armlet and a finger ring that Dinga always touched to recognize his eldest. Then he bound a piece of goatskin to the young man's arm before leading him into his father's presence.

Sightlessly, the old man reached for his son's arm and was reassured by what he felt. And so it came about that he passed on the chieftaincy to Djabe Sisse and not to his elder brother, who had expected it as his birthright.

The Gift of the River King

For many early peoples supernatural forces were everywhere – in mountains, rivers, lakes and forests. A story from Lesotho in southern Africa shows how these so-called local spirits could reward good behaviour and punish those who refused to comply.

Selekana was a beautiful young woman, and her good looks won her the admiration of all the young men – and the undying hatred of the other village girls. Eventually the girls' envy grew too much to bear, and they decided to get rid of Selekana by throwing her into a neighbouring river.

But she did not drown as they had expected. Instead she was seized by the god of the river, who took the form of a ferocious crocodile. Taking Selekana to his realm on the river-bottom, a magical place where she could live and breathe as easily as in the human world, he set her to work as a servant for his consort, River Woman.

Selekana proved to be as patient and industrious as she was pretty, and she carried out her many duties without complaining. Her forbearance so impressed River Woman that eventually the spirit decided to let her return to the human world, giving her a gift of precious stones from the riverbed as a leaving present.

The young woman's enemies were startled when she reappeared in the village, and after they had seen the valuable treasures she had brought back with her they were consumed by jealousy too. Her greatest foe was the chief's daughter. So covetous was she of her rival's wealth that she resolved to throw herself into the same river in the hope of winning even more beautiful jewels still.

But where Selekana had been patient and diligent, the newcomer was haughty and uncooperative. When the River King instructed her to serve his wife, she refused point blank. And so the giant crocodile swallowed her up, handing out the summary justice that folktales generally reserved for arrogant, greedy people.

A Dog's Life of Ease

A tale from Angola set out to explain how dogs came to be domesticated while jackals remained in the wild. As the storytellers told it, it was the dogs that took the initiative, realizing the advantages to be gained from a partnership with humans.

Modern science takes the view that the impetus behind the domestication of dogs may well have come from the canine side. The argument goes that in hunter-gatherer times wolves that approached most closely to campfires may have benefited evolutionarily from the scraps provided, winning out over their more savage cousins. The tamer the creatures became, the more their human hosts too saw the benefits of cohabitation, with the domesticated animals serving both as camp guards and as hunting partners.

The Angolan story focused on the contrasting fates of dogs and jackals. It described how Jackal and Dog originally lived as kinsmen deep in the bush. When they passed by the villages of the Mbundu people, they smelled the rich odours of meat cooking and saw men and women squatting around blazing fires. Jackal wanted fire for himself, so that he and Dog could also cook their meat. He therefore sent Dog into the village to fetch it.

When Dog arrived he ran up to a hut where a woman was scraping leftovers out of her cooking pot. She fed them to Dog and he found that they tasted good – and he realized that life in the village with food aplenty would be better than roaming the bush with Jackal, where most days hunger ruled. So Dog stayed put.

In the bush Jackal howled, as he does to this day, lamenting the fact that Dog had abandoned him and settled down with the villagers. Jackal never got fire, and now is frightened by it. He roams, hunting and scavenging, and has to eat his meat raw.

Australasia

Australasia comprises Australia itself and the islands of Oceania, and its two different parts have had very different histories. While the Australian landmass has been inhabited for at least 40,000 (and perhaps even 65,000) years, large swathes of Oceania were only populated much more recently. The Maoris arrived in New Zealand little more than a thousand years ago, making that country the last of the world's major landmasses to be settled by humans, Antarctica alone excepted.

Even so, the myths of the two regions had some common features. All reflected an animist belief in a world filled with spirits. With their long hinterland of continuous occupation, Australia's Aborigines traced the origins of these unseen presences to the Dreamtime, a primal age when ancestor beings had stalked the land, shaping the landscape and filling it with animal and plant life. Many of these mythic creators took non-human form, the giant Rainbow Snake being perhaps the best known. Siblings also played a significant role, sometimes in human guise but also in animal shape like the Melatji Law Dogs of the Bunuba people or like Kurukadi and Mumba, hybrid iguana-men credited with leaving their traces across the whole continent (see page 296).

Much of the Australian interior was dry, making the weather a central focus of the mythmakers' concern. So the occasional flooding of the Tambo River in what is now the state of Victoria was explained in terms of a slight offered to Kaboka the thrush long ago in the Dreamtime (see page 292), while for one Cape York group the rainbow got the red band in its spectrum from the blood of a murdered son of the primeval snake spirit Taipan (see page 293). Other stories addressed specific features of the natural environment. A rock rising from the sea off Tasmania's southern coast marked the fall of a star thrown down from the heavens by a victorious rival (see page 294), while a distinctive patch of ochre on a hillside in the Flinders Range was all that remained of an emu hounded to its death by a pack of Dreamtime dogs (see page 295).

The Aborigines used the word *djang* to describe the spiritual energy that attached to spots hallowed by their connections with the legendary past, seeking to tap it through rituals and dances that linked the living to their remote ancestors. The Oceanian equivalent was *mana*, a concept particularly developed in Polynesia, the archipelago's easternmost extension. (Its other components were Melanesia, incorporating New Guinea and the surrounding islands, and Micronesia, to the north of Melanesia.) *Mana* could exist in people as well as in places and objects, and anyone or anything that possessed it had to be respected and feared.

In some of the larger islands *mana* served to underpin a highly stratified society based on clans tracing their genealogy back to ancestors venerated as gods. Chiefs were chosen from the direct line of descent and ruled in the name of their deified forebears. Their divine extraction gave them sacred power, and an elaborate system of prohibitions known as *tapu* – the origin of the English word "taboo" – maintained their special status. In Hawaii, commoners could be put to death for failing to bow down before their sovereign. Something of the terror people must have felt in the rulers' presence comes over in the story of Eleio, a royal messenger who feared for his life when he was delayed in carrying out one of his master's commissions (see page 303).

One feature of the islanders' stories that has long fascinated mythographers is the odd echoes they contain of plots familiar from far distant lands. Vanuatu, for example, had its own version (see page 300) of the swan maiden motif known from many parts of the world, including Ireland (see page 70) and Mongolia (see page 173). Similarly, a tale from Tonga strangely paralleled the Greek legend of Pandora's box, repeating its theme of a woman whose fatal curiosity to know forbidden knowledge unleashed untold evils in its wake (see page 305).

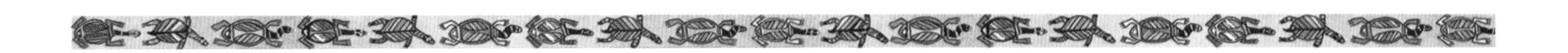

The Thrush & the Flood

Floods have always been a recurrent danger in Australia, a predominantly dry land in which periods of drought are often broken by brief outbursts of torrential rain. Myth provided a variety of explanations for the phenomenon, most of them involving Dreamtime creatures.

Some myths spoke of a great Dreamtime flood that swept away the original creation. Different stories were told to explain its onset; according to one version the Wandjina weather spirits sent it as retribution after a group of children captured and tortured an owl, a bird that was sacred to the spirits.

Other folktales had a more limited resonance. One told by the Gunai people from the Gippsland region of Victoria blamed a local deluge on Tiddalick the frog, who once became feverish and drank so much that he emptied all the watercourses in the world. The other creatures were at a loss as to how to make him disgorge the water, until someone persuaded No-Yang the eel to dance on his tail. The spectacle was so droll that Tiddalick burst out laughing. As he did so, water gushed from his mouth, causing a flood in which many creatures drowned.

Another story from Victoria blamed Kaboka the thrush for the first flooding of the Tambo River. After an unsuccessful day's hunting he returned to camp with nothing to show for his efforts but a single, scrawny wallaby. Still, he made ready to cook it and share it out just the same. But his companions scorned his offering, complaining about such a meagre meal.

Angered by his friends' ingratitude, the thrush took the food back and told them to catch their own. Furious, he lit a sacred fire and danced round it for hours until he had raised a storm of wind and rain. He danced on and the rain kept falling down until the whole country was awash and his companions were all drowned. When the Tambo floods today, people say it is due to Kaboka remembering his day of rage.

Taipan, the Shaman-Snake

The snake was invested with deep symbolic significance in Australian myth. Its bite could bring death but its furious coilings carried a suggestion of the quickening impulse of life at creation's heart.

Among the Wik Kalkan of the Cape York Peninsula in northern Queensland, the story of the snake-deity Taipan is told. A powerful magician, he could cure the sick – or kill the healthy – at will. He could control not only human life and death but the elements: the lightning flashed and the thunder rumbled at his command. For wives he had the watersnakes Uka and Tuknampa, and Mantya the death-adder. Only one child had been born of these alliances, however: a fine son, whom Taipan loved above all things.

One day the youth decided to go hunting downriver. He saw the watersnake Tintauwa, wife of Wala the blue-tongued lizard, and immediately fell in love with her. She seduced him, and they ran away together into the bush.

Wala gave chase and murdered Taipan's son. The magician was left desolate by his loss. Calling his family together he daubed them all with the blood of his child, before sending them down to take up residence in the earth in whose depths he himself soon joined them. His two sisters, meanwhile, he sent off to the highest heaven, telling them to add their nephew's red blood to the other colours of the rainbow. It can be seen there to this day, richest colour in the spectrum of the arc of life, in which it stands symbolically for the regenerative blood of menstruation.

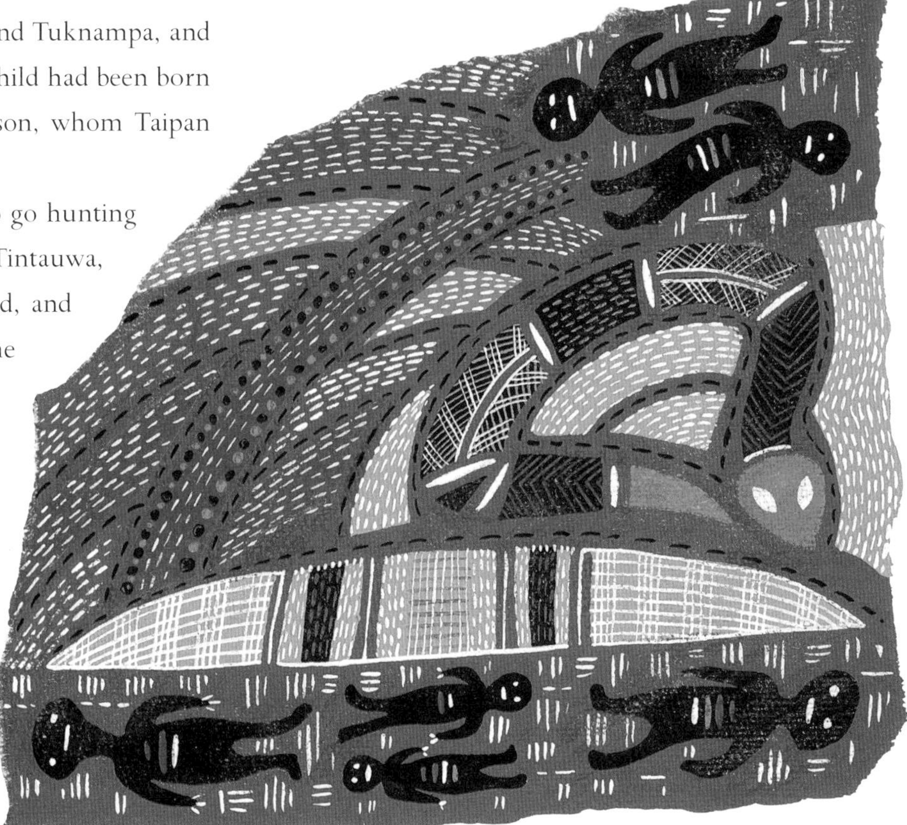

The First Tasmanians

The making of men and women has no part in most Aboriginal traditions. So close were the Aborigines to nature that they were able to see themselves as just another part of the landscape. One of the few accounts of the origins of humankind comes from Tasmania.

Long ago, the two brightest stars in the firmament were Moinee and Dromerdeener, rivals for supreme mastery of the sky, who resolved to fight it out after epochs of tension and bickering. The other stars looked on helplessly until the duel was over: Moinee was defeated and cast out of the heavenly realm. Dromerdeener stormed across the sky on his victory trail as his rival fell forlornly to Earth. He came to rest off the southern Tasmanian coast, and can still be seen, a large boulder in the sea at Sandy Bay.

Before he died, however, Moinee bestowed a great gift on his earthly home, creating the first Tasmanians to occupy its empty spaces. In his haste, however, he gave them tails like kangaroos – worse still, he neglected to give them jointed knees. They had to spend their whole lives standing up, quite unable to lie or hunker down: soon they cried to the heavens to take pity on their plight. Dromerdeener finally heard their call: ruthless though he was, he was moved by what he saw. Descending from heaven, he chopped off their tails and rubbed healing grease upon the wounds. Then to the middle of each leg he added a hinge-like knee: the people were now free to squat or lie down as they wanted.

The Emu & the Ochre

Many Aboriginal stories had the function of explaining distinctive features of the Outback landscape. One such traced the origins of a patch of ochre on a southern Australian hillside to a hunting incident that took place in the Dreamtime.

When Europeans arrived in Australia, one of the many surprises the native fauna held for them was the emu, a large, flightless bird that had survived for millennia for want of predators. That situation changed with the advent of firearms; within decades two island species and the Tasmanian subspecies had become extinct, although the mainland birds are still thriving.

Prior to the coming of the Europeans, Aborigines had hunted the birds, as a Dreamtime story indicated. It told how one day a man was out walking with his dogs in the Flinders Range when the animals suddenly stiffened, startled by a rustling in the undergrowth. They had disturbed an emu, which fled headlong in terror.

Over hills and mountains the bird ran with the dogs in pursuit, fording rivers, leaping streams and scrambling over rocks. Slowly, the dogs gained on their quarry, which was visibly tiring. Yet at the final moment they were cheated of their prey. The emu ran straight into a hillside where it remains to this day – a rift of finest ochre, as red as gushing blood.

The Iguana-Men

Sibling pairs, both animal and human, played a great part in the mythology of the Dreamtime. Kurukadi and Mumba, the iguana-men, were merely one example of a common mythic type found in Aboriginal tales from across the Australian continent.

One strand of Aboriginal myth told of the brothers Yuree and Wanjel, who ended up ascending into the night sky as the twin stars known in the West as Castor and Pollux. Another concerned the Melatji Law Dogs, two dingoes who travelled south across the continent, digging waterholes and spreading knowledge of the fundamental laws of nature on the way.

The prevalence of siblings in myth may in part reflect the Aboriginal habit of using the terms "brother" and "sister" to cover most close relatives of the same generation. Yet it also highlighted a recurring dualism in traditional thought. So Kurukadi and Mumba were not just brothers but also had twin identities, part human and part lizard. The stories told how they travelled southeast from the Kimberley region, naming plants and creatures and fashioning the landscape across much of the western desert. They hurled their magic boomerang as they went: as it soared across the wastes, the land took on form and definition beneath its flight.

The iguana-men's journey is thought not to have ended until they had crossed the continent, their travels having taken them across the lands of many peoples. As so often happens in Aboriginal culture, each tribe knows its own section of the "songline" and remains more or less in ignorance of the rest. To the outside observer it is clear, however, that the myth of the iguana-men is one of those tales that spans all Australia, bringing its various peoples together in an unwitting cultural union.

The Blackening of the Crow

Only seven wise women originally understood the mystery of fire, say the Aboriginal people of Victoria: all through the Dreamtime they guarded their secret jealously. The cunning crow-man was no respecter of other people's property: he resolved to find out what they knew.

First ingratiating himself with the sacred guardians by flattery and gifts, he was soon sharing their conversation and assisting them in their work. He noticed that they carried flames of fire on the tips of their digging-sticks; and that they loved to eat termites but were terrified of snakes. So, carefully concealing a knot of coiling serpents in a termites' nest, he went to see his new friends and invited them to join him in a banquet. They followed him eagerly to the termite mound and broke it open with glee – only to fall back in horror when the snakes spilled forth in a writhing mass. Laying about them in a panic, the women failed to notice the flames falling from their sticks. The crow-man gathered them up, and nursed the fire in some soft bark kindling. Now it was he who hugged the secret to himself, refusing to share it with anyone. Beset by constant questions from men anxious to acquire fire for themselves, his selfishness was almost his undoing. Losing his temper with one man who seemed unprepared to take no for an answer, he hurled a burning coal at him, but the missile fell short and set fire to the very patch of ground on which the crow himself was sitting. It seemed to those who saw the resulting blaze that he must surely be burned to a crisp – till suddenly they saw his blackened body stir in the smoke and flame and take wing to a nearby tree. From there he cawed at them mockingly, the sooty-feathered crow that he has remained ever since.

The Boomerang & the Sun

From the Aborigine people of the Flinders Range of southern Australia comes the astonishing story of how the distinction first arose between night and day – for in the world's infancy, it seems, all was light and sunshine, with no intervening darkness.

The trouble started one Dreamtime day when the goanna lizard and the gecko discovered that their neighbours had been massacred: with one voice they vowed vengeance upon those responsible. It had, it soon transpired, been the sun-woman and her dingo dogs who had attacked and killed the defenceless community: she was a formidable foe, but the goanna and the gecko were quite undaunted. As the sun-woman stormed and shouted her defiance, the lizard hurled his boomerang – and dashed the sun clean out of the sky. It plummeted over the western horizon, plunging the world into darkness – and now the lizard and the gecko really were alarmed. They must do everything they could to restore the sun-woman to the heavens. The goanna took another boomerang and hurled it westward with all his might to where he had seen his target disappearing. It fell ineffectually to ground so he threw two others to the south and north, but they too drifted back without hitting anything. In despair, the goanna took his last boomerang and launched it into the eastern sky – the opposite direction from that in which he had seen the sun-woman sinking. To his astonishment it returned, driving before it the sun's burning sphere, which tracked westward across the sky before disappearing. From that day on the sun maintained this course, rising in the east and setting in the west – lighting up the day for work and hunting, and casting the night into shade for sleeping. All agreed this was an ideal arrangement, and the Aborigines of the Flinders have felt a debt of gratitude to the goanna and the gecko ever since.

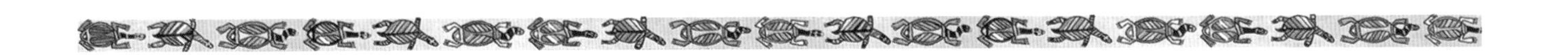

Yam-Woman & Arrowroot-Man

A staple for many Aboriginal peoples, the yam inevitably had a special place in their myths. Cultivated and cooked by the women, it tended to be identified with the feminine principle in general and pregnancy in particular, as a story from the Cape York Peninsula showed.

The local Wik Munggan people enjoyed an environment that was rich in foodstuffs, at least in comparison with those available to the desert-dwellers of the Red Centre. Yams and arrowroot grew there naturally, and the Aborigines had a story that not only commemorated the plants' origins but also reminded people where to find them.

It claimed that in the Dreamtime, before things had taken on their present forms, the yam was a woman herself. Not far from her lived the arrowroot – then a man. The two met and fell in love, living together as man and wife: but their relationship was always quarrelsome, and in the course of time they parted.

Before long, however, the woman started to feel queasy and out of sorts. Pregnant, she scraped out a little hollow in the ground in the hope of making herself more comfortable. She had to dig herself in deeper and deeper to accommodate her bulging figure, but the further down she sank, the more claustrophobic and hot she felt. The sun beat down and she thirsted for water. She was desperate now to escape, but the sides were steep and she could not climb them. In time she resigned herself to her imprisonment, recognizing it as a part of her reproductive function: from this hole would issue an abundance of yams for future women to cook for food.

Meanwhile, without Yam-Woman to look after him, Arrowroot-Man grew old and helpless. Soon he could hardly walk without a stick. One day he staggered to the waterside in search of a drink, but collapsed on the bank and was swallowed up by the ground. Only his stick remained, protruding as the arrowroot's stalk to remind future generations where to find the plant's starchy tubers.

Swan Maidens

The story of the swan maidens was widespread throughout Melanesia. The main character, to whom the heavenly women appeared, could be one of the islands' culture heroes or sometimes – as among Vanuatu's Efate people – a simple human.

There was a divine race of women who visited Earth in the guise of swans. They came down at night, when the tide was out, and discarded their wings to go fishing. When dawn came and the tide turned they would pick up their wings and fly home. One night, however, a man saw them at work. He stole a pair of wings which he buried under the main post of his house. Come daybreak the swan maidens flew home – all save one beautiful woman who could not find her wings. The man seized her and made her his wife. They had two children, both boys, whose names were Tafaki and Karisi Bum.

In time, however, the man grew tired of his wife and began to beat her. She wept bitter tears that washed away the earth floor of their home. The more she wept the more the soil ran away until, one day, she spotted the wings her husband had hidden. She put them on and flew up to the sky, telling her sons to find her when they were able.

The boys became rich and clever men. Their powers were such that they climbed a palm tree armed with clubs in order to beat the winds into submission. Although unsuccessful, they managed nevertheless to turn the southwest wind into a whimpering, soon-forgotten thing.

When the two sons were out hunting they fired an arrow at a bird flying high in the sky. It missed its target and hit a celestial banyan tree. They fired more arrows, each of which hit the other until there was a chain leading down to Earth. Climbing up it, they discovered not their swan-maiden mother but their blind grandmother, who was tending yams. They were able to cure her blindness and descended the arrow-ladder with a basket containing her thanks: pigs, fowl, yams and every plant that could possibly be of use to humankind.

Male Prestige

In Melanesia men claimed the social high ground. They reinforced their status by carrying bags which contained – so they said – myths of origin available only to males.

This quasi-masonic system was echoed throughout Melanesia, resulting in secret societies which acted both as stepping stones to social advancement and repositories of ancient lore. Shrouded in mystery, their proceedings were accompanied by elaborate rituals that were spiritual in intent but which often led to periods of mayhem and debauchery.

In the Banks Islands, male prestige revolved around the Suque, a secret society that involved several grades. An initiate would be proposed by his uncle – to whom he would give a pig – who would then hold a feast for fellow Suque members. Each step up the ladder involved larger payments and more elaborate feasts until the member's status was made plain to all.

The practice was encapsulated in a myth involving a hero called Ganviviris and his sponsor, the sea spirit Ro Som. The sea spirit sponsored Ganviviris so fulsomely that in a single feast he was able to buy his way through two grades of Suque. With Ro Som's help Ganviviris leaped from stage to stage, buying his way with extraordinary pigs whose tusks formed perfect circles.

Once he had reached the top, however, Ganviviris turned his eyes to other Suques, one of which Ro Som had forbidden him to join. Disaster struck: one of Ganviviris's feasts was interrupted by the arrival of a woman smeared with red earth and wearing pigs' tails in her hair. The men looked on aghast as the apparition made her way to Ganviviris's house. No sooner had she entered the door than they rushed after her. But she was gone. And so was Ganviviris's wealth. Unable to maintain his status, Ganviviris was thrown out of the Suque and died five days later.

Hina, the Eel & the Coconut

Hina (translating simply as "young woman") was the Polynesian goddess of women and women's work. In a culture where the writing of love poems and the initiation of courtship were a female prerogative, some of Hina's tales were practical and others blatantly sexual.

Hina enjoyed bathing in a sea pool full of eels. Normally they fled at her approach, but one more daring than the rest got into the habit of wrapping itself round her legs. Hina treated it as a pet until one day it magically turned into a handsome young man called Tuna. The two became lovers, but Tuna changed back to eel form after every visit so nobody would suspect their liaison.

Eventually Tuna brought the affair to a close. He announced that a great rain would come, causing a flood that would rise to the door of Hina's house. But she was not to be afraid, for he would swim up to her home and lay his head on the threshold. She was then to cut off his head, bury it on high ground and see what happened next.

Everything occurred as Tuna had predicted, and Hina did as she was told. When the waters subsided, two green shoots appeared where she had buried the head that grew into the very first coconut tree. Lest people forget their benefactor, they had only to remove the husk of a ripened coconut to find markings recalling the two small eyes and mouth of an eel.

The Maoris of New Zealand told a similar tale, but with a less uplifting moral. In their version, Hina was the wife of the trickster Maui, who found out about her infidelity. In revenge, he constructed a channel provided with canoe skids and tempted Tuna to swim up it. Having trapped him with no easy way out, he proceeded to chop his rival into pieces.

The Cloak, Alu Hula

Cloaks made of red feathers epitomized majesty on Hawaii. They were believed to descend from Alu Hula, the first such garment to be brought to the Hawaiian Archipelago, which was given to a man named Eleio, the fastest of the chief of Maui's messengers.

It was said that Eleio could run around Maui in the time it took to cook one side of a fish. He also had the gifts of seeing otherwise invisible spirits and returning life to a corpse.

Eleio's job was not always easy. His chief threatened him with death if he was late, and sometimes he would be taunted by spirit-women who sought to delay him. When that happened he would call upon his sister to shame them with a display of her naked bottom. Once, however, Eleio came across a spirit so beautiful that he had to chase her. He finally caught her at the entrance to a cave. In return for her life she pointed out her parents' home and agreed to bring him their cloak of red feathers, Alu Hula. Having pledged her word she disappeared.

Disgruntled, Eleio went to find the cloak himself. He met the spirit-woman's parents and made a deal: he would revive their daughter in return for the cloak. Eleio was given not only the cloak but the spirit-woman as a wife. Yet there was one big problem: Eleio was late.

Evading the sentries, he presented his master with a beautiful wife – the resurrected spirit-woman – and Alu Hula. The chief accepted the gifts and spared Eleio. From that time Hawaiian royalty wore a cloak of red feathers and claimed descent from the spirit world.

The Rat & the Bat

Unlike the inhabitants of the rest of Polynesia, whose myths revolved mainly around the sea, the people of Tonga and Samoa also recounted tales of land mammals – among them the rat that cheated the fruit bat.

Over the course of the centuries rats found their way to all the larger Polynesian islands. Sea voyagers travelling by raft to new homes may in some cases have deliberately carried them, for in lands that were short of meat they served as food. Although Tonga and Samoa had no greater variety of the creatures than other places save the relatively barren Chathams, their mythological presence may have reflected a distant memory of life on the mainland.

One story that carried a rather depressing warning against being overtrustful toward friends told how, in the primeval time before creatures' identities were firmly fixed, the rat and the fruit bat changed roles. The rat was envious of the fruit bat's wings and devised a stratagem whereby it could acquire them. Watching the fruit bat to see which berries it liked best, the rat positioned itself under an ifi tree, and when the bat came to eat there the rat asked it why it was trespassing on its personal food supply. Sweeping aside the bat's apologies, the rat said it did not mind too much and that they should both be friends. As a sign of their friendship the rat would let the bat eat from the ifi tree; all it asked in return was to borrow the bat's wings so that it could experience flight.

The bat reluctantly handed over its wings with the warning that the rat must not take too long in returning them. The rat gave the bat its paws and tail to look after, then soared into the sky, never to be seen again. Thereafter, whenever one Samoan chief cheated another, the people would say, "But did you not know of the friendship of the bat and the rat?"

The Sun's Unwanted Gift

The awe inspired by nature's elemental forces was a wellspring of world mythology, and Polynesian myth was no exception. A story from Tonga warned of the devastating legacy of a union between the sun god and a mortal woman.

Crossing the heavens one day, the sun's gaze fell upon a beautiful, half-naked woman who was catching fish. Immediately attracted to her, he decided to approach her in human form, and nine months later she bore him a son, Sisimatailaa. The boy grew up a handsome youth, and when the time came to marry he had no trouble finding a bride. But he wanted his father's blessing on the union, so at his mother's suggestion he climbed to the top of the island's highest mountain to beg the sun's permission for him to take a wife.

His appeal did not go unanswered. Two bundles dropped down from the sky, and with them came a warning – only one should be opened, while the other must remain untouched. He returned home with the packages, and when he unwrapped the first he found a treasure of gold and silver inside.

He kept close watch on the other bundle to make sure that the god's instructions were obeyed, and it lay unopened for months. But then one day he and his wife went out together fishing. In the heat of the afternoon, the young man fell asleep; and while he dozed, his wife came across the mysterious package. Like her Greek counterpart Pandora, she was consumed by curiosity to know what might be inside, and the consequences of her inquisitiveness were to prove just as dire. For in opening the bundle she released storms and tempests into the world, and she and her husband became their first victims when the savage winds capsized their boat, sending them to a watery grave beneath the waves.

Glossary

Ahura Mazda
The creator god of Persia's Zoroastrian faith and the embodiment of truth and universal order.

Angra Mainyu
The spirit of destruction in the Zoroastrian worldview, a figure of evil constantly seeking to undo the creative work of the benevolent Ahura Mazda.

Anzu
A huge bird of Mesopotamian myth, sometimes portrayed as an eagle with a lion's head. Its best-known exploit was to steal the Tablet of Destinies from the sky god Enlil.

Apophis
In Egyptian myth, the cosmic serpent that swallowed the sun at the end of its daily journey across the sky. Each evening the sun god Re had to defeat Apophis to proceed on his nocturnal journey through the Underworld. Yet, as a god himself, Apophis could not be killed; so the struggle repeated itself endlessly, with the future of the world depending on Re's continued victories.

apsu
In Mesopotamian mythology, fresh water, conceived as coming from an underground ocean. This subterranean aquifer was seen as a counterpart to the saltwater seas.

Asgard
The home of the gods in Norse mythology.

Avesta
The holy book of the Zoroastrian religion. The oldest portions are thought to have been written by the prophet Zoroaster himself.

Bochica
The culture hero of the Chibcha people of Colombia, who taught humans how to grow crops and work metals, and introduced the moral code and the rule of law. He was portrayed in legend as a bearded man who came from the east; when his work was done, he disappeared westward to devote himself to an ascetic life.

bodhisattva
In Buddhist parlance, a future Buddha who puts the attainment of enlightenment on hold to enable him (or her) to assist suffering humankind. In the Mahayana tradition followed in Tibet, Mongolia and the Far East, *bodhisattvas* have a role equivalent to Christian saints, and are themselves objects of veneration. For followers of Theravada Buddhism, the dominant faith of Sri Lanka and much of Southeast Asia, the term simply implies someone on the path to enlightenment.

Bon
The native religion of Tibet, predating the arrival of Buddhism in the country. An animist faith, Bon profoundly influenced the development of Tibetan Buddhism and still has practitioners, known as *bonpos*, within Tibet to this day.

bylina

An early form of Russian epic poetry, describing supposedly historical events in blank verse. Initially the *byliny* were passed down orally.

centaurs

Hybrid creatures from classical mythology, with the head, torso and arms of men and the bodies of horses.

Chibchachum

The creator god of the Chibcha people, responsible for the shaping of the Earth. A mother goddess named Bachué was credited with giving birth to the human race.

codex (pl. codices)

A hand-written manuscript in book form, generally predating the invention of printing. Mesoamerican codices were mostly produced on a single long sheet of fig-bark paper, folded concertina-style.

Coyote

A leading figure in the myths of the Native American peoples of the Great Plains and Far West, Coyote often featured in stories as a trickster, but also played a wider role as a creator or culture hero. Despite his name, Coyote generally walked and talked like a human, although he could take animal form if he chose.

culture hero

A figure familiar from mythologies around the world who introduces essential survival skills such as cooking, weaving, hunting, fishing or agriculture to the human race. Culture heroes may be human but are most often divine; frequently they take the guise of legendary early rulers.

Djabe Sisse

A legendary ruler of the Soninke people of West Africa, said to have been the son of the empire-builder Dinga. Having used trickery to cheat his elder brother of the throne, Djabe subsequently had to strike a Faustian bargain with an earth-serpent that allowed him to rule only in exchange for the annual sacrifice of the most beautiful maiden in his capital.

Dobrynya

One of the best-known of the *bogatyrs*, heroes of the medieval Russian epics known as *byliny*. He was particularly reputed for his courage.

domovoi

The domestic spirits of Slav tradition, playing a similar role to that of Germany's kobolds or the boggarts and brownies of British folklore.

Dreamtime

For Australia's aboriginal peoples, a mythical era in the remote past when spirit beings shaped the landscape.

earthdiver

In Native American myth, a creature – often a bird – dispatched to the bottom of the primeval ocean to bring up mud subsequently used by a creator god or culture hero to create land.

El Cid

A legendary Spanish hero of medieval times, famed for his battles with the Moors. The stories drew their inspiration from a real-life figure, Rodrigo Díaz de Vivar, who lived in the eleventh century and served as the chief general of King Alfonso VI of Castile.

Elysian Fields

The paradise of classical myth, a part of the Underworld reserved for the souls of the virtuous, who wandered there among shady groves and fields of asphodel.

Eshu

A Yoruba god who presided over travellers and over good and bad fortune as well as personifying death. Eshu was a trickster figure who delighted in causing trouble; some stories quoted him as saying "Bringing strife is my greatest joy". Belief in Eshu travelled to the New World on the slave ships, and he is invoked today by followers of the Candomblé and Santería religious traditions in the Caribbean and on the American mainland.

Fates

The Moirae of classical mythology, three sisters who determined the destiny of new-born children, appearing three nights after the birth to set the course of the infant's future life. They were usually depicted as sinister hags, unresponsive to the hopes of parents and merciless in their judgments.

Fields of Aaru

Literally the Fields of Reeds, the ancient Egyptian paradise where the souls of the righteous dead enjoyed a happy afterlife under the protection of the god Osiris in a fertile land resembling the Nile Delta. Only souls that survived judgment in the Hall of the Two Truths were allowed to proceed to this Egyptian Elysium.

Firbolg

One of the early groups to inhabit Ireland, identified by some scholars with the Belgae, a Celtic tribe based in northern France.

Hades

The Underworld of classical myth and also the name of its ruler, alternatively known as Pluto. Hades was generally regarded as a sad and gloomy place, although one section, the Elysian Fields, represented a kind of pastoral Arcadia, while another, Tartarus, was a place of torment similar to the Christian Hell.

Hero Twins

Known individually as Hunahpu and Xbalanque, the chief protagonists of the *Popol Vuh*, which presents them as champions of cosmic order battling the evil forces of the Mayan underworld that had been responsible for the deaths of their father and uncle.

Honingi

Also known as Ninigi-no-Mikoto, one of the gods of Shintoism and a grandson of the sun goddess Amaterasu, who dispatched him with the imperial regalia to Japan, where he married a human princess. Jimmu, the first emperor of Japan, was the couple's great-grandson.

Izumo

A province of ancient Japan, located in the southern part of the island of Honshu, that played an important role in the nation's legendary history. To this day the Izumo Shrine is one of the most sacred sites of the Shinto faith.

Jotunheim

The home of the giants in Norse myth, also sometimes known as Giantland.

Kali

The Hindu goddess of death and destruction, described in myth as dancing on battlefields where she became intoxicated by drinking the blood of the corpses. Yet Kali also had a maternal aspect, providing the blessing of her protection to those who showed her proper respect.

klu

Water spirits that performed much the same function in Tibetan myth that the *naga* serpent-kings played in Indian legend. Both were semi-divine creatures of great power that guarded springs, wells and rivers. Humans needed to propitiate them to avoid rousing their anger.

Langobards

The Latinized name of the Lombards, a Germanic people who invaded Italy in 568 CE, subsequently giving their name to the region of Lombardy.

Lianja

Culture hero of the Mongo-Nkundo of central Africa, born fully-grown and armed, who led his people to their ancestral homelands.

maat

The ancient Egyptian principle of order and harmony, sometimes personified as a goddess. Her symbol was a feather, which played a crucial role in the judgment faced by the souls of the dead when seeking admission to the afterlife. In the Underworld Hall of the Two Truths they had to make the so-called Negative Confession, denying having committed a list of wrongs while their heart was weighed in the balance against Maat's feather. Those who failed the test were swallowed up forever.

maenads

Female devotees of the Greek god Dionysus (known as Bacchus to the Romans) who were known for the ecstatic frenzy of their rites. The name means literally "raving ones".

mana

The name that Oceanian peoples gave to the spiritual power that pervades the universe, manifesting itself in animals, plants and inanimate objects as well as in exceptional individuals. People possessing *mana* could achieve great feats.

Midgard

The human realm in Norse myth. It was thought to be encircled by an band of ocean, the home of the monstrous Jormungand, also known as the Midgard Serpent.

Milesians

In Ireland's legendary prehistory, the last wave of settlers to arrive on the island, where they defeated the Tuatha de Danaan, driving them underground. They were said to have come from Iberia, and are now generally regarded to have been the forebears of the Gaelic Celts.

Ometeotl

The Mesoamerican creator god, having both male and female attributes, who was held responsible for sending the seeds of those about to be born down to Earth. Unlike such other leading deities as Quetzalcoatl or Tezcatlipoca, Ometeotl was a remote figure rarely represented in art and with no cult dedicated to him/her.

Perun

The chief god of the pagan Slavs, linked with thunder and lightning and also with war and weapons. He was thought of as a bearded figure wielding an axe or hammer and riding a chariot drawn by a goat.

Popol Vuh

A sacred manuscript of the Quiché people of Guatemala and the principal surviving source for Mayan myth.

Quatre Fils Aymon

The title of a twelfth-century French *chanson de geste* (epic poem describing heroic deeds), also sometimes known by the name of its hero, Renaud de Montauban.

Saami

Indigenous people of the northern parts of Sweden, Norway, Finland and the Kola Peninsula of Russia, a cultural area often referred to by outsiders as Lapland although it is correctly known as Sápmi.

Sage Kings

A trio of rulers in China's distant past who provided good governance and introduced vital arts of civilization. Named Yao, Shun and Yu the Great, they were praised by Confucius as models for subsequent emperors to follow.

Sedna

Also known as Arnakuagsaq and as Nerrivik, an Inuit sea goddess who presided over the creatures that live in the oceans, particularly the seals, walruses and whales. In times of hardship, shamans made spirit journeys to her underwater domain to persuade her to release her charges so that human hunters could catch them.

Shahnameh

Persia's national epic, a work in rhyming couplets seven times the length of Homer's *Iliad* written by the poet Ferdowsi between 977 and 1010 CE. It recounts the story of Iran from the nation's mythical origins up to the time of the Muslim conquest.

Sigurd

The central figure of the Norse *Volsung Saga* and the Norse equivalent of Germany's Siegfried, hero of the *Nibelungenlied*, a Middle German epic that drew much of its plot from the earlier work. Sigurd's most famous exploit was to kill the dragon Fafnir and take possession of the golden hoard of the dwarf Andvari, cursed to bring misfortune on whoever possessed it.

soma

The drink of the gods in Hindu myth, from which they drew their divine power and energy. There was also a real-life drink of the same name that played a central part in Vedic rituals, where it was thought to convey godlike qualities on those who consumed it.

songlines

In aboriginal myth, the tracks followed in the Dreamtime by the totemic spirit creatures who shaped the Australian landscape. As they went, they sang out the names of the animals, plants, rocks and other natural features that they created or passed on their way. Aboriginal groups still preserve some of the songs, thereby celebrating and renewing their bond with their ancestral lands.

Swerga

The Hindu heaven, thought to lie on and above Mt Meru. It provided a temporary abode for the souls of the righteous while they awaited either rebirth or else assumption into the godhead if they had attained *moksha* – liberation from the eternal cycle of death and rebirth.

Tablet of Destinies

Taking the form of a clay table inscribed with cuneiform writing, a legal document that in Mesopotamian myth was considered to bestow supreme authority over the cosmos on its possessor. Various gods contested its ownership.

Taira

With the Minamoto, one of two warrior clans that competed for domination in twelfth-century Japan. The Taira went down to defeat at the naval Battle of Dannoura in 1185 CE, after which the Minamoto chief Yoritomo took power as Japan's first shogun, or military leader.

tengri

A name applied to the gods of Mongolia's native, pre-Buddhist religion, shared with other Turkic peoples and sometimes referred to as Tengriism. The principal deity of this animist faith was himself called Tengri.

Tuatha de Danaan

Legendary early inhabitants of Ireland who are thought to reflect folk memories of the island's ancient Celtic gods, transformed into historical figures by chroniclers writing at a much later date. The name literally meant "People of the Goddess Danu". After their defeat by the Milesians they took refuge underground in the *sidhe* or fairy mounds, where they formed an alternative society alongside the human world.

Valhalla

In Norse myth, the hall where warriors who had died in battle enjoyed an eternity of alternate fighting and carousing. It belonged to the god Odin.

valkyries

Minor divinities of Norse myth who escorted the souls of dead heroes either to Valhalla or else to Folkvangr, a similar hall in the possession of the goddess Freyja.

Vedas

The scriptures of Hinduism and India's most ancient literary texts. Hindus regard them as divinely revealed, and many elements from them feature in prayers and rituals. They survive in four collections: the Rigveda, Yajurveda, Samaveda and Atharvaveda.

Viracocha

The supreme creator god of the Incas and the father of the sun god Inti, from whom the empire's rulers claimed descent.

Wagadu

The legendary capital of the ancient empire of Ghana, which flourished in sub-Saharan West Africa in the final centuries of the first millennium CE. Myth claimed that the city owed its prosperity to annual sacrifices made to a seven-headed snake; when a hero finally killed the serpent, drought ensued, the capital had to be abandoned, and the empire eventually collapsed.

Yellow Emperor

Known as Huang Di in Chinese, this legendary early ruler of China was said to have ruled in the twenty-seventh century BCE. He was credited with incredible feats of valour as well as with introducing essential benefits to the nation, among them silk weaving, traditional Chinese medicine and the Chinese calendar. On his death, Huang Di ascended to heaven to become the chief god of the Daoist pantheon.

Zoroaster

Also known as Zarathustra, the prophet of the Zoroastrian religion and the composer of its oldest liturgical texts, preserved today in the *Avesta*.

Further Reading

Alexander, H.B. *The Mythology of All Races: Latin America.* Kessinger Publishing: Montana, 1920.

Ashe, Geoffrey. *The Discovery of King Arthur.* The History Press: Gloucestershire, new ed., 2005.

Ashkenazi, Michael. *Handbook of Japanese Mythology.* Oxford University Press USA: Maryland, 2008.

Barber, Richard. *Myths and Legends of the British Isles.* Boydell Press: Suffolk, 1999.

Baring-Gould, Sabine. *Myths of the Middle Ages.* Blandford Press: Dorset, new ed. 1996.

Belcher, Stephen (ed.). *African Myths of Origin.* Penguin Classics: London, 2005.

Bierhorst, John. *The Mythology of North America.* Oxford University Press: Oxford, new ed., 2002.

Birrell, Anne. *Chinese Mythology: An Introduction.* John Hopkins University Press: Maryland, new ed., 1999.

Black, Jeremy and Green, Anthony. *Gods, Demons and Symbols of Ancient Mesopotamia.* British Museum Press: London, 1992.

Byock, Jesse L. (trans.). *Sagas and Myths of the Northmen.* Penguin Classics: London, 2006.

Courlander, Harold. *A Treasury of African Folklore.* Marlowe & Co.: New York, 1996.

Crossley-Holland, Kevin. *The Penguin Book of Norse Myths: Gods of the Vikings.* Penguin Books: London, new ed., 1996.

Curtin, Jeremiah. *Myths and Folk Tales of the Russians, Western Slavs, and Magyars.* Dover Publications Inc.: New York, 2003.

Curtis, Vesta Sarkhosh. *Persian Myths.* British Museum Press: London, 1993.

Dalley, Stephanie (trans.). *Myths from Mesopotamia.* Oxford World Classics: Oxford, new ed., 1998.

Davies, Sioned (trans.). *The Mabinogion.* Oxford University Press: Oxford, 2007.

Davis, Dick (trans.). *Shahnameh: The Persian Book of Kings.* Penguin Classics: London, 2007.

Ellis Davidson, H.R. *Gods and Myths of Northern Europe.* Penguin Books: London, 1990.

El-Mahdy, Christine. *Mummies, Myth and Magic in Ancient Egypt.* Thames & Hudson: London, 1991.

Erdoes, Richard and Ortiz, Alfonso (eds.). *American Indian Myths and Legends.* Random House Inc.: London, 1990.

Grant, Michael. *Myths of the Greeks and Romans.* Weidenfeld & Nicolson: London, new ed., 2001.

Graves, Robert. *The Greek Myths.* Folio Society: London, 1996.

Green, Miranda J. *Dictionary of Celtic Myth and Legend.* Thames & Hudson Ltd: London, new ed., 1997.

Guppy, Shusha. *The Secret of Laughter: Magical Tales from Classical Persia.* I.B. Tauris: London, 2005.

Hadland Davis, F. *Myths and Legends of Japan.* Dover Publications Inc.: New York, new ed., 1992.

Hardin, Terri (ed.). *Legends and Lore of the American Indians.* Barnes & Noble: New York, 1993.

Heissig, Walther. Samuel, Geoffrey (trans.). *The Religions of Mongolia.* University of California Press: California, 1992.

Karmay, Samten G. and Watt, Jeff (eds.). *Bon: The Magic Word – The Indigenous Religion of Tibet*. Philip Wilson Publishers: London, 2007.

Knappert, Jan. *African Mythology*. Diamond Books: London, 1995.

Knappert, Jan. *Pacific Mythology*. Diamond Books: London, 1995.

Kononenko, Natalie O. *Slavic Folklore: A Handbook*. Greenwood Press: Connecticut, 2007.

Krueger Roberta L. (ed.). *The Cambridge Companion to Medieval Romance*. Cambridge University Press: Cambridge, 2000.

Loomis, R.S. & L.H. (eds.). *Medieval Romances*. The Modern Library: New York, 1957.

Mackenzie, Donald. *Indian Myth and Legend*. Adamant Media Corporation: Boston, 2004.

March, Jennifer R. *The Penguin Book of Classical Myths*. Allen Lane: London, 2008.

McAlpine, William and Helen. *Japanese Folk Tales and Legends*. Oxford University Press: Oxford, new ed., 1989.

Miller, Mary and Taube, Karl. *The Gods and Symbols of Ancient Mexico and the Maya*. Thames & Hudson Ltd: London, 1993.

Narayan, R.K. (trans.). *The Ramayana*. Penguin Classics: London, new ed., 2006.

Norman, Howard. *Northern Tales: Stories from the Native Peoples of the Arctic and Subarctic Regions*. Pantheon: New York, 1998.

O'Flaherty, Wendy Doniger (trans.). *Hindu Myths*. Penguin Classics: London, 1975.

Orbell, Margaret. *The Illustrated Encyclopedia of Maori Myth and Legend*. Canterbury University Press: Christchurch, 1995.

Osborne, Harold. *South American Mythology*. Hamlyn: London, 1990.

Pinch, Geraldine. *Egyptian Mythology: A Guide to the Gods, Goddesses and Traditions of Ancient Egypt*. Oxford University Press USA: New York, 2004.

Price, Simon and Kearns, Emily. *The Oxford Dictionary of Classical Myth and Religion*. Oxford University Press: Oxford, 2004.

Reed, A.W. *Aboriginal Myths, Legends and Fables*. Reed Natural History: Sydney, new ed., 1999.

Riordan, James (trans.). *The Sun Maiden and the Crescent Moon: Siberian Folk Tales*. Canongate Books Ltd: Edinburgh, 1989.

Sandars, N.K. (trans.). *The Epic of Gilgamesh*. Penguin Books: London, new ed., 2006.

Seidelman, Harold and Turner, James. *The Inuit Imagination: Arctic Myth and Sculpture*. University of Alaska Press: Alaska, reprint ed., 2001.

Shaw, Ian. *The Oxford History of Ancient Egypt*. Oxford University Press: Oxford, new ed., 2003.

Storm, Rachel. *Illustrated Guide to Latin American Mythology*. Studio Editions: London, 1995.

Taube, Karl. *Aztec and Maya Myths*. British Museum Press: London, 1995.

Tedlock, Dennis (trans.). *Popol Vuh*. Simon & Schuster: New York, rev. ed., 1996.

Vernant, Jean-Pierre. Asher, Linda (trans.). *The Universe, the Gods, and Mortals*. Profile Books Ltd: London, new ed., 2002.

Waley, Arthur (trans.). *Monkey* (an abridged translation of Wu Cheng'en's *Journey to the West*). Penguin Classics: London, new ed., 2006.

Walters, Derek. *Chinese Mythology: An Encyclopaedia of Myth and Legend*. Diamond Books: London, 1995.

Yeats, W.B. (ed.). *Fairy and Folk Tales of Ireland*. Picador: London, 1979.

Index

Acknowledgments

The publisher would like to thank the following people, museums and photographic libraries for permission to reproduce their material. Every care has been taken to trace copyright holders. However, if we have omitted anyone we apologize and will, if informed, make corrections to any future edition.

Key
AA: The Art Archive, London
BAL: Bridgeman Art Library, London
BM: British Museum, London
RHPL: Robert Harding Picture Library, London
RMN: Réunion des Musées Nationaux, Paris
V&A: Victoria & Albert Museum, London
WFA: Werner Forman Archive, London

Page 7 Private Collection/Christie's Images; **8–9** Irish Image Collection/Axiom; **11** Joe Beynon/Axiom; **13** Museum of Fine Arts, Boston, Massachusetts/BAL; **14** Fitzwilliam Museum, University of Cambridge/BAL; **15** Private Collection/AA **16** Dagli Orti/AA; **21** Louvre, Paris/AA; **22** BM/Michael Holford; **23** Michael Holford; **24** The Egyptian Musuem, Cairo/Jurgen Liepe; **25** Louvre, Paris/AA; **27** BM/Michael Holford; **30** The Egyptian Museum, Cairo/Jurgen Liepe; **31** The Egyptian Museum, Cairo/RHPL; **44** BM/Michael Holford; **45** Archaeological Museum, Naples/AA; **46** BM; **47** Archaeological Museum, Genoa/Scala; **48** Ancient Art & Architecture; **49** Sonia Halliday; **51** Dagli Orti/AA; **52** Museo Pio Clementino, Rome/Scala; **53** Dagli Orti/AA; **54** Dagli Orti/AA; **56** Erich Lessing/akg-images; **60** Villa Romana del Casale, Sicily/BAL; **62** Olsannburg, Oslo/AA; **67** BM/WFA; **71** National Museum of Ireland, Dublin/WFA; **72** Danish Natural Museum, Copenhagen/Erich Lessing; **74** BM/akg-images; **78** Herzog Anton Ulrich Museum, Braunschweig; **79** Bibliothèque Nationale, Paris/BAL; **80** British Library, London/BAL; **81** British Library, London/BAL; **85** Private Collection/CM Dixon; **86** Royal Library, Copenhagen/BAL; **95** akg-images; **96** akg-images; **97** akg-images; **121** Private Collection, © Frank C. Pape/Jean Loup Charmet; **124** BM; **129** Elizabeth Warner, Mike Smith/DBP; **130** Gavin Hellier/RHPL; **137** BM; **138** Louvre, Paris/RMN; **139** BM; **141** BM; **142** Private Collection/ Christie's Images; **150** V&A; **151** Private Collection/Christie's Images; **152** Dinodia, Bombay/BAL; **168** Musée Guimet, Paris/ John Bigelow-Taylor; **172** Choijin-Lama Temple Museum, Mongolia; **173** Louvre, Paris/RMN; **204** WFA; **222** Museum of the North American Indian, New York/BAL; **223** University of Pennsylvania, Philadelphia/University Museum Archives; **226** Smithsonian Institution, Washington D.C./Peter Furst; **228** American Museum of Natural History, New York/Steve Myers; **231** Schindler College, New York/WFA; **234** Robinson Museum, South Dakota/WFA; **235** Field Museum of Natural History, Chicago/WFA; **237** Smithsonian Institution, Washington D.C./Peter Furst; **238** Private Collection/BAL; **239** Buffalo Bill Historical Center, Cody, Wyoming/WFA; **240** Smithsonian Institution, Washington D.C./Peter Furst; **246** Justin Kerr; **247** Private Collection, New York/WFA; **249** Justin Kerr; **250** Anthropological Museum of Mexico, Veracruz University/ WFA; **253** National Museum of Anthropology, Mexico City/ WFA; **257** Private Collection/WFA; **258** National Museum of Archaeology, Lima/AA; **264** The Metropolitan Museum of Art, New York/Art Resource/Scala; **267** WFA; **269** E.Z. Smith; **270** E.Z. Smith; **274** Karl Lehmann/Lonely Planet Images